W9-ARH-867

THE HOLY LAND

FROM THE PERSIAN TO THE ARAB CONQUEST

THE HOLY LAND

FROM THE PERSIAN TO THE ARAB CONQUESTS

(536 B.C. to A.D. 640)

A HISTORICAL GEOGRAPHY

by
MICHAEL AVI-YONAH
Professor of Archaeology
The Hebrew University, Jerusalem

BAKER BOOK HOUSE
Grand Rapids, Michigan

Library of Congress Catalog Card Number: 65-18260

PHOTOLITHOPRINTED BY CUSHING - MALLOY, INC.
ANN ARBOR, MICHIGAN, UNITED STATES OF AMERICA
1966

Preface

The beginnings of this book go back to 1931. The author, then on the staff of the Department of Antiquities, Government of Palestine, was asked to prepare the Palestinian part of the Cairo sheet in the 1:1 000 000 Map of the Roman Empire, published under the auspices of the Union Académique Internationale. The sheet was duly issued by the Department of Surveys of Egypt. The material collected for the purpose of our contribution exceeded, however, by far the original need and it was decided to publish a separate "Map of Roman Palestine," with the cooperation of the Department of Surveys. This map (1:250-000 in scale) was prepared in consultation with the three outstanding authorities on the subject, Prof. Albrecht Alt, Père Francois Marie Abel (both now dead) and Professor William Foxwell Albright. The text and map appeared in 1935 in the fifth volume of the *Quarterly of the Department of Antiquities, Palestine,* pp. 139-193. A second, revised edition, was issued in 1940. Both editions have now been out of print for many years.

The rising interest in the past of the Holy Land among the Hebrew speaking population in Israel made a Hebrew edition desirable. This was planned on a larger scale than the original English edition. A historical introduction of 93 pages was added, recording the evolution of the political geography of the country within its traditional boundaries, i.e. comprising those parts of it east of the Jordan which were not included in the Cis-Jordanian Palestine under British Mandate. The descriptive list of sites, arranged by cities, in the original edition was expanded into a comprehensive description of the territory of each city or region, with an enumeration of all the identifiable localities within its boundaries. The Hebrew edition was first published by the Bialik Institute, Jerusalem, in 1949, with a map in two sheets (1:330 000); a second, revised edition, was issued in 1951. The third edition, with an appendix bringing it up to date, was made in 1962.

In the meantime the author had prepared an English translation of the addenda included in the Hebrew edition, with new chapters on the economic geography of the Holy Land, and the composition and number of its population in antiquity. This part of the work was submitted to the University of London in 1957 and accepted by it as a thesis for the degree of Doctor of Philosophy.

The present edition represents a revision of the original translation, brought up to date with all the available information which has come to light since 1956 in the caves on the shores of the Dead Sea, whether in Israel or in Jordan, and from other excavated sites. The material obtained by recent surveys on the surface has also been included, as well as the results, if acceptable, of recent publications on the subject.

The author wishes to thank Prof. J. Vardaman of the Southern Baptist Theological Seminary, Louisville, Kentucky, who carefully read and revised the first part of the manuscript. I am also greatly obliged to Prof. A. H. M. Jones, Cambridge, for his corrections.

The maps in the English edition have been prepared by Miss Yael Avi-Yonah.

In conclusion the author would like to remind the readers of two facts. Historical geography is not an exact science; many of the identifications given in this volume and many of the boundaries indicated are based on logical conclusions and on readings of sources, which might prove erroneous in the light of later discoveries or interpretations. We have here a subject which is in a state of rapid development, with new facts constantly modifying the old assumptions. Nevertheless, a study of the geographical environment of the Scriptures and of later periods in the history of the Holy Land is essential for the proper understanding of our texts and thus remains a matter of supreme interest.

MICHAEL AVI-YONAH

Jerusalem

Contents

List of Maps

Map

Preview

This book is divided into three parts

PART ONE deals in chronological order with the historical factors which have affected the map of the Holy Land in the periods under discussion. *Chapter I* treats of the administrative divisions of the Persian period, in particular with the boundaries and districts of Judaea under Nehemiah and the Phoenician cities of the coast. In *Chapter II* the changes made by the Ptolemies are discussed, in particular the Hellenization of cities and the establishment of Greek colonies. *Chapter III* is devoted to the period under Seleucid rule, especially as regards the administrative divisions of Coele-Syria and the arrangements made in consequence of the revolt of Judas Maccabaeus and his brethren. *Chapter IV* deals with the rise of the Hasmonaean state, the causes and phases of its expansion and the changes it effected in the population of the country. *Chapter V* describes the consequences of the Roman conquest of the country in 63 B.C., the revival of the Greek cities and the diminution of the Hasmonaean state. *Chapters VI-VIII* describe the gradual formation of the kingdom of Herod, its internal divisions ("king's country," cities, colonies, fortresses etc.), its partition among Herod's sons and the other territorial changes down to A.D. 70. *Chapters IX-X* describe the way in which the Roman government re-arranged the administration of Palestine after the First and Second Jewish Revolt, the consequent urbanization of the country, its division into three provinces in the Byzantine period, the problems of frontier defence (the *limes Palaestinae* and its date) and the ecclesiastical divisions as reflecting political developments.

In PART TWO the boundaries of each one of the territorial units making up the country are analyzed in detail, with the available evidence assessed in each case.

PART THREE consists of three chapters: *Chapter I* deals with the development of the Roman road system. *Chapter II* attempts a summary of the economic geography of the country by regions, reviewing in each case the natural resources, agricultural produce (wheat, wine, oil, etc.) of each region, its cattle breeding and fisheries, mineral and other resources. *Chapter III* deals with the composition of the population, as reflected in literary and epigraphical sources. In conclusion an attempt is made to estimate the total population of the country in the Roman and Byzantine periods.

Parts One and Two are illustrated with twenty-four sketch maps.

PART ONE

Chapter I

JUDAEA UNDER PERSIAN RULE

THE Assyrian and Babylonian empires, which preceded the rule of Persia in the Ancient Orient, had effectively put an end to the congeries of small independent Kingdoms, which had previously flourished in this area in the political vacuum created by the decline of Egyptian power in the twelfth century B.C. The Assyrian conquest beyond the Euphrates in the eighth and seventh centuries B.C. caused the native dynasties to be replaced with Assyrian governors (*bêl-pahati*). The only exceptions to this process were the Phoenician and Philistine coastal cities and the Kingdom of Judah. The destruction of the latter was accomplished in 586 B.C. by Nebuchadnezzar II, the Babylonian successor of the Assyrians. When Babylon fell to Cyrus of Persia fifty years later, the Syrian and Palestinian provinces submitted at once to their new ruler and were incorporated within the framework of the Persian Kingdom.

According to the administrative reorganisation of the Persian empire into twenty provinces (satrapies), as undertaken by Darius I (522-485 B.C.) and described by Herodotus,[1] the fifth satrapy included all the country from the city of Posidium (modern Basit in Northern Syria[2]) to the borders of Egypt. "All Phoenicia, Palestine, Syria[3] and Cyprus, were herein contained," "excluding the district which belonged to Arabia

[1] *Historiae*, III, 89-97.

[2] R. Dussaud: *Topographie historique de la Syrie antique et médiévale,* Paris, 1927, p. 419.

[3] Herodotus visited only the coastal areas of Southern Palestine, to which he applies the name *palaistinē syrinē* (I, 105; II, 106; VII, 89) and to which he assigns the area between Gaza (Cadytis) and Phoenicia (III, 5). The mention, however, of the "Syrians of Palestine" who practiced circumcision (II, 104) must refer to the Jews, the Philistines being always contemptuously referred to in the Bible as *arelim* "uncircumcised" (Judges 14:3; 15; 18; I Samuel 14:6, etc.), Herodotus thus seems to extend the area of Syria Palestine well inland.

and was free of tax."[4] The official name of this satrapy was '*Ebirnâri,*' "the land beyond the river" (*scil.* Euphrates) (Heb. 'Eber ha-nahar, Aram. 'Abar-nahara),[5] which was originally derived from Assyrian usage;[6] it reflects, of course, the point of view of a King residing at Babylon and Susa. The Governor (*satrapēs,* Heb. *Ahashdarpan* from the Old Persian *khshathra-pavan*) resided at Damascus.[7]

The vast extent of the Persian empire made it necessary that its primary subdivisions should be correspondingly large. A further subdivision into secondary and tertiary units was obviously necessary. The former was supplied by the Assyrian and Babylonian governorates, which now formed the provinces of the Persian empire. In the official Aramaic of the Persian administration they were known as *medînah,* a term adopted into Biblical Hebrew. These are the "an hundred and seven and twenty provinces"[8] over which Ahasuerus reigned "from India even unto Ethiopia;" their actual number must have varied from time to time. Each province was presided over by an official (*pihat*), known as "His Excellency" (*tirshathâ*).[9] The provinces themselves were further subdivided into districts ("parts" A.V. *pelakhim* in Hebrew), which corresponded in general with the administrative areas in use under the Kings of Judah and Israel. The districts themselves consisted of one or two principal localities,[10] and a number of villages, which were the lowest administrative unit. In addition to the governorates, each satrapy included a number of cities or regions ruled by local dynasties, as well as territories of tribes, some of them semi-independent, royal fortresses, etc.[11]

In accordance with the general scheme outlined above, the area of

---

[4] Rawlinson's translation.

[5] Neh. 2:7, 9; Ezra 8:36 (Hebrew); Ezra 4:10, 11, 16, 17, 20, etc.

[6] Luckenbill: *Ancient Records of Assyria.* II, No. 901, referring to 'the governors, the kings of Ebir-nâri' in a text of Assurbanipal describing his campaign against Egypt.

[7] Strabo XVII, 2, 20-756.

[8] Esther 1:1; in Ezra 8:36: 'the governors on this side of the river' the plural refers to the provinces subject to the satrap; cf. also Neh. 1:3; 11:13; Ezra 2:1.

[9] Nehemiah 10:2; cf. Ezra 2:63; Neh. 8:9. It means: 'He who is to be feared'. (Scheftelowitz: *Arisches im AT,* p. 93f.)

[10] See below, pp. 19-23.

[11] O. Leuze: *Die Satrapieneinteilung in Syrien von 520-320,* Halle a/S, 1935.

Palestine was divided into several such provinces, city areas, royal fortresses and tribal areas.

JUDAH

Judah (officially known as *Yehud, yhd*)[12] was one of the provinces under the satrap of Ebirnari. Some doubts have been recently cast upon this fact[13] and the theory has been advanced that originally Judah was dependent politically upon Samaria. The basis of this hypothesis is the interference of the Samaritan authorities in the affairs of Jerusalem, as reported in the Book of Ezra.[14] However, the slackness of Persian rule was such that there were often disputes between various administrative units, and civil wars between the satraps were nothing unusual. That the rulers of Samaria denounced the authorities of Jerusalem to the King, and then sent in troops to enforce a royal order, need not necessarily imply that they were legitimately entitled to do so. The fact that even before the days of Nehemiah, Zerubbabel the son of Shealthiel is called by the prophet Haggai[15] "governor (*peha*) of Judah" also weakens this theory. Haggai was a contemporary of Zerubbabel and would hardly address him otherwise than by the correct official title. The fact that Judah was a province at least from the reign of Darius I onwards does not, of course, imply that there were no gaps between one governor and another.[16] In fact, we know only six names of governors in the four hundred years of Persian rule: (1) Sheshbazzar "whom he (Cyrus) had made governor,"[17] (2) the Zerubbabel mentioned above; (3) Nehemiah the son of

[12] This form appears on the coins struck by the province; A. Reifenberg: *Ancient Jewish Coins,* Jerusalem, 1940, pp. 1f, 27.

[13] In particular by A. Alt in the *Proksch Festschrift,* 1934, p. 21ff; cf. K. Galling, *PJb,* 1938, p. 75.

[14] Ezra 4:7-23.

[15] Haggai 1:1 etc.

[16] The absence of a governor in the negotiations preceding the surrender of Judah to Alexander the Great does not therefore prove anything. A Persian official might well have absented himself from his post in the crisis, his place being easily supplied by the High Priest. Josephus, *Ant.* 11:8:2/7, 306-347; cf. J. Touzard, *RB,* 1923, p. 62; Abel, *RB,* 1935, pp. 48-57; Galling, *PJb.,* 1938, p. 75.

[17] Ezra 5:14; it is doubtful in how far this Sheshbazzar, who is elsewhere (Ezra 1:8) called 'prince of Judah' and who was apparently a descendant of King Jehoiachin, was a regular

Hachaliah in the time of Artaxerxes I (465-425 B.C.);[18] (4) Bigoai, or Bagohi, who is addressed as governor of Judah by the Jews of Elephantine in a letter written in the seventeenth year of Darius II (408 B.C.)[19]; (5) Yehoezer and (6) Ahio are named, with the addendum *peha* (*phwa*), on jar-handle stamps found at Ramat Rahel near Jerusalem.[19a] The coins struck by the provincial authorities with the legend *yhd* certainly prove that Judah was a full-fledged province towards the end of the Persian rule; the stamps on jar-handles inscribed *yhd* seem to begin in the time of Nehemiah at the latest.[20] The governor was assisted by the High Priest and a Council of Elders (*sabey yehûdayê*).[21]

Having established the fact of an autonomous province of Judah, we must next consider its boundaries. Our principal source for these is the Book of Nehemiah. In using the material from this source we should, however, distinguish between the area settled by Jews and the area included within the boundaries of their own province. Thus the list of those returning from the Babylonian captivity[22] or that of the "villages with their fields" of the children of Judah[23] should be used with caution. As regards the latter list, it includes places "from Beersheba to the valley of Hinnom," such as Hebron (Kirjath-arba), En-rimmon, Lachish, etc.—localities clearly situated outside the province of Judah, as we shall see

---

governor; especially as under Cyrus the Persian administration was still in a fluid state. More likely the appointment of Sheshbazzar is regarded in the nature of a first step towards a restoration of the Davidic dynasty. Later on this attempt was given up by the Persian kings after Zerubbabel's failure to dissociate himself from the Messianic movement in the crisis preceding the accession of Darius I.

[18] Neh. 5:14; 5:18, etc.

[19] A. E. Cowley: *Aramaic Papyri of the Fifth Century B.C.,* Nos. 30-32, pp. 108-124. The Persian name does not in itself prove that he was a Persian. The "children of Bigvai" appear in the lists of those who went up out of the captivity (Ezra 2:14; Neh. 7:19). Josephus (*Ant.* 11:7:1, 297-301) mentions a Bagoses, general (*stratēgos*) of the second Artaxerxes, who exercised authority over the Jews. This Bagoses was certainly a non-Jew; his going up to the Temple is termed a defilement. He might perhaps be identical with the Bagohi of the Elephantine letters; but it seems much more likely that his authority was superior to that of a governor, i.e. that he was either a satrap or a military commander.

[19a] Y. Aharoni: *Excavations at Ramat Rahel,* Roma, 1962, pp. 32-34.

[20] See supra, n. 12. As regards their dating, cf. Y. Aharoni, *IEJ,* 6, 1956, p. 150.

[21] Ezra 6:7.

[22] Ezra 2:21-34; Neh. 7:26-37.

[23] Neh. 11:25-35.

later. The view, occasionally expressed,[24] that the boundaries of Judah originally included Idumaea and parts of the coastal plain—in particular Lod, Hadid and Ono[25]—implies a subsequent reduction of this area to the limits known from later sources, in particular the Books of the Maccabees. Such a "Greater Judah" would contrast strangely with the well-known weakness of the province immediately after the Return. There is, moreover, no known historical event which would justify such a drastic reduction of the area of Judah. The late Roman historian Solinus[26] refers certainly to a destruction of Jericho, the "capital" of Judah after the destruction of Jerusalem by Artaxerxes (which?), and Eusebius[27] repeats his story, but it is an undatable story and seems unhistorical. (Jericho is given there as the capital of Judah!) It is much more likely that the list in Nehemiah refers to Jewish towns and villages which had kept a foothold after the Babylonian exile among foreign nations in the former area of Judah.

We have to base our information as regards the boundaries of Judah under the Persians on three sources: first and foremost the list of the places whose people helped in Nehemiah's reconstruction of the walls of Jerusalem[28]; secondly, the lists of those returning from the Captivity,[29] used critically and lastly, the places of the 'sons of the singers' who came to Jerusalem on the occasion of the dedication of the wall.[30]

From these sources we learn that the northern boundary of Judah included Gibeon[31] Mizpah,[32] Bethel,[33] and Beeroth.[34] The identifications

---

24 Abel: *Géographie de la Palestine,* II, 1938, p. 120, refers to a "canton détaché"; cf. also B. Mazar (Maisler): *Historical Atlas,* 1941, map 29, p. 35 (Hebrew).

25 See below, p. 17f.

26 C. Iulius Solinus: *Collactanea rerum memorabilium,* § 4, XXXV: Iudaeae caput fuit Hierosolyma, Sed excisa est. Successit Hierichus: et haec desivit, Artaxerxis bello subacta.

27 Chronicon, *PG* 19, c. 186.

28 Neh. 3:2-27.

29 See n. 22 above.

30 Neh. 11:25-35.

31 Neh. 3:7.

32 Ib., 15, 19.

33 Ezra 2:29; Neh. 7:32; Zechariah 7:2.

34 Ezra 2:25; Neh. 7:29.

of these sites now commonly accepted are el-Jib, Tell en Nasbe,[35] Beitîn and el Bîre. As regards Gibeon and Mizpah some doubts have arisen, because according to Nehemiah 3:7, the mention of the men of Gibeon and of Mizpah is followed by the words "unto the throne of the governor on this side of the river." Some interpreters[36] have understood this to mean that these villages were directly dependent on the satrap. On the one hand, it is by no means certain that the "throne of the governor" does not refer to some building in Jerusalem,[37] and moreover, the fact that the satrap possessed an estate in Judah does not exclude it from the area of the province; especially so as Mizpah is mentioned in another verse of this chapter[38] as the capital of a district of Judah. The northern boundary corresponds, therefore, roughly to that of the Kingdom of Judah after the division of the monarchy under Rehoboam; of all the conquests of Hezekiah and Josiah Judah kept only Bethel. On the other hand, the area of Jewish settlement extended far beyond the political boundary, as we shall see later.[39]

On the east the natural boundary of Judah was the Jordan. The plains of Jericho[40] including Beth ha-Gilgal[41] and Senaah[42] formed one of the Judaean districts. Here, too, Jewish settlement (under the Tobiads, for

---

[35] This site should not be confused with the Mizpah of I Macc. 3:46, which, it seems, suits better to locate at en-Nabi Samwîl. Cf. Albright, *AASOR,* IV, p 90 foll. as against Abel, *RB,* 1924, p. 360 sqq.

[36] E. Meyer, *Die Entstehung d. Judenthums,* p. 108 n; Mitchell, *JBL,* 1903, p. 148ff.

[37] *IEJ,* 4, 1954.

[38] See n. 32 above.

[39] See pp. 19, 55 below.

[40] Ezra 2:34; Neh. 3:2; 7:36.

[41] Neh. 12:29.

[42] This name, which occurs in Neh. 3:3 "the sons of Hassenaah" appears in Ezra 2:35 and Neh. 7:38, in the list of those returning from captivity as 'The children of Senaah', the largest group among those enumerated (3630 in Ezra, 3930 in Nehemiah). Some interpreters have, therefore, suggested that this group did not come from a specific locality, but represents the common people or the people of Jerusalem (ha-Senuah- 'the hated one')—cf. W. Rudolph: *Esra u. Nehemia* (Hdt. z. A. T. 20), Tübingen, 1949, p. 9 ad loc. and the authors quoted there. On the whole, however, Abel's suggested identification of Senaah with the Migdalsenna of Eusebius (*On*: 154:16 identified with Kh el Beiyudât) seems more suitable than such fanciful interpretations. Cf. Abel: *Géographie de la Palestine,* II, 1938, p. 455, and Guthe *MN,* 1911, p. 68f. The fertility of the Jordan valley would explain the elevated number of this group in the list of those returning from captivity.

which below) extended east of the river, into the land of the Ammonites.

The southern boundary of Judah reflected the huge reduction of its area caused by the Edomite occupation of the whole south of the old Kingdom of Judah, including Hebron. Here the Judaean area was limited to Netopha,[43] Tekoah[44] and Beth-Zur.[45] In the south-western corner Judah had kept the district of Keilah[46] which included the valley of Elah and Azekah.[47] From this south-western extremity the border turned northwards, including Zanoah,[48] Kirjath-jearim,[49] Chephirah.[50] As regards the two Beth-horons, the Upper and the Lower, it has been suggested that these villages were outside Judah, because in one passage[51] Sanballat, the governor of Samaria and one of Nehemiah's most inveterate enemies is called 'the Horonite.' On the other hand, one should remember that a Samaritan might after all have been born in a Judaean village, and that the Horon mentioned in this passage is not bound to be the Beth-horon of Judah; the god Horon, after whom it is called, was worshipped over wide areas.[52] Finally, the evidence of the Books of the Maccabees[53] is definitely in favour of including Beth-horon in Judah; and the same applies to Emmaus, lower down in the plain.[54] From Beth-horon the boundary returned eastwards towards Gibeon.[55]

An interesting problem of the western boundary of Judah are the three cities Lod, Hadid and Ono. They appear towards the end of the two

---

[43] Ezra 2:22; Neh. 7:26; 12:28. For the identification see Y. Aharoni, *IEJ*, 6, 1956, p. 152.

[44] Neh. 3:5, 27 (Kh. Taqû').

[45] Ib. 15 (Kh. Tubeiqa near Burj es-Sûr).

[46] Ib. 17, 18 (Kh. Qeila).

[47] 4 Ezra, 5:15 (Tell Zakariya).

[48] Neh. 3:13.

[49] Ezra 2:25 (where MT has "arim" for Jearim); Neh. 7:29.

[50] Ib.

[51] Neh. 13:28.

[52] J. Gray, *JNES*, 8, 1949, pp. 27-34; the Horonaim in Moab, Isa. 15:5; Jerem. 8:3, 5, 34; Antiq. 13:15:4-397; 14:1:4-18.

[53] I Macc. 3:24.

[54] Ib., 42.

[55] For a discussion of the boundaries of Judah under Persian rule see: E. Meyer: *Entstehung d. Judentums*, pp. 107ff.; R. Kittel: *Geschichte d. Volkes Israel*, III, 2, pp. 341ff.; G. Hölscher: *Palästina i. d. pers. u. hellenist. Zeit*, p. 34; F. M. Abel: *Géographie de la Palestine*, II, p. 121.

parallel lists of those returning from the Babylonian captivity,[56] but are not mentioned in the list of the builders of Nehemiah's wall. Their attachment to the province of Judah would add to this province a narrow and inconvenient strip reaching into the coastal plain. We might therefore either make an exception in this case to the general rule implied in the lists of Ezra-Nehemiah, viz. that those returning from the Exile returned each to his own place, and assume that the original inhabitants of these places settled elsewhere, or we can list Lod, Hadid and Ono with the Judaean villages dispersed through Edom, which are to be excluded from the province of Judah.[57] Two other sources seem to support the exclusion of these three cities: firstly, when Sanballat proposes to meet Nehemiah in a kind of no-man's land between their respective provinces, he suggests a village in the plain of Ono,[58] obviously on the assumption that it was outside both Samaria and Judah. Secondly, the prophet Zechariah, in comparing the present decay of Judah with its former prosperity, speaks of the old times when its people "inhabited the South and the plain," thus implying that they no longer did so.[59]

The boundaries of Judah, as delimited above, seem to have remained unchanged, possibly from the time of Nebuchadnezzar,[60] and certainly from the time of Nehemiah to that of Jonathan the Hasmonean, i.e. for the three centuries from the middle of the fifth to the middle of the second century B.C.[61] This stability allows us to draw retrospective conclusions from the time of the Hasmoneans to the earlier periods, Seleucid, Ptolemaic and Persian. We may include in Persian Judah whatever was included in it at a later time, and vice versa.

The province of Judah had roughly the shape of a rectangle. It extended from north to south along the watershed of the Mediterranean

---

56 Ezra 2:33; Neh. 7:37.

57 Neh. 11:25-35.

58 Neh. 6:2. The MT has *bakefîrîm,* which some interpreters (cf. W. Rudolph: *Esra u. Nehemia,* Hdb. Z. AT, 20, ad.loc.) identify with Chephirah or some other place name; the AV, following the Septuagint, has 'in the villages' meaning one of the villages. In any case Ono is outside *both* provinces.

59 Zechariah 7:7.

60 Kittel, *op. cit.* (above, n. 55), p. 341.

61 See p. 55f. below.

and the Jordan Valley, from Ramallah to the neighbourhood of Hebron; and in the east-west direction it stretched from the Jordan to the foot of the Mediterranean versant of its mountains. Its extent from north to south was about 25 miles, from east to west about 32 miles. The total area was about 800 square miles, of which about one third was an uncultivable desert. Even in the Jericho Valley, cultivation had not yet reached the peak it achieved in Herodian and Roman times with the introduction of Hellenistic irrigation methods. The smallness of the cultivable area and the long period of peace under Persian rule produced in Judah a surplus of population. (The Greek historians noted with astonishment that the Jews reared all their children, not exposing any as was the Greek custom).[62] This population surplus explains the extension of Jewish settlement into the coastal plain and the mountains north of Judah, and in particular into the districts of Accraba, Apharaema, Thammah and Lod, as well as into Galilee[63] and Gilead. In the Persian period emigration into foreign parts was by no means as common as it became under the Hellenistic kingdoms; there were however military colonies of Jews in Egypt, the best known of which was on the island of Yeb (Elephantine); the Babylonian provinces might also have absorbed some of the surplus.

Judah as thus constituted formed a strategically strong body: the approaches to Jerusalem on the west and east were in Jewish hands from the mountain base upwards, as well as the upper part of the Elah Valley, the south-western approach. In the north the heights of Bethel and Mount Asor blocked the way to any invader. Only in the south did the border cut across the watershed and make it easy for an enemy to advance into the heart of Judaea.[64a]

The list of those who helped to build Nehemiah's wall also furnishes some information on the internal division of the province into districts. In this list five districts or "parts" (pelakhim) are mentioned: Jeru-

[62] Hecataeus of Abdera (*Fragm. gr. Hist.* II, p. 392, §§ 4, 8); cf. Josephus: *Contra Apionem,* I, 199; II, 202.

[63] I Macc. 5:14.

[64] Ib., 5:9.

[64a] For the historical consequences of this fact, see below, p. 52.

salem,[65] Beth-haccerem,[66] Mizpah,[67] Beth-Zur,[68] Keilah.[69] To this we must certainly add Jericho. The fact that Nehemiah was the governor of Judah, acting under a royal order,[70] certainly precluded the absence of any district in his province; a single case of insubordination on the part of the nobles of Tekoah is carefully noted.[71] The above list therefore represented in its original form the complete administrative division of the province, and any lacunae must be due to a later corruption of the text. We may, however, complete the obvious lacunae in the list from the other place-names mentioned there, as it appears likely that these localities were expressly listed as headquarters of sub-divisions. In several instances the districts appear sub-divided into two halves,[72] which supports the view that the second locality mentioned in each district (and no third one is ever, as will be seen), represents the administrative centre of the other half. We shall now list each district, with its probable boundaries:

1. *Jerusalem* naturally included the vicinity of the city as well as the places listed in the 'plain country round about Jerusalem and from the villages of the Netophathi' . . . Geba and Azmaveth.[73] As a secondary administrative centre we would suggest the newly discovered fortress at Ramath-Rahel, which was very rich in jar-handle stamps such as "Yhd" "Yrshlm" (Jerusalem) dating from the time of Nehemiah.[74] Its identification with Nethopha has been denied, on what seem to us insufficient grounds.[74a]

II. *Keilah*. This district occupies the south-western part of Judah. Its

---

[65] Neh. 3:9, 12.
[66] Ib. 14.
[67] Ib. 15, 19.
[68] Ib. 16.
[69] Ib. 17-18.
[70] Neh. 2:7.
[71] Neh. 3:5.
[72] Ib. 9, 12 (Jerusalem); 16 (Beth-Zur); 17, 18 (Keilah).
[73] Neh. 12:28-29; cf. 16, iii, 22.
[74] Y. Aharoni, *IEJ,* 6, 1956, p. 148ff.
[74a] Ib., p. 152. It is based on an *argumentum ex silentio* i.e. the absence of Iron Age I pottery, so far. For the proposed identification with Beth-Haccerem see below.

two halves are mentioned in the list,[75] but not its second capital. A comparison with the list of the districts of Judah under Josiah (on which see below, p. 22) suggests that the secondary capital was Adullam[76] which appears in Maccabean times as a Jewish city.[77]

III. *Mizpah.* This northern district presents certain difficulties: (a) in two passages referring to it it is assigned to two different persons, in v. 15 to Shallum the son of Col-hozeh 'the ruler of part of Mizpah' and in v. 19 to Ezer the son of Jeshua 'the ruler of Mizpah'; (b) the 'men of Gibeon and Mizpah' are mentioned separately in v. 7[78] in connection with 'the throne of the governor this side of the river.' We may, however, assume that even if part of the district belonged to the satrap (an assumption by no means certain; see above, p. 16), the whole district was organized normally with its capitals at Mizpah and Gibeon, as set out in v. 7, and that the 'ruler of Mizpah' refers to the residence at Mizpah itself, while the expression 'ruler of part of Mizpah' refers to part of the district by its official name.

IV. The fourth, western, district is *Beth-Haccerem.* Most interpreters identify it with 'Ain Karîm or a site in its vicinity.[79] It is not necessarily identical with the Karem which the Septuagint adds to Jos. XV, 59,[80] but even this would not preclude such an identification, as the list includes names south-west of Jerusalem, such as Bether (Battîr), Sores (Sâris), Manahat (Malha), Gallim (Beit Jâlâ).[81] It should be noted that only half of this district is mentioned in the list (v. 14), the other half being missing. However, if this district extended westwards to the foot of the

---

[75] Neh. 3:17-18.
[76] Jos. 15:35. cf. Alt. *PJb,* 1925, p. 114.
[77] 2 Macc. 12:38.
[78] Melatiah the Gibeonite and Jadon the Meronothite mentioned in the same verse seem to have been local "nobles" not identical with the governors of the district.
[79] Jerem. 6:1 suggests that Beth-Haccarem was situated on a hill, from which a sign of fire would be visible. The mention of Tekoa and of the children of Benjamin in the same verse shows that we cannot determine the direction of Beth-Haccerem in relation to Jerusalem from this poetical passage.
[80] Cf. Y. Aharoni, *op. cit.* (supra, n. 74). It appears doubtful, however, if an administrative centre could be set up 4 km. from Jerusalem and in plain view of the city.
[81] The confused text of the Septuagint (Jos. 15:59) makes it quite possible to assign *theko, ephratha, phagor* and *aitan* to one district, *sorēs, karem,* etc. to another.

mountains, there is a likely candidate for a secondary capital in Zanoah, mentioned in the preceding passage (v. 13). The fact that Hanun and the inhabitants of Zanoah repaired a gate—a task usually left to a community rather than an individual, suggests that part of a district is meant here, with Hanun as its 'ruler.'

V. The fifth district is that of *Beth-Zur,* half of which is mentioned in v. 16 and the other half omitted. We would suggest that the secondary capital was at Tekoah (v. 5), whose inhabitants worked on the wall (although their 'nobles' did not). Since Tekoah was later chosen as one of the fortresses in Bacchides' chain of forts round Judah,[82] since its area was called 'the desert of Tekoah'[83] and since otherwise the whole south-east of Judah would remain an administrative vacuum, this is a plausible view.

VI. To these districts, which are named in our text, we must obviously add the Judaean part of the Jordan Valley, the district of *Jericho.* Its principal locality, mentioned in Nehemiah's list, is Jericho itself;[84] its secondary capital seems to be Senaah.[85] We note that the inhabitants of both places built side by side on the walls of Jerusalem.

To sum up: Judah was divided into six districts and twelve sub-districts.[86] The division was based on Josiah's administrative arrangements, but there were naturally many changes resulting from the historical development from the seventh to the fifth century B.C.[87] The districts of Nehemiah in their turn formed the basis of the later division into toparchies, again *mutatis mutandis.*[88]

The map, Fig. 1, illustrates the proposed division of Judah.

---

[82] Josephus, *Ant.* 13:1:3 16 in MS version W and Lat. (cf. below, p. 53f.).
[83] 2 Chron. 20:20; I Macc. 9:33.
[84] Neh. 3:2.
[85] Ib. 3; see also above, n. 42.
[86] Whether the intention was to reproduce the number of Josiah's districts in a diminished Judah must remain doubtful. The number twelve was the consecrated number of the tribes of all Israel, to which Judah felt itself heir.
[87] Cf. Alt, *PJb,* 1925, pp. 100-116; Abel, *Géographie,* II, p. 93. The districts of Beersheba, Libnah, Lachish, Debir, Ziph, Hebron and Engaddi were lost.
[88] See below, p. 95f.

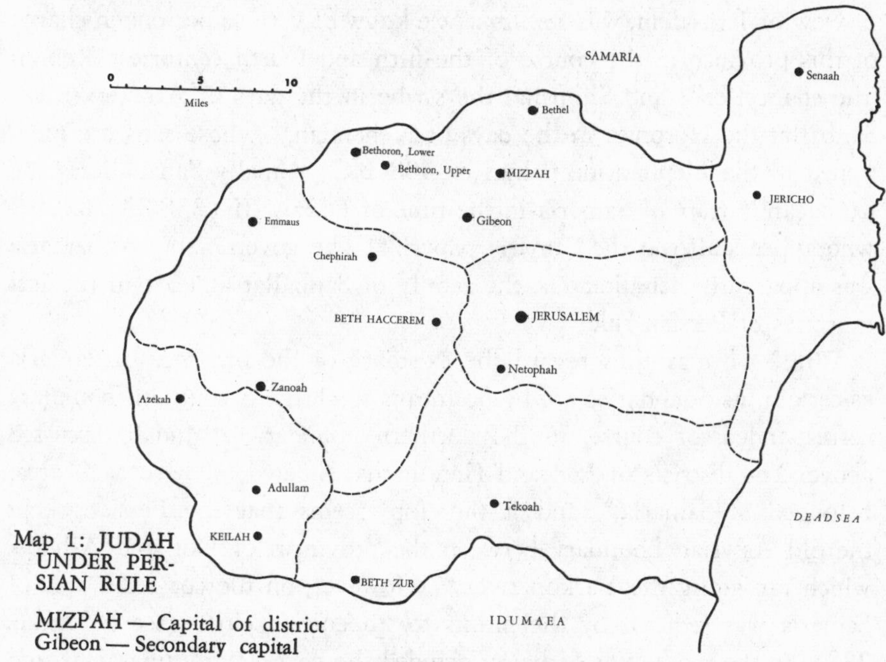

Map 1: JUDAH UNDER PERSIAN RULE

MIZPAH — Capital of district
Gibeon — Secondary capital

THE OTHER PROVINCES

While the biblical record throws at least some light on the boundaries and subdivisions of Judah, we grope in almost total darkness as regards the other provinces. We may conclude both from what is known about the Assyrian provinces[89] and from the Elephantine papyri, that the system of provinces existed in other parts of the country. In the Book of Nehemiah we find allusions to at least four other provinces. Among his enemies Nehemiah lists Sanballat head of 'the army of Samaria,'[90] Tobiah 'the servant the Ammonite,'[91] Geshem the Arabian[92] and the Ashdodites.[93]

The head of these, and the most important province from the point

---

[89] Forrer: *Die Provinzeinteilung des assyrischen Reiches*, pp. 62-63.
[90] Neh. 2:10; 3:34.
[91] Neh. 2:10— the AV translation given above does not reproduce the Hebrew correctly: Tobiah is called *ha 'ebed ha-'Ammoni* i.e. the Ammonite servant.
[92] Neh. 2:19; 6:1. On this Geshem or Gashmu see below, p. 26.
[93] Neh. 4:7.

of view of Jerusalem, was *Samaria.* We know of various persons in charge of this province in the course of the fifth and fourth centuries: Rehum 'the chancellor'[94] and Shimshai the scribe in the days of Artaxerxes I;[95] Sanballat the Horonite in the days of Nehemiah,[96] whose sons are mentioned in the Elephantine papyri of 408 B.C.;[97] finally Sanaballetēs the Cuthaean 'satrap' of Samaria in the time of Darius III (338-331 B.C.),[98] who appears also in the Samaria papyri.[98a] The governorship of Samaria was apparently hereditary in the family of Sanballat at least in the last centuries of Persian rule.

While we may thus regard the existence of the province of Samaria as certain, its boundaries are by no means so clear. Its southern boundary corresponded, of course, to the northern boundary of Judah discussed above. The districts of Lod and Haramatha, situated in the coastal area, belonged to Samaria,[99] and it therefore seems that the Persians kept the old Assyrian boundary between the provinces of Dor and Ashdod, which ran along the Yarkon river.[100] However, on the coast the area of Samaria was reduced by the grants to Phoenician cities (see below, p. 28f.). In the mountains Samaria included the districts of Apharaema and Acraba, which had a considerable Jewish population, mixed with Idumaeans.[101] The mountains of Ephraim naturally formed the bulk of the province, reaching down to the plain of Sharon on the west and the middle Jordan on the east. The mountains of Gilboa and the inner Carmel would be included within the boundaries of Samaria, considering that they form morphological outshoots of Mount Ephraim. If the subdivision into districts was adopted also in this province, Samaria itself, Sichem and Aruboth (Narbata) would be almost certainly district

[94] Lit. *ba'al t'em,* the Aramaic translation of the Persian *framatar* 'commander', cf. Andreas in Marti: *Aramäische Grammatik* p. 56.
[95] Ezra 4:8.
[96] Neh. 2:19.
[97] Cowley: *Aramaic Papyri of the Fifth Century B.C.,* No. 30 (end).
[98] Josephus: *Antiq.* 11:7:2-302.
[98a] P. Lapp, *Archaeology,* 16, 1963, pp. 204-206.
[99] 1 Macc. 10:30; 11:34; *Antiq.* 13:4:9-127.
[100] Forrer, *op. cit.* (supra, n. 89), pp. 60-61.
[101] See below, pp. 73, 216.

capitals. A Sidonian colony already lived in Sichem in Persian times.[102]

The northern boundary of the province of Samaria is problematical. Documents from the Seleucid period[103] suggest that at that time Samaria included *Galilee,* and some scholars have concluded therefrom that the two were also united in Persian times. This argument is fallacious: in Seleucid times Samaria included Judaea, and in the Persian period Judah was certainly independent of it.[104] We should therefore conclude with Alt[105] that Samaria and Galilee were separate provinces under the Persians; especially since in Assyrian times there was a province of Magîddu (Megiddo) i.e. Galilee. Settlement at Megiddo continued into Persian times,[106] but we cannot tell whether it remained the headquarters of the provincial administration; the poor remains in the Persian level rather suggest that the capital was elsewhere. The Assyro-Persian palace, recently discovered at Hazor, suggests by its similarity to the Lachish palace that the governor of Galilee resided there, thus restoring an old Canaanite tradition (Jos. 10:10).

If Galilee was part of Samaria, the Valley of Jezreel lying between the two would be included in the combined province. If, however, the two were separate, as suggested above, the Valley would belong to Galilee, as it did in Assyrian times (for Megiddo at its Southern border was capital of the province); in any case its fertile lands constituted a royal domain perhaps since the times of the Israelite Kings.[107]

South of Judah was the province of *Idumaea,*[108] inhabited by Edomite Arabs who moved there after the fall of Jerusalem in 586 B.C. It included all Southern Judah, from Beth-Zur to Beersheba, except for the coastal plain. Its capital may have been Lachish, where a big palace stood

---

[102] *Antiq.* 11:8:6-344. We learn on the extension of Sidonian colonization inlands also from the Marissa tomb inscriptions, see below, p. 37.

[103] 1 Macc. 10:30; *Ant.* 12:4:1-154.

[104] See p. 13 above.

[105] A. Alt, *PJb,* 1938, pp. 90-92.

[106] Lamon & Shipton: *Megiddo I-V,* Chicago, 1939, p. 91.

[107] Cf. the story of Naboth and Ahab's winter palace at Jezreel. 1 Kings 18:45, 46; 21:1, etc.

[108] Diodorus XIX, 95, 2; 98, 1.

in Persian times,[109] or perhaps Maresha, the capital of Idumaea in Ptolemaic times,[110] or even Hebron, the ancient capital of Judah. Nehemiah omits to refer to the ruler of this province, unless we see in him 'Geshem the Arabian.'[111] A "Gashmu" appears as King of the Qedar in recently discovered dedicatory inscriptions on a vase.[112] We know of Arabs 'free from tax' from Herodotus[113] possibly their rulers also had some authority over the Idumaeans who were of Arabian stock.

West of Idumaea extended the province of *Ashdod*,[114] another creation of the Assyrian empire.[115] Its area comprised ancient Philistia (excluding, however, Ashkelon and Gaza)[116] from the Yarkon southwards, as well as Gezer. The Ashdodite dynasty of Assyrian times[117] seems to have ceased to exist in Persian times.

We know very little about the territorial divisions of Trans-Jordan in the Persian period. If there were no changes after Assyrian times, we might assume in the northern part of this area two provinces: *Qarnînî* (Karnayim i.e. Bashan and Golan, possibly also Gilead) and *Haurîna*, i.e. the Hauran.[118]

As regards the area to the south of Gilead, Nehemiah mentions several times Tobiah the Ammonite servant (*'ebed*).[119] In fact, this Tobiah was the descendant of a noble Judaean family, which at one time disputed the throne with the Davidic dynasty.[120] *'Ebed* "servant" (of the King) is the title of a high Judaean official and Tobiah was perhaps the governor of a province of *Ammon*. We may assume that many Jews began to

---

109 O. Tuffnell *et al.*: *Lachish III*, pp. 131-141; 196ff.; cf. Galling, *PJb*, 1938, p. 77; Abel, *Géographie* II, p. 123.

110 See below, p. 37.

111 Neh. 2:19; 6:1.

112 I. Rabinowitz, *JNES*, 15, 1956, pp. 6-7.

113 III, 91.

114 Neh. 4:1; 13:23-24.

115 Forrer, *op. cit.*, (n. 89 above); Herodotus, II, 157. On the history of Ashdod under Assyrian and Egyptian rule see A. Malamat, *IEJ*, 1, 1950-51, p. 150; *ib.* 3, 1953, p. 29.

116 Ashkelon belonged to the Tyrians, Gaza was a royal fortress (see below, p. 31).

117 B. Mazar. *Encycl. Miqra'it*, s.v. (Hebrew).

118 Forrer, *op. cit.* (n. 89 above), pp. 62-64.

119 Neh. 2:19; 4:1; 6:1.

120 B. Maisler, *Tarbiz*, XII, pp. 109-122 (Hebrew); *IEJ*, 7, 1957, pp. 137ff., 229 ff.

settle beyond the Jordan under the protection of the Tobiad family. Naturally, they tended to occupy the western parts of the province, i.e. the Jordan Valley and the mountain slopes adjoining it. These areas were the nearest to their homeland Judah. They were also, of all lands beyond the Jordan, the most fertile and the easiest to irrigate.[121] In the Persian period, these settlers formed as yet no political unit.

The greatest change of all (in comparison with the Assyrian period) was effected by the Persians in the coastal area. The Assyrians had gradually subjected almost all the coastal cities to the rule of their governors, grouping them into three provinces. Accho was included in the province of Magîddu (Megiddo);[122] the Sharon—from Cape Carmel to the Yarkon river—was formed into the province of Dûrû (Dor).[123] Philistia became subject to the governor of Asdûdu (Ashdod) at least for a time.[124] Only Ashkelon and Gaza escaped incorporation into a larger unit. With the Persian conquest all this changed. The provinces were replaced by the rule of the Phoenician cities Tyre and Sidon, which obtained alternate patches of the coastal plain right down to and including Ashkelon.

We have to seek the reason for this change in the international situation of the period. The Kings of Assyria did not as a rule aim at extending their power beyond the seas. Their Persian successors, however, having once subjugated the Greek cities of the Ionian coast, became entangled with the Greeks of the islands and the mainland. Naval power thus became of vital importance to the Persians. Of all their subjects only the Phoenician cities (and in a smaller degree the Egyptian) were able and willing to supply the ships and the men for this purpose.[125] The wars with Greece ended in a series of Persian defeats, and it became then

---

[121] The slope of the Trans-Jordan mountains in the Jordan Valley faces the Mediterranean and its rainfalls are comparatively abundant, whereas the opposite slope of Judah faces the desert and is barren.

[122] Alt, *PJb,* 1937, p. 65.

[123] Luckenbill: *Ancient Records of Assyria,* II, Nos. 589, 590; Forrer, *op. cit.* (n. 89 above), p. 60.

[124] A. Malamat, *IEJ,* 1, 1950-51, pp. 150-51; Luckenbill, *op. cit.* (above, n. 123), p. 439.

[125] Herodotus, III, 19; VII, 89ff., 96.

almost as vital for the Achaemenid Kings to prevent the Greeks from penetrating into the eastern basin of the Mediterranean. Such an invasion could fan into open flame the smouldering resentment of various Persian possessions, especially Egypt. Later events showed how justified were their apprehensions. In this point the interests of the Persians were identical with those of the Phoenicians, for the latter were the principal trade-rivals of the Greeks, fighting them on a front reaching from Spain through Sicily to Cyprus. The Phoenicians were the most willing allies of the Persian Kings who, in their turn, were only too pleased to help their trusty allies. The Phoenician cities were confined to the narrow coastal strip of the Lebanon. Their greatest need was for more cultivable land to feed their teeming populations. Here the flat Palestinian coast came in most helpfully, and the Persian Kings granted Tyre and Sidon almost the whole of this area. For obvious political reasons these grants were, however, not made in one block, but distributed alternately along the coast. The cordial relations with Persia were interrupted in Sidon by the repressive measures of Artaxerxes III in 351. In Tyre they persisted till the end of Persian rule and beyond.

Our main source for the state of the coast in Persian times is the *Periplus* attributed to Scylax of Caryanda. This famous Greek seafarer was employed by Darius I.[126] An examination of the *Periplus* attributed to Scylax, has shown that this text was composed in the second half of the fourth century B.C.[127] Unfortunately, the text of this Pseudo-Scylax is badly preserved, but it suffices to give us a general picture of the coastal area.

The Palestinian part of this account begins (after Tyre) with "the city of the . . . (a lost name) and its river" followed by "the city of Ace." The city whose name is missing can only be Achzib-Ecdippa, which was apparently independent of Accho at that time. Both were Phoenician cities, not dependent on either Sidon or Tyre. We learn from Strabo

---

[126] *Ib.*, IV, 44. Cf. Alt, *PJb*, 1937, p. 72.

[127] No mention is made of the *basileia* of Sidon, hence the text was composed after 354 B.C. For the text and date cf. C. Müller: *Geographi graeci minores* I, p. 78ff., c. 104; K. Galling, *ZDPV*, 1938, pp. 66-87; cf. also Rosenberg s.v. Scylax in Pauly-Wissowa's *Realencyclopädie.*

and Diodorus that Accho was a royal fortress and the Persian military base in their wars against Egypt.[128]

After Accho begins a string of cities, alternatively Sidonian and Tyrian. The text of Ps-Scylax continued: *exô pē polis ty . . . .* Galling[129] has preferred to complete it: *exô tou kolpou sy{kaminôn polis}* 'Beyond the bay the city of Sycaminum.' But the next item refers to Cape Carmel. Sycaminum is almost certainly to be identified with Tell es Samak and its vicinity *south* of this Cape. This solution, therefore, does too much violence to the text. Galling's second suggestion (which he himself rejects) seems preferable, viz.: *ex(ēs) hēpha polis ty{riön}*—'Next after (scil. the bay) Haifa city of the Tyrians.' This might refer to the remains at Tell Abu Hawâm in Haifa Bay which go back to the fourth century B.C.[130] Its anchorage was inferior to that of Acre, but was certainly sufficient for the smaller vessels in ancient times. Then follows 'Carmel the sacred mountain of Zeus.' The sacred character of Mount Carmel appears already in the lists of Thutmosis III. There it is called *rôsh qadôsh* (the sacred cape).[131] Its god or Baal was identified by a recently discovered inscription with the Jupiter Heliopolitanus, i.e. the old Canaanite god Hadad.[132] Cape Carmel is followed by *arados polis sidôniôn* 'Aradus city of Sidonians' and *dôros polis sidôniôn* 'Doros city of Sidonians.' The similarity of the two names and the fact that both were "Sidonian" suggest that the first line was a dittography.[133] The attribution of Dor to Sidon is supported by the Eshmunazar inscription (see below, p. 38). The next item is again marred by a lacuna: *{polis} kai potamos tyriôn* "X, city) and river of the Tyrians." The completion suggested by Galling is

---

128 Strabo XVI, 2, 25; Diodorus, XV, 41, 3; cf. Galling, *op. cit.* (n. 127 above) as against U. Kahrstedt: *Syrische Territorien in hellenistischer Zeit,* p. 38.

129 *Op cit.* (n. 127), p. 79.

130 Hamilton, *QDAP* IV, pp. 2-5.

131 J. Simons, *Handbook for the study of Egyptian topographical lists,* Leiden, 1937, p. 122.

132 *IEJ,* 2, 1952, pp. 118-124.

133 Galling, *op. cit.* (n. 127 above) p. 80 suggests the reading *adaros* for *arados* and identifies it with the *bovkolôn* polis of Strabo XVI, 758, which he places at Atlit. However, the name *'Atlit* appears to be ancient—the Phoenician letters *'t* were found cut in one of the rock passages leading to it from the coastal plain; the site was probably also called *qrt,* the Mutatio Certha of later days (*Itinerarium Burdigalense* 19, 10, Johns, *QDAP,* III, p. 151; VI, p. 138); possibly it is identical with the Magdiel of *Onom.* 130, 21.

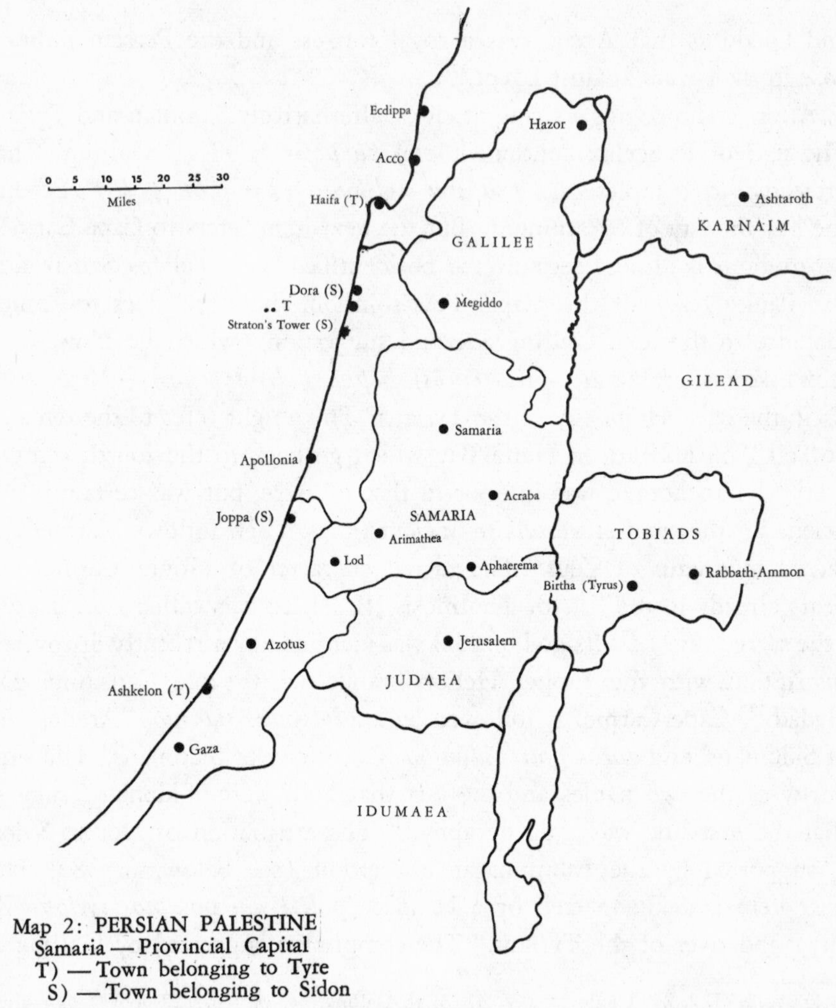

Map 2: PERSIAN PALESTINE
Samaria — Provincial Capital
T) — Town belonging to Tyre
S) — Town belonging to Sidon

krokodeilôn polis (Crocodilopolis, a city mentioned by Strabo and Pliny[134] and identified with Tell el Malât on the Difla river). The next city on the coast-line, not mentioned in Ps-Scylax, is the Tower of Straton. This harbour town already existed in the early Hellenistic period.[135] We may assign its foundation to the Straton, King of Sidon ('Abd-

[134] Strabo XVI, 2, 27; Plinius, *Nat. Hist.* V, 18.
[135] *Pap. Zenon,* Cairo 59004.

Ashtart in Phoenicia) who lived in the second half of the fourth century B.C.[136] Such a late foundation date might explain why Straton's tower was omitted from the Periplus. The next city, Rishpûna (Arsuf)—possibly Tyrian,[137] is also passed over.

The next item in Scylax's list is "the city of (Joppa) where—they say—Andromeda was abandoned to the sea-monster." The town name is missing, but the completion is certain. According to the Eshmunazar inscription Joppa belonged to Sidon. This state of things, might well have begun in the Persian period. The last item in the periplus is Ascalon "city of the Tyrians and royal palace" *(basileia)*. Here ends the list of Scylax. South of Ascalon was the city of Gaza, which was outside Phoenician control.[138] It was apparently another royal fortress.[139] It was also the Mediterranean port of the Nabateans, whose caravans reached it from Elath on the Red Sea, or from Petra across the desert. The Qedarite Arabs also had possession of the coast between Gaza and Ienysus,[140] but without a harbour.

The administrative division of Palestine in the Persian period reflects the wisdom of Persian rule. Under the general supervision of the satrap at Damascus autonomous nations governed by native governors or dynasts, lived side by side with trading cities and royal fortresses, while around them, on the edge of the desert, roved nomad tribes, free allies of the King.[141]

---

[136] Perhaps even Straton I (370-358 B.C.)? cf. Honigmann, Pauly-Wissowa: *Realencylopädie* s.v. Sidon, c.1221; cf. also A.H.M. Jones; *Cities of the Eastern Roman Provinces,* 1937, p. 231.

[137] Clermont-Ganneau, *Archaeol. Researches,* II, p. 79.

[138] According to Iliffe, *QDAP,* III, pp. 132-135, Gaza was the Mediterranean outlet of the Nabatean caravans from Elath, and the plenty of Attic sherds found at Tell Jemme, and south of it down to Tell el Kheleifi on the Red Sea, show that the Greco-Nabatean commerce went both ways (Iliffe, *QDAP,* II, p. 15ff.); Gaza was also the first city in Palestine to abandon the Phoenician standard of coinage and adopt the Attic (Hill, *Brit. Museum Catal.,* Palestine, p. XXXV).

[139] Arrian II, 25, 4; cf. Galling, *PJb,* 1938, p. 78; Abel, *RB,* 1935, p. 48.

[140] Herodotus III, 5, "from Cadytis (Gaza) . . . the marts upon the coast till you reach Jenysus are the Arabian King's."

[141] *Ibid.,* III, 88; The Arabians were never subject as slaves to the Persians, but had a league of friendship with them.

Chapter II

THE BEGINNINGS OF THE HELLENISTIC PERIOD; PTOLEMAIC RULE

THE brief sojourn of Alexander in Palestine in 332 and 331 was a hurried one and he was unable to make any substantial change in the administrative arrangements he had inherited from the Persians. Alexander's only significant measure was the replacement of the Persian satrap at Damascus by a Macedonian; Alexander's veteran general Parmenio was the first ruler of Syria.[1] His successor Andromachus (for whom see below, p. 36) was followed by Menon, son of Cardimas, who was succeeded by Ariames and then Asclepiodorus. At the same time Koiranes was placed in charge of the revenues of Syria. In 328 Asclepiodorus was replaced by Bessus.

In the course of the wars between Alexander's successors the country passed several times from one hand to another. The day-to-day administration certainly continued in its old routine. Only the titles of the rulers were changed into Greek. This is reflected in the assembly convened by Antigonus Monophtalmus of "the Kings and the hyparchs (i.e. governors) of Syria."[2] With the reestablishment of Ptolemaic rule in 301 B.C., a period of relative political stability began.

The northern boundary of the Ptolemaic possessions in Asia has been much disputed.[3] It is certain, however, that the whole of Palestine was in their hands. In order to understand the principles of Ptolemaic rule outside Egypt, it is necessary to keep in mind the general character of their kingdom.[4] It was by nature conservative, for the supreme aim of the

---

[1] H. Berwe, *Das Alexanderreich,* 1926, pp. 258, 315; cf. *ib.,* pp. 76, 114, 167, 213, 441, 484, 514.

[2] Diodorus XIX, 58, 1.

[3] Polybius V, 45, 7-8; 46, 2; 68, 7-8; cf. Tscherikover, *Mizraim,* IV-V, 1937, pp. 32-36; Kahrstedt, *Syrische Territorien,* pp. 20-24.

[4] W.W. Tarn, *Hellenistic civilization*[2], 1930 p. 179f.

Ptolemies' policy was to preserve their rule in Egypt against the rival Hellenistic powers of Macedonia and Syria. To keep the status quo at all costs was the guiding principle of the Ptolemies—and they followed it even when their rule extended beyond the Nile Valley into the Mediterranean islands and the Asian mainland. Palestine was in their eyes an external bulwark, protecting Egypt on its vulnerable eastern side. The rule of the first Ptolemies was at one and the same time energetic and cautious, orderly and bureaucratic, concerned first and foremost with its own security. With this aim in view, the Ptolemies created a strong army; while a strong navy was even more vital to guarantee their sea-power and assure them against hostile incursions. Such instruments of policy were costly; hence the constant pre-occupation of the Ptolemies with money matters. The spread of Hellenism in the territories under their rule was a matter of secondary importance. They founded relatively few Greek colonies, but accorded many existing communities a Greek name and some of the rights of a Greek city. The area under Ptolemaic rule in Asia was comparatively small, but it was easily defensible. They did not, it seems, entrust it to a governor-general similar in function to the Persian satrap of Eber-nahara, but governed it from Alexandria.[5] Special offices were set up there for this purpose. The most important of these was probably the supervisor of "the revenues of Syria and Phoenicia" (*tas kata Syrian kai Phoinikēn prosodous*) who seems also to have resided in the capital. His title has been preserved in a tax-decree of Ptolemy II.[6] The whole area under Ptolemaic rule in Asia was officially called Syria and Phoenicia[7] but in common usage there prevailed the unofficial 'Coelesyria.'[8]

A first-hand source concerning the state of things in Palestine under Ptolemaic rule are the papyri from the archives of Zenon. Zenon, a native of Caunos in Caria, was a high official in the service of Apollonius, the finance minister of Ptolemy II. He visited Palestine in 260-58 B.C., and

[5] Tscherikover, *op cit.* (n. 3 above), p. 39.

[6] Pap. PER, Inv. No. 24, 552 gr.; Liebesny, *Aegyptus,* 16, 1936, p. 259ff.

[7] Ib.

[8] Kahrstedt, *Syrische Territorien,* pp. 12, 20-21; Galling, *ZDPV,* 61, 1938, pp. 85-87; Bickerman, RB, 1947, pp. 257-261.

his letters and accounts contain much information on the state of the country at that time.[9] Another important source is the tax-edict mentioned above, dating from the time of Ptolemy II. The fragmentary accounts of the campaigns of Antiochus III in Palestine refer to the various administrative centres in the last quarter of the third cenury B.C.[10]

The Egyptian unit of administration was the *nomos*, which was subdivided into smaller units, called *topos*. These in their turn consisted of groups of villages.[11] A similar system of administrative nomenclature was used in the Ptolemaic possessions in Asia. It was there adjusted to the earlier (Persian) usage in those parts. The primary unit was a *hyparchy*,[12] which corresponded to the Persian province (*medinah*). It was subdivided into secondary units called *toparchy* which paralleled the former district (*pelekh*).[13] The latter consisted, as before, of groups of villages. The Greek colonies established within a hyparchy seem to have remained within its administrative framework. They were not exempted from its jurisdiction, unless granted the special status of a *polis*. The Ptolemies were, however, notoriously wary of granting autonomous rights to the cities under their control.

Another typical tendency of a strongly centralized government can be observed in the Ptolemaic administration of Palestine: the big units were split into smaller ones. (Small districts are less independent and easier to govern from a centre).

Each of the Ptolemaic districts formed an economic unit as well. Beside the governor (*hyparchus*) resided the oeconomus who dealt with economic matters, in particular the collection of taxes and of goods for the royal monopolies. A third official on the spot was in charge of the police. All these were Greeks.[14] The ruler of a village, the comarch was, of course, a native.[15] This type of administrative structure is attested for

---

[9] Vincent, *RB*, 1920, p. 182f; Abel, *RB*, 1923, p. 409ff; 1924, p. 566ff.; 1927, p. 145f., 475f.

[10] Polybius V, 70, 71; Josephus, *Ant.*, 12:3:3-136.

[11] W.W. Tarn, *JHS*, 1926, p. 129.

[12] Liebesny, *op. cit.* (n. 6 above), p. 266.

[13] In Seleucid official documents the toparchy is sometimes called by the Egyptian term *nomos*, cf. 1 Macc. 10: 30; 11: 57, etc.

[14] Cf. Liebesny, *op. cit.* (n. 6 above); Tscherikover, *op. cit.* (n. 3 above), pp. 41-42.

[15] Liebesny, *op. cit.*, p. 267.

Idumaea. In districts where there was a tradition of native rule, more latitude was allowed, in the case of Judaea under the high-priests, the territory of the Tobiads beyond the Jordan, and various tribal areas.

One of the hyparchies of Coele-Syria was *Judaea,*[16] although its name does not appear in the extant official documents. Its area was already so small that no changes were made in its boundaries. The Ptolemies seem to have left more or less intact the autonomy granted by the Persians. A coin found at Beth-zur is stamped on the reverse with the name of the province *Yhd* and the personal name Hezekiah (*Hzqyh*);[17] it has been assumed that this was the Ezechias mentioned by Hecataeus (quoted by Josephus)[18] as "chief priest" (*archiereus*) of the Jews, who followed Ptolemy I into Egypt and encouraged his countrymen to do likewise. No such high priest appears on the list given by Josephus at the end of his *Antiquities.*[19] Nor is he to be found in the various references to the holders of this office scattered throughout his works.[20] We are obliged to follow Thackeray and Marcus[21] in assuming that *archiereus* in this particular case was *a* high priestly official, an associate of *the* High Priest. Ezechias might have been the chief financial officer (*dioikētēs*) who put his name on the coins minted in Jerusalem.[21a] We know of another case in which a person other than the high-priest obtained a kind of chief magistracy (*prostasia*) of the people. This was Joseph the Tobiad in the time of the high priest Onias II.[22] The autonomous Jewish authority was also limited by the commander of the Egyptian troops garrisoning the

[16] Polybius XVI, 39, 1, 3 ; Josephus, *Ant.* 12:3:3-138, 141.

[17] O. Sellers, *The citadel of Beth-Zur,* p. 73; Galling, *PJb,* 1938, p. 76; Reifenberg, *Ancient Jewish Coins*², 1947, p. lf., 27; N. Avigad, *EIJ,* 7, 1957, pp. 148-149.

[18] *Against Apion* I, 187-189.

[19] XX, 234-251.

[20] Collected by R. Marcus in his translation of Josephus, Loeb ed. VII, p. 733; cf. also his note on *Antiq.* 12:1:1-9, where he follows Sellers in his reading "Jehohanan" for "Jehud" (*Yhd*).

[21] *Against Apion,* Loeb ed. I, p. 238, and *Antiq.* Loeb ed. Appendix B, p. 733;

[21a] N. Avigad, *IEJ,* 7, 1957, p. 148f.

[22] *Antiq.* 12:4:2-161; as against Marcus *ad loc.;* the decisive argument seems to be 2 Macc. 3:4, where a prostatēs tou hierou appears in opposition to the high priest. The influence of the Egyptian usage of appointing a civil administrator of temples should also be considered in this connection; in the eyes of the Greeks Judaea was a kind of temple estate, similar to the temple principalities of Asia Minor.

fortress (Acra) of Jerusalem,[23] who naturally exercised the military authority in this area.

The fate of the province of *Samaria* differed from that of Judaea in several respects. Judaea submitted to Alexander peacefully and accepted Ptolemaic rule without much difficulty.[24] The Samaritans revolted against Andromachus, the governor appointed by Alexander over Coelesyria and burnt him alive.[25] As a punishment Alexander (according to Curtius Rufus) or more probably the regent Perdiccas, took away their capital Samaria and founded there a colony of Macedonian veterans. The hyparchy of Samaria henceforth included two territorial units: the city of Samaria and the people (*ethnos*) of the Samaritans, whose religious (and probably also political) centre was the temple on Mount Gerizim.

North of Samaria extended the hyparchy of *Galilee.* This name appears for the first time in Greek in one of the Zenon papyri, in the form "Galila".[26] Under Ptolemaic rule the changes in this area surpassed even those made in Samaria. The town of Beth-Shan became a Greek settlement named Scythopolis.[27] It received an extensive territory and a great deal of autonomy.[28] It may also have served as administrative centre of the whole of Galilee, but it is possible that this centre had been established at the fortress on Mount Tabor, for Antiochus III later-on cap-

[23] This Acra, mentioned in connection with Antiochus' III capture of Jerusalem (*Antiq.* 12:3:3-138) is identical with the temple fortress (*Baris, ha-Birah* of Nehemiah 7:2) and distinct from the Acra erected in Jerusalem by the Seleucids at a later date (1 Macc. 1:35-38).

[24] Arrian II, 25,4; *Antiq.* 11:8:3/6-313/345. Ptolemy I captured Jerusalem by a stratagem on a sabbath and carried many citizens into Egypt; but Ptolemy II released them (Josephus, *Antiq.* 12:1:1-3-7; 2:3-26-28); the troubles under Ptolemy III (3 Macc.)—if historical—were transient. As a consequence the conservative Jews and the majority of the people seem to have favoured Ptolemaic rule, as against the Hellenizing aristocracy, who tended to the Seleucids.

[25] Curtius Rufus IV, 8,9; Eusebius: *Chronicon,* p. 197, 199; Hieronymus, *Chronicon,* p. 123, 128.

[26] W.L. Westermann and E.S. Hasenoehrl, *Zenon Papyri,* 1934. Pap. 2, p. 6-8.

[27] A.H.M. Jones, *op. cit.* (see Chap. I, n. 136 above), p. 242 and note 20. The Scythian invasion of 609 B.C. (A. Malamat, *IEJ,* 1, 1950-51, pp. 155-157) is a fact, but its connection with the name of Scythopolis (Syncellus, I, p. 405, ed. Bonn) is improbable, see M. Avi-Yonah, *IEJ,* 12, 1962, pp. 123-128.

[28] Josephus, *Ant.,* 12:4:5-183; Polybius V, 70—on the latter cf. Jones, *op. cit.* p. 449, n. 20 end.

tured a Ptolemaic commander there.[29] Hazor, in any case, had lost all its importance in the Hellenistic period. Its name only remained attached to a plain in Northern Galilee.[30] The Ptolemaic rulers naturally kept in their hands the royal estates in the Valleys of Jezreel, the Jordan and the Huleh,[31] which they had inherited from the former Kings (see above, p. 25).

In *Idumaea* things remained as before under Hellenistic rule. Diodorus, writing of the events at the end of the fourth century B.C., calls Idumaea once a satrapy and once an "*ep*archy."[32] The papyrus published by Liebesny[33] shows that the official name of a Ptolemaic district was *hyp*-archy. Diodorus mentions the Dead Sea as situated in the middle of Idumaea. He obviously refers to its geographical position in relation to the northern and southern limits of the province. An extension of Idumaea east of the lake is improbable.[34] It seems, however, that the capital of the hyparchy was transferred in Hellenistic times from Lachish to nearby Mareshah (Marissa), which contained a strong element of Hellenized Sidonians. Their family tombs show the extent to which Greek influences penetrated their family and religious life, usually the two spheres most resistant to alien cultures.[35] The existence of such Hellenized families must have rendered more agreeable the sojourn of the Greek officials stationed in Marissa. Zenon visited them and addressed to them several letters.[36] Another district centre was at Adoraim, the capital of Eastern Idumaea.[37]

The capital of the province of Ashdod was transferred to *Jamnia*

---

[29] Polybius V, 70, 3. The earlier assumption that Philoteria was an administrative centre of Galilee—based on Polybius' phrase tēn *hypotetagmenēn chōran tais* with its reference to Scythopolis and Philoteria—has been disproved by the fact that in ancient times the supposed site of Philoteria i.e. Beth Yerah (Kh.Kerak) was situated *east* of the Jordan, that is outside Galilee; see p. 138 below.

[30] 1 Macc., 11: 67.

[31] Alt, *PJb*, 1937, pp. 81, 84, 86.

[32] Diodorus XIX, 95, 2 ; 98, 1.

[33] *Aegyptus* 16, 1936, p. 266.

[34] Diodorus *loc. cit.*

[35] Thiersch and Peters, *The Painted Tombs of Marissa*, 1905; *OGIS*, 593.

[36] *Pap. Zenon*, Cairo 59006, 59015, 59537.

[37] *Ibid.*, 59006.

(Hebrew Yabneh), where it remained in Seleucid times.[38] Ashdod (Azotus) apparently declined subsequently, in favour of its epineion, Azotus Paralius (Ashdod-yam). We learn from Zenon's letters that a frontier guard (*horophylax*) was stationed at Pegae.[39] He probably supervised the boundary between the district of Jamnia, that of Samaria (which reached down to the Sharon Plain) and the Sidonian properties in the lands of Joppe.

The coastal plain underwent a thoroughgoing reorganization in Ptolemaic times. At the beginning of their rule, the holdings of the Phoenician cities seem indeed to have been respected, and in some cases even extended, as we learn from the epitaph of Eshmunezer King of Sidon. According to this the 'Lord of the Kings, (*adôn melakhim*) had given him "Dor and Iafo, wide wheat lands in the field of Sharon" in the measure of the great deeds which he had done. They were "added to the boundaries of the lands to belong to the Sidonians for ever."[40] The date of this inscription has been much disputed.[41] At first sight it seems to fit the extension of Phoenician rule over the whole coast in Persian times, of which we learned from Ps.-Scylax. On the other hand, the title 'Lord of the Kings 'appears many times in Semitic epigraphy, and always in connection with the Ptolemies.[42] The Persian Kings, on the other hand, were called "King of Kings" (*malkâ di malkayâ*).[43] We may assume, therefore, that the earlier Ptolemies still favoured the Phoenician cities. A change of policy came only with the consolidation of Ptolemaic rule over Palestine and Phoenicia, when the local dynasties were allowed to die out gradually. The line of Sidonian Kings, re-established in the time of Alexander, came to an end in 278 B.C.[44] Tyre became a republic in 274 B.C.[45] Concurrently the Palestinian coast ceased to be subject to

[38] *Ibid.*, 59006 1. 63f.; *Ant.* 12:7:4,308.
[39] *Ibid.*, 59006 and *PSI,* 406.
[40] G.A. Cooke, *North Semitic Inscriptions,* 1903, p. 30ff.
[41] Ginsberg, *JBL,* 1937, p. 142 ; Lidzbarski, *Ephemeris,* I, p. 149; II, pp. 49-55.
[42] Cooke, *op. cit.* (n. 40) 10, 5 (222 B.C.), 27, 1 (254 B.C.), 29, 4 (132 B.C.).
[43] *Ib.*, 71, 3 (482 B.C.).
[44] Arrian II, 15, 6; Tarn, *JHS,* 1926, p. 158; cf. *IG* II, Suppl. No.1355 b.
[45] They began to date their inscriptions "in the year of the people of Tyre". Cooke, *op. cit.* (n. 40 above) p. 47.

Phoenician rule. Ascalon was emancipated from Tyre before 318 B.C.[46] Only Accho (which from ca. 261 B.C. was renamed Ptolemais and kept this name till the end of antiquity) remained connected with the province of Phoenicia.[47] South of Ptolemais, a new hyparchy was apparently created in the Sharon, reviving the Assyrian province of Dûrû. In this area were situated two cities, called on the Egyptian model Crocodilonpolis and Bucolonpolis.[48] The capital of the province was in all probability the Tower of Strato (later Caesarea), where Zenon landed in 259 B.C. and whence he proceeded directly to Jerusalem.[49] Dor was taken from the Sidonians and became a royal fortress.[50] Joppa became an autonomous harbour town, with a Ptolemaic mint coining money there.[51] Gaza[52] and Ascalon certainly had the same status. Thus, the Phoenician rule over the coast came to an end in the Ptolemaic period; their former possessions became a series of autonomous cities. This change was in conformity with the policy of the Ptolemies to split up the great territorial units into a series of small areas. The Hellenized coastal cities remained loyal to the Kings of Egypt and helped them to consolidate their sea-power. The ancient rivalry between Greeks and Phoenicians ended in a Greek victory. Paradoxically, however, the victors exercised their power from the former bases of their enemy, with whom they now joined forces.

The process of splitting up the larger administrative units and the establishment of Greek colonies found more favourable ground east of the Jordan. There was less density of settlement in this area than west of the river. A. H. M. Jones has suggested that the districts whose name ends in *-itis* (the ending common in the names of the Egyptian nomes) were set-up in Ptolemaic times.[53] Such names are most common east of the Jordan. If we accept this plausible suggestion, then the Assyrian-Persian

---

46 Cf. the inscriptions of an Ascalonite, *ib.*, p. 93.

47 Diodorus XIX, 93, 7; Hill, *Brit.Mus.Cat. Greek Coins, Phoenicia,* p. lxxviii.

48 Strabo XVI, 2, 27; Plinius, *Nat. hist.*, V, 18 ; see above, p. 29.

49 *Pap. Zenon,* Cairo 59004.

50 1 Macc. 15: 11-14; *Ant.* 13:7:2-224; *War*-1:2:2-50.

51 Hill, *BMC Palestine,* p. xxiv; Diodorus XIX, 93, 7.

52 Hill, *op. cit.*, p. xxiv.

53 *Op. cit.* (Chap.1, n. 136 above) pp. 241, 448-9.

governorates must have been split up into smaller areas under the Ptolemies. This was effected sometimes by the division of one administrative unit into two provinces. In other cases the foundation of a Greek city led to the diminution of a former unit by its territory. We find accordingly that the province of the Hauran was now divided into the districts of Trachonitis[54] and Auranitis,[55] Karnaim into Bataneia (biblical Bashan),[56] Gaulanitis (the biblical Golan)[57] and the territory of the city of Dium (Tell Âshtari),[58] which was founded by Alexander (?) or, more likely, Perdiccas.[59] The former province of Gilead was diminished by the separation of the city lands of Pella (now Tabaqât Fâhil), which was for some time called Berenice[60] and of Gerasa (now Jerash), the foundation of which was also attributed to Alexander.[61] The reduced district of Gilead, now called Galaaditis,[62] had its capital at Gadara (Umm Keis).[63] Abila (Tell Âbil) also remained with its boundaries.[64] The city of Philadelphia ('Ammân) was made independent of Tobiad rule.[65] The remaining lands of the Tobiads were consolidated into a separate territorial unit with a predominantly Jewish population. Its capital was at the castle of Tyrus ('Irâq-el-Âmîr), which Zenon calls the Birtha of the Ammonitis.[66] Here a military colony was formed by the Tobiads under the protection of the Ptolemaic kings and on the model of their cleruchies, with a mixed population of Persians, Macedonians and

---

54 *Ant.* 16:9:2-285 etc.

55 *Ib.,* 15:10:1-343 etc.; Zenon Pap. *PSI,* No. 406.

56 Polybius V, 71, 2.

57 *Ant.,* 13:15:4-396.

58 Steph. Byz. s.v. *Diōn;* Abel, *Géographie,* II, p. 306f.

59 V. Tscherikover, *Die hellenistischen Städtegründungen,* 1927, p. 26.

60 Steph.Byz. s.v. *Berenike;* Tscherikover, *op. cit.,* p. 75ff.

61 Steph.Byz. s.v. *Gerasa; Etym. magn.* s.v. *Gerasēnos;* Tscherikover, *op. cit.,* p. 67.

62 1 Macc. 25:6-13; *Ant.* 12:8:1-330; 13:6:6-209.

63 Polyb. V, 71, 2.

64 *Ibid.*

65 Eusebius, *Onomasticon* (ed. Klostermann), p. 16.

66 Pap. Zenon, Cairo, No. 59003; *Ant.,* 12:4:9-222; Syncellus, I, p. 558 ; cf. B. Mazar, *IEJ,* 7, 1957; for the ruins Lapp, *Basor,* 165, pp. 16-34; 171, pp. 8-55.

Jews.[67] South of the Tobiad principality were two new districts: Moabitis[68] and Gabalitis,[69] possession of which was disputed between the Ptolemies and the Nabataeans. The latter remained independent in Ptolemaic times and all attempts to subdue them came to naught.[70] However, they temporarily lost the port of Elath, which became Ptolemaic under the name of another Berenice.[71]

67 Pap. Zenon, Cairo, No. 59003; 2 Macc. 4:26-27. In *Ant.* 12:4:11-233, Josephus states that the Birtha of the Tobiads was not far from 'Essebonitis', i.e. the district of Heshbon. However, in *Ant.* 13:15:4-397, we find Heshbon listed among the cities of Moabitis. It seems, therefore, that we should correct in *Ant.* XII to Esebôn (the city).

68 *Ant.* 13:14:2-382; 13:15:4-397; Syncellus, I, p. 558.

69 *Ant.* 18:5:1-113 (corrected from Gamalitis).

70 Diodorus Siculus XIX, 97-98.

71 *Ant.* 8:6:4-163.

Chapter III

PALESTINE AS PART OF THE SELEUCID KINGDOM

IN 302 B.C. the year preceding the battle of Ipsus, a coalition directed against Antigonus Monophthalmus, was made between Ptolemy I, Seleucus I Nicator and Lysimachus. According to the coalition agreement, Palestine was to fall to Seleucus, but after the allies' victory at Ipsus, Ptolemy refused to hand it over. Seleucus I did not wish to fight his old comrade in arms, and acquiesced in the *status quo*. He reserved his rights, however, considering Palestine his lawful possession. His successors were naturally less scrupulous. In consequence, the country became an apple of discord between four generations of Seleucids and Ptolemies. Almost the whole of the third century B.C. was filled with wars between the rival dynasties. Four Syrian wars (276-272, 260-255, 246-241 and 221-217 B.C.) were fought and still the Ptolemies kept their grip on the country. Finally, Antiochus III succeeded in beating the Egyptian army at Paneas in 198 B.C. and in occupying the whole of the disputed area. His rule and the rule of his dynasty continued (in theory at least) for nearly a century, i.e. till 104 B.C.

The new dynasty ruled over a much greater area than their predecessors. The Seleucid administration could not, therefore, be as close-meshed as that of the Ptolemies. The Seleucids in fact continued the Persian system of satrapies. Their kingdom was divided into large provinces, which contained many and varied subdivisions. Such were the 'Kings, dynasts, towns and peoples,' whom Seleucus II addressed in his letter, preserved on stone.[1] Huge as it was, the Seleucid empire was yet smaller than the Persian. The Achaemenids ruled over 'an hundred and seven and twenty provinces'; the Seleucids over only seventy-two "satrapies."[2]

The difference between Ptolemaic and Seleucid rule was, however, qualitative as well as quantitative. The Ptolemies were cautious and prudent, intent on consolidating their rule in Egypt and preserving things as

[1] *OGIS*, 229 (I, p. 336).
[2] Appianus, *Syr.* 62.

they were. The Seleucids, on the other hand, felt themselves the heirs of Alexander the Great. Their task was to unite the peoples of Asia under the aegis of Hellenic culture. They looked for support in this policy to the Greek and Hellenized cities of their realm. Consequently, the kings made great efforts to multiply cities as much as possible, to develop in them the ideals of the Greek polis. With this aim in view, they were prepared to grant the cities a great deal of autonomy. In return, these cities were the most loyal supporters of their rule.

Our evidence for Ptolemaic administration is derived to a great extent from first-hand sources, viz. the papyri. As regards the Seleucids, a few documents on parchment have been preserved,[3] but they are as naught compared with the vast mass of papyri. We have to rely, therefore, mostly on secondary sources. Another difficulty in evaluating the Seleucid administration lies in the political circumstances of the period. A short time after its annexation of Palestine, the Seleucid Kingdom began to decline and then to fall apart. In the course of its disintegration the instruments of government, including the administrative arrangements, changed with great rapidity. It is very difficult now to follow these changes, especially if one has to distinguish between measures intended to last and those taken provisionally to meet a transient situation. A third source of confusion is the excessive use of the title *strategus* to designate officers of various kinds. Its original meaning is 'officer' or 'commander.' In the administrative terminology of the Seleucids, however, it stands sometimes for a viceroy, ruling over half the kingdom. In other cases 'strategus' designates the ruler of a "strategia," a province corresponding to the Persian satrapy. Occasionally the term designates the governor of an *eparchy* (the substitute for a Persian *medinah* i.e. a secondary unit). From time to time it is used to describe a military commander without any civilian functions.[4] Because of the many meanings of this title, our sources often add to it some qualifying term. Thus we find a "strategus protarches,"[5]

---

[3] At Dura-Europos and Avroman, cf. Rostovtzeff & Welles, *Yale Classical Studies,* II, p. 43ff.

[4] 2 Macc. 12:2.

[5] 2 Macc. 10:11. There Lysias is called the strategus protarches of Coele-Syria and Phoenicia. From comparison with 1 Macc. 3:32 (a more reliable source) it appears that the competence of Lysias exceeded that of an ordinary provincial governor.

a "strategus and meridarches" i.e. the ruler of a *meris,* the subdivision of an ordinary "strategia" etc.

When Antiochus III conquered Palestine, his rule extended from Persia to the shores of the Aegean. The primary administrative units of this wide empire were correspondingly large. In times of crisis the Seleucid Kings entrusted all the lands 'beyond the river' to a viceroy 'from the river Euphrates to the borders of Egypt.'[6] This viceroy was entitled "strategus protarches," to raise him above the ordinary provincial governors. We know of two such viceroys within the period of Seleucid rule in Palestine: Lysias[7] and subsequently Bacchides.[8] Both were appointed to deal with an emergency resulting from the Maccabean revolt.

In times of peace the ordinary *strategia* was the principal unit of Seleucid administration. This was a large unit. Its proportion to the whole Seleucid kingdom corresponded to that of a satrapy to the Persian empire. Thus, all Syria was one strategia, called 'Seleucis.'[9] After conquering the Ptolemaic provinces in Asia, Antiochus III formed them into a new *strategia,* calling it 'Coelesyria and Phoenicia.'[10] Here the name Coelesyria appears for the first time in official terminology. Various authors had, indeed, used it before,[11] but the official name of the Ptolemaic possessions was (as we have already seen) 'Syria and Phoenicia.'[12] The Ptolemies ruled over only this part of Asia, and hence used the general term 'Syria' which sounded better. The Seleucids, however, had been the possessors of the real 'Syria' for over a century. They therefore found more useful to add the qualifying adjective 'Coele-' 'the hollow,' in order to distinguish the newly-won province from their earlier possessions. Our sources give six names of governors of this province: Ptolemy son of

---

[6] 1 Macc. 3:32.

[7] 1 Macc. 3:32; Ant. 12:7:2-295.Cf. also n. 5 above.

[8] 1 Macc. 7:8. Josephus (*Ant.* 12:10:2-393) calls him by mistake "governor of Mesopotamia"; cf. R. Marcus note *ad loc.* (Loeb ed. VII, p. 205, n.c).

[9] Strabo, *Geographica,* XVI, 2, 21.

[10] 2 Macc. 3:5; 4:4; 8:8.

[11] Bickermann, *RB,* 1947, pp. 261-3.

[12] PER Inv. 24.552 g; Liebesny, *Aegyptus,* 16, 1936, pp. 258-9.

Thraseas, 'strategus and priest' in the time of Antiochus III;[13] Apollonius son of Thraseas[14] and Apollonius son of Mnestheus,[15] both under Seleucus IV; Seron[16] and Ptolemy[17] in the reign of Antiochus IV Epiphanes, and Apollonius (Daus?), who was nominated by Demetrius II.[18] We should perhaps add Lasthenes the Cretan, to whom Demetrius II addressed his edicts.[19]

The *strategia* of Coele-Syria and Phoenicia was in its turn divided into a number of provinces called *eparchia,* parallel to the Persian *medinah* or *pahati.*[20] This is the administrative unit that Appianus[21] refers to when he says that the Seleucid ruled over seventy-two 'satrapies.' Any of the larger units would not make up this number, even at the time when the Seleucid kingdom reached its greatest extent. Diodorus Siculus sometimes calls Idumaea an eparchy and sometimes a satrapy.[22] As we shall see, the eparchy was also occasionally called a *meris* i.e. a subdivision, 'part' of a strategia.

According to Strabo[23] the whole of Coele-Syria was divided into four 'satrapies' (i.e. eparchies). However, we seem to be able to identify four eparchies in Palestine alone. Strabo apparently excludes from the divisions of 'Coele-Syria' Phoenicia and the eparchy of 'Coele-Syria' in the restricted sense, which included Damascus and the Valley between the Lebanon and the Anti-Lebanon. It formed part of the *strategia* of Coele-Syria in the larger sense, together with the five other eparchies of this province.

The Seleucids thus tended to create large-sized administrative units. They combined several Ptolemaic *hyp*archies into one single *ep*archy.

---

[13] *OGIS* 230 (I, p. 376).
[14] 2 Macc. 3:5.
[15] Ib., 4:4.
[16] 1 Macc. 3:13; *Ant.* 12:7:1-288.
[17] 2 Macc. 8:8.
[18] 1 Macc. 10:69; *Ant.* 13:4:3-88.
[19] Ant. 13:4:9-126 and Marcus' note *ad loc.* in the Loeb edition.
[20] Cf. Tarn. *Proced. Brit. Acad.,* 16, 1930, pp. 125-135.
[21] *Syr.* 62.
[22] Diodorus XIX, 95, 2; 98, 1.
[23] *Geogr.* XVI, 2, 4.

The Seleucid eparchies in Palestine were four in number:[24] Samaria, Idumaea, Paralia (the coastal plain) and Galaaditis. All the other provinces, which may possibly have retained their former designation of hyparchy,[25] were reduced to tertiary units from their previous status of secondary ones.

JUDAEA was one of these; it was now subject to the authority of the *eparchos* residing at Samaria. This would explain what happened at the beginning of the Maccabaean revolt. In 167 B.C. the rising, which had started at Modiin near Lydda, had spread all over Judaea. The first commander to march against the insurgents was not, however, the governor of that province. It was one Apollonius, who led against Israel—in the Biblical phraseology of the First Book of Maccabees—"the Gentiles" (*ethnē*) "and a great force from Samaria,"[26] the latter phrase recalling the 'army of Samaria' of Sanballat.[27] One could presume that the intervention came from Samaria for these two reasons: 1) the place where the revolt originated (Modiin in the district of Lydda),[28] and 2) the place to which the insurgents had fled (the mountains of the district of Gophna)[29] was situated within the district of Samaria. However, Josephus in his parallel account definitely calls Apollonius governor (*stratēgos*) of Samaria.[30] He is probably identical with Apollonius the meridarch, who is mentioned in a letter of the Samaritans (the 'Sidonians in Sichem,' as they called themselves) to King Antiochus IV,[31] but hardly with Apollonius the Mysarch, the commander of the Mysian guard.[32] The fact that the next Seleucid official to advance against the Jews was the governor of Coele-Syria in person[33] also seems to show that the de-

[24] See p. 34.
[25] Tarn (*op. cit.* n. 20 above), n. 95.
[26] 1 Macc. 3:10.
[27] Neh. 4:2.
[28] For the much later transfer of Lydda to Judaea see below, p. 55f.
[29] The district of Aphaerema, subsequently that of Gophna, was transferred at the same time as that of Lydda. Josephus (*War* 1:1:5-45) mentions anachronistically the Gophanitice in the time of Judas Maccabaeus.
[30] *Ant.* 12:7:1-287.
[31] 12:5:5-261.
[32] Cf. 2 Macc. 5:24; contra R. Marcus *ad loc.* in the Loeb edition VII, p. 248, note e.
[33] 1 Macc. 3:13.

feated governor of Samaria was his immediate substitute. The officers residing in Jerusalem, who took no active part in the fighting, were two. One of them was Philippus the superintendent (*epistatēs*),[34] i.e. a royal commissioner sent there on special duty dealing with Temple affairs. The other was the military commander in Jerusalem, one Sostrates, who was the governor of the citadel.[35]

As the fighting progressed, the need was felt to raise the status of the province of Judaea. It was apparently considered necessary to entrust the rebellious province to a special officer, releasing the eparch of Samaria from the double duty of administering his province and fighting the rebels.[36] Judaea was therefore raised to the rank of an eparchy. Its first governor was Nicanor.[37] He was defeated twice and finally killed by Judas Maccabaeus. His successor, Bacchides, was a viceroy with extended powers over all Trans-Euphratene;[38] his authority naturally superseded that of a mere provincial governor. After Bacchides' departure there is a gap of several years. Finally Jonathan the Hasmonaean, the brother of Judas Maccabaeus, was appointed in 150 B.C. governor of Judaea[39] two years after his appointment as high priest.[40] At that time the disintegration of the Seleucid Kingdom was already far advanced. Jonathan was *de facto* an independent ruler, who oscillated from one pretender to the throne to the other. Yet throughout this stormy period the official boundaries of Judaea underwent no change. Jewish settlements continued to extend in the districts of Apharaema, Lydda (Lod), and Ramathaim (Arimathaea). Without being formally attached to Judaea, they were closely bound to the national sanctuary at Jerusalem. As is usual in border regions, their religious and national zeal exceeded that of the inhabit-

---

[34] 2 Macc. 5:22.

[35] 2 Macc. 4:28.

[36] A similar phaenomenon could be observed in Roman times. As one revolt in Judaea followed another, the province was gradually raised from a procuratorial to a praetorial, and from that to a consular one; cf. below, pp. 110, 114.

[37] 2 Macc. 14:12.

[38] 1 Macc. 7:8.

[39] 1 Macc. 10:65.

[40] Ibid., 21.

ants of the interior. The Maccabean revolt broke out in Modiin, which formally did not belong to Judaea at all.

The eparchy of SAMARIA (or Samaritis)[41] also included Galilee. This we learn from the passage in I Maccabees, according to which Demetrius II transferred to the Judaea of Jonathan three toparchies from "Samaria and Galilee."[42] Josephus, paraphrasing this statement, adds in one place "Joppa"[43] and in another[44] "Peraea." Joppa (Jaffa) could have been part of the province in order to supply Samaria with an outlet to the sea. Peraea (the part of Trans-Jordan which formerly constituted the domain of the Tobiads) was attached to Samaria (together with Judaea) when the eparchy was first set up by Antiochus III. It remained under Samaria after Judaea became a separate eparchy. Apollonius, the adversary of Judas Maccabaeus,[45] is the only known governor of this province.[46]

South of Samaria (enlarged by Judaea) extended the eparchy of IDUMAEA.[47] Like Samaria, it was enlarged by the province of Jamnia (formerly Ashdod, cf. p. 27 above). Gorgias, who commanded the army against Judas Maccabaeus, is called strategos of Idumaea;[48] his command included Azotus and Jamnia, for after its defeat near Emmaus the Syrian army retreated to the plain of "Idumaea and Azotus and Jamnia."[49] The Hellenized city of Marissa was included in this province,[50] and the royal fortress of Gezer, a Seleucid strongpoint commanding the road to Jerusalem from the West. Here the army beaten at Emmaus first halted in its flight.[51] Nicanor's army fleeing from Adasa, north of Jerusalem, also

---

[41] 1 Macc. 10:38; 11:28, 34.
[42] 1 Macc. 10:30.
[43] *Ant.* 13:4:9-125.
[44] Ib. 13:2:3-50.
[45] 1 Macc. 3:10.
[46] He appears also as "Apollonius the meridarch" in the Samaritan petition to Antiochus IV, as quoted by Josephus *Ant.* 12:5:5-261, 264; 12:7:1-287.
[47] Diodorus XIX, 95, 2.
[48] 2 Macc. 12:32.
[49] 1 Macc. 4:15; *Ant.* 12:7:4-308.
[50] 2 Macc. 12:35.
[51] 1 Macc. 4:15.

directed its march towards Gezer.[52] Gezer seems to have been connected particularly with Azotus.[53] Possibly it had been already included in the Persian province of Ashdod.

In the coastal plain the same system of unification of several smaller units into a larger one was pursued. The various coastal cities were combined into one eparchy, PARALIA, "the sea-coast." This extended from the "Ladder of Tyre to the border of Egypt."[54] We know of three governors of this eparchy: Hegemonides,[55] who ruled "from Ptolemais to Gerar (?)," Simon the Hasmonaean[56] and Cendebaeus the "viceroy" (*epistratēgos*) of the Paralia under Antiochus VII Sidetes.[57] We first hear of this province in the time of Antiochus V. It is thus possible that it was only created during the Maccabaean revolt in order to put the coastal cities under one governor. The province was cut in two by the territories of Joppa, Jamnia and Azotus. These belonged to Samaria and Idumaea respectively.[58] It continued with the lands of Ascalon and Gaza. Dora was a royal fortress in this province.[58a]

Beyond the Jordan several Ptolemaic provinces were also joined by the Seleucid Kings into one eparchy, called GALAADITIS from the name of one of the units composing it. The greater extension of Seleucid Gilead (in comparison with the territory so called in biblical and Ptolemaic times) is evident from I Maccabees. Judas Maccabaeus captured several cities in what is called Gilead,[59] or Galaaditis.[60] The cities he conquered are, however, all situated in the Gaulanitis and the Batanaea.[61] Timotheus, who apparently was governor of the eparchy of Galaaditis

---

[52] I Macc. 7:45. The Andronicus who commanded at Garazin' while Philippus governed Jerusalem (2 Macc. 5:23) was probably a commander of the fortress of Gezer; cf. the version *Garazan* for *Gazaran* in 1 Macc. 14:34.

[53] 1 Macc. 14:34.

[54] 1 Macc. 11:59; *Ant.* 13:5:4-146.

[55] 2 Macc. 13:24 has *Gerrēnōn,* apparently for *Gerrarēnōn* a reminiscence of the biblical boundaries of Canaan in Gen. 10:19.

[56] Cf. n. 54 above.

[57] 1 Macc. 15:38.

[58] See above, p. 48.

[58a] See 1 Macc. 15:25.

[59] 1 Macc. 5:9.

[60] Ib., 20, 26, 27, 37, 45.

[61] Ib., 26.

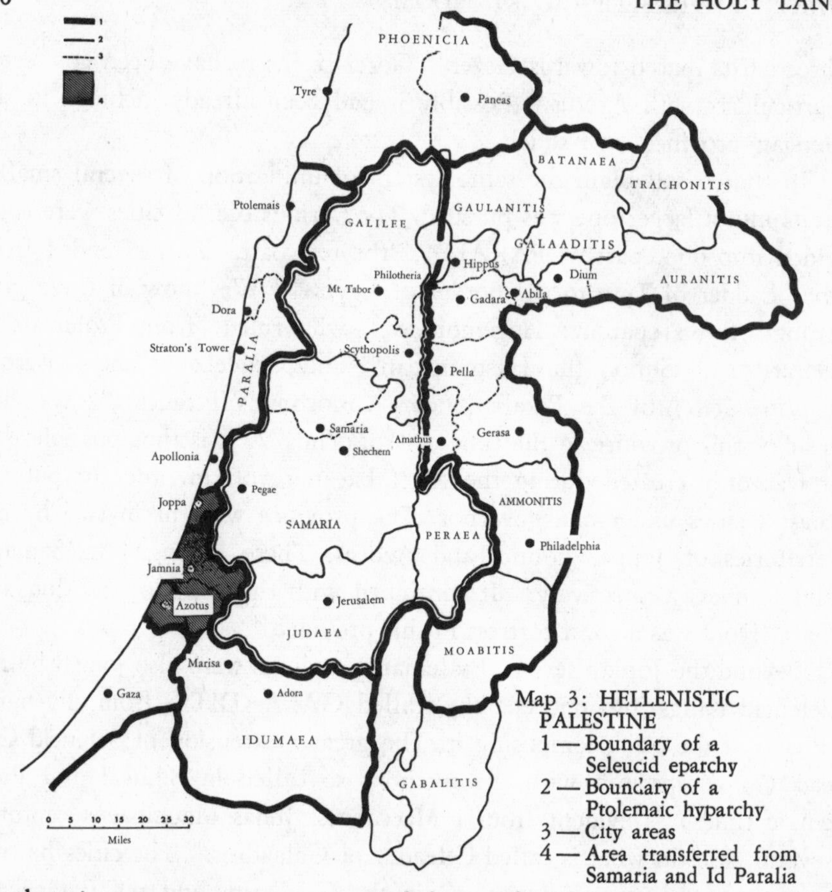

Map 3: HELLENISTIC PALESTINE
1 — Boundary of a Seleucid eparchy
2 — Boundary of a Ptolemaic hyparchy
3 — City areas
4 — Area transferred from Samaria and Id Paralia

at that time, appears at one time fighting at the head of the Ammonites[62] and then in the "Gilead"[63] i.e. the Gaulan, which was included in Greater Galaaditis.

The only part of Trans-Jordan not included in Seleucid Gilead was the domain of the Tobiads. At the accession of Antiochus IV, the last ruling member of this dynasty, Hyrcanus, committed suicide.[64] As we have seen above, this territory was attached to Samaria; perhaps because of its Jewish population it was made to share the fate of Judaea.

The situation in Southern Trans-Jordan remained fluid. The Arab

[62] 1 Macc. 5:6.
[63] Ib., 11.
[64] *Ant.* 12:4:11-236.

tribes on the border stayed under the authority of their phylarchs, who were either allied with, or were under the supervision of the governor of the province bordering the desert.[65]

The Seleucids were eager to foster city life in their territories. In or beside many of the older oriental cities they founded Hellenistic communities which formed separate political bodies. This happened at Jerusalem, where the inhabitants of the new Greek city, bordering on the old, received the name of Antiochenes.[66] In Ptolemais too, we find local "Antiochenes." No doubt the city was glad to adopt this additional appellation, which weakened the associations with the former régime evoked by its name.[67] In Gaza, too, we find a "Seleucid demos."[68] The people of Hippus called their city 'Antioch.'[69] In Galilee Scythopolis received the additional name Nysa, in honour of a princess of the Seleucid house from the time of Antiochus Epiphanes at which time it might officially have received the status of a *polis.*[70] Nysa happened to be also the name of the nurse of the god Dionysus and of the place where he was reared. The worship of Dionysus was therefore officially adopted by the city.[71] Another Antiochia was founded at Dan in the Northern Huleh.[72] Cities with royal names were especially plentiful beyond the Jordan. There was a Seleucia in the Gaulan[73] and another Seleucia at Abila.[74] Gadara became Antiochia Seleucia[75] and Gerasa was henceforth pompously known as "The city of the Antiochenes on the Chrysorrhoas, formerly the city of the Gerasenes."[76]

---

[65] 2 Macc. 8:32.

[66] 2 Macc. 4:9; ib., 19; cf. Tscherikower in *Tarbiz* XX, 1950, pp. 61-7 (Hebrew).

[67] Hill, *BMC Phoenicia,* pp. LXXIX, 129.

[68] *Ib., Palestine,* pp. LXIX, 143.

[69] B.V. Head: *Historia numorum,* p. 786.

[70] A.H.M. Jones: *Cities of the Eastern Roman Provinces,* p. 252; M. Avi-Yonah, *IEJ,* 12, 1962, p. 129.

[71] A. Rowe: *History and Topography of Beth-Shan,* p. 44f.

[72] Cf. the *antiochou pharanx* of *Ant.* 13:15:3-394, *War* 1:4:8-105, and apparently also of *Ant.* 17:2:1-24 in spite of the misleading 'Syria' Q as Vlatha (the Hule) is mentioned in the same passage, cf. Talmudic sources quoted *BJPES,* 10, pp. 19-20 (Hebrew).

[73] *Ant.* 12:15:3-393-4; *War* 1:4:8-105.

[74] Head, *op. cit.,* n. 69 above.

[75] Ib.

[76] Welles ap. C. Kraeling, ed.: *Gerasa,* 1938, p. 600.

Chapter IV

THE FORMATION OF THE HASMONAEAN KINGDOM

FOR about four hundred years after the Return from Exile the borders of Judaea remained static. During this long period of relative quiet forces were accumulating within the province which finally burst out in the second century B.C. The cruel challenge of religious persecution and the reaction following it were the propelling factors of expansion. The political constellation was especially favourable: the Seleucid Kingdom was collapsing under its own weight, while the Roman menace, which had threatened it since the loss of the battle of Magnesia in 188 B.C., became more and more evident. The magnitude of the task of Hellenizing Asia and defending their western border at one and the same time proved too much for the dynasty. The inward and outward conflicts found expression in a struggle between the two branches of the dynasty—the descendants of Seleucus IV and those of Antiochus IV. Their conflict favoured every disruptive force latent in the Kingdom, as well as every external enemy.

At the beginning of the Maccabean revolt, however, the Seleucid empire looked solid enough. The first twenty years of the struggle (167-147 B.C.) passed in *vigorous* combat, with many changes of fortune. During this period almost all the fighting took place within Judaea, only occasionally extending outside the province, into the coastal plain, Galilee, Gilead and other parts beyond the Jordan. The events described in the Books of the Maccabees prove that the borders of Judaea had not changed since the days of Nehemiah. Beth-Zur was still a border strongpoint facing Idumaea;[1] whoever came from these parts arrived at Beth-Zur on Judaean soil.[2] Adullam, which was situated in the district of Keilah, was

---

[1] 1 Macc. 24:33.

[2] Ib. 6:31;2; 9:29,61; 2 Macc. 11:5.

a Jewish city.[3] Hebron,[4] Adoraim,[5] Marissa,[6] Azotus,[7] Jamnia[8] and Joppa[9] were all Gentile, although there were Jewish communities in the two last-mentioned towns. Outside Judaea was the royal fortress of Gezer[10] and the districts of Lydda, Arimathaea in the West, and Apharaema in the North.[11]

We have yet another source for the boundaries of Judaea in the first period of the Hasmonaean revolt. This is the list of fortresses built by Bacchides to keep the country under control. This list as it stands, obviously requires some amendments. As found in our principal source, is contains the following seven place-names: Jericho, Emmaus, Beth-Horon, Bethel, Thamnatha, Pharathon and Tephos.[12] The first four names are certainly within the boundaries of Judah as outlined above. The other three places would, if we accept the usual identifications,[13] fall outside the boundaries of the province. These identifications are: 1) Thamnatha = Timnath Heres, now Kh. Tibne near Arimathaea; 2) Pharathon = biblical Pirathon = Far'atâ, 8 kms. WSW of Nablus;[14] 3) Tephos = biblical Tappuah = esh-Sheikh Abu Zared.[15] All these are outside the boundaries of Judaea, and the two later, Fara'tâ and esh-Sheikh Zared, were never included in Judaea, not even in the days of its greatest extent. We have therefore to look for other possibilities: 1) Thamna(tha) = the Timnah of Judah, now Kh. et Tibbâne East of Beit Nattif,[16] in the district of Keilah; 2) Pharathon—in the Wadi

[3] 2 Macc. 12:38.
[4] 1 Macc. 11:65.
[5] 1 Macc. 13:20; *Ant.* 13:6:5-207.
[6] 1 Macc. 5:66 according to La and *Ant.* 12:8:6-353; (the SA variant *samarian* is certainly wrong; 2 Macc. 12:35.
[7] 1 Macc. 5:68; 16:10; *Ant.* 12:8:6-353.
[8] 2 Macc. 12:8-9.
[9] Ib., 12:3-4.
[10] 1 Macc. 19:34; cf. ib. 4:15; 7:45.
[11] See below p. 55f.
[12] 1 Macc. 9:50; *Ant.* 13:1:3-15-16.
[13] Abel, *RB,* 1925, pp. 202-205; Id., *Les Livres des Maccabées,* Paris, 1949, p. 172f.
R. Marcus in Loeb ed VII, p. 235, nn. c-h.
[14] Judges 12:15.
[15] Jos. 12:17; Abel, *RB,* 1936, pp. 103-112.
[16] Abel: *Géographie,* II, p. 481.

Farah, 8 kms. north-east of Jerusalem; the biblical Brook of Perath, the Valley of Pheretae of Josephus;[17] 3) as for Tephos, one prefers the version of "Tekoah" preserved in one of the MSS of Josephus.[18] The archaeological survey of Kh. et Tibbâne has not so far produced evidence of settlement in the Hellenistic period.[19] The two other sites were certainly inhabited at that time. The remains of a stronghold have been observed at Kh. Farah.[20] Tekoah was inhabited both in biblical and later times.[21] If we accept these corrections, we obtain a logical line of fortifications intended to protect the approaches to Jerusalem on all sides: Thamna on the south-west, Emmaus and Beth-Horon in the west, Bethel in the north, Pharathon in the north-east, Jericho in the east, Tekoah in the south-east and Beth-Zur (which is mentioned in a separate list in the same passage)[22] on the south. The Acra of Jerusalem and Gezer are also listed there separately. These three strongpoints constituted in the eyes of the Seleucid government royal fortresses separated from the rest of Judaea.[23]

The struggle for Judaea came to an end in 152 B.C. with the appointment of Jonathan the Hasmonaean as high-priest and de facto ruler of the province.[24] Two years later he was formally nominated governor of the *meris*.[25] Shortly afterwards he began to enlarge the boundaries of his province.

This process of enlargement went through three stages. In the first Judaea was still an autonomous province of the Seleucid Kingdom, not only in the eyes of the Syrian Kings, but also in the eyes of Jonathan himself. Territorial changes had therefore to be authorized by the kings and were effected by royal decree, usually for political reasons.

---

[17] Jerem. 13:4 (AV has wrongly: Euphrates); *War* 4:9:4-512.

[18] Marcus in Loeb ed. VII, p. 234, n. 10.

[19] *BIES*, 16, 1951, p. 51 (Hebrew). Z. Kallay has however remarked that this negative result does not prove that the site was uninhabited in earlier period (*ib.*, 17, 1952, p. 63f.).

[20] Abel: *Géographie*, II, p. 404, s.v. Para.

[21] Sütterlin, *PJb*, 1921, pp. 31-46; Beyer, *ZDPV*, 1931, p. 219.

[22] 1 Macc. 9:52.

[23] See p. 41 below.

[24] 1 Macc. 10:20-1.

[25] Ib., 65.

In the second stage (after 141 B.C.) Judaea was already an independent state. Its conquests were conquests *de facto,* which had to be confirmed by a peace treaty with the King formally ceding the disputed territories. During this period the Hasmonaeans occupied much territory when acting on behalf of one or another Seleucid pretender to the throne; the territory they could rightfully call their own grew but slowly.

The third stage began with the death in 129 B.C. of Alexander VII Sidetes. Thenceforth the various Seleucid Kings were almost powerless in Palestine, and the country relapsed into anarchy. Only a few cities remained loyal to the Kings until 104 B.C. The Hasmonaeans treated the various pretenders to the throne with the contempt they deserved.[26] The later conquests of John Hyrcanus I, Judah Aristobulus I, and Alexander Jannaeus were at once incorporated into Judaea by force of the fact itself.

The first increase of Judaean territory took place in 147 B.C. Alexander Balas then granted to Jonathan "Accaron (Ekron) and all its boundaries as 'distributed land' "(*klērodosia*).[27] It is by no means clear whether the land was granted to Jonathan in his private or his public capacity. However, the use of the terms *klērodosia* or *klērouchia* 'land for settlement'[28] show that this territory was meant to serve as land to be distributed among the dependents of the ruler of Judaea. We might therefore regard the transfer of territory as a private and not a political transaction, especially as both Judaea and Idumaea (from which Accaron was taken) remained, in theory at least, Seleucid provinces.

In the meantime, Hasmonaean rule extended *de facto* over the *nomes* of Lydda (Lod), Haramatha (Arimathaea), Apharaema and the Tobiad domains beyond the Jordan. These areas bordered Judaea on the west, north-west, north and east. They were apparently inhabited mainly by Jews, who joined the revolt as soon as they were able to do so, and

---

[26] *Ant.* 13:10:1-273-4.

[27] 1 Macc. 10:89.

[28] This is the term used by Josephus in the parallel *Ant.* 13:4:4-104. The description of the estate as a 'toparchy' is an anachronistic use of a term common in Josephus' time. The Books of the Maccabees use the term *nomos* when quoting official documents and toparchia only in descriptive passages.

who accepted the authority of its leaders. We should remember that Modiin itself, the home-town of Mathatias and his sons, was situated in the district of Lydda, and was thus formally outside Judaea.

The actual authority in these districts was exercised by Jonathan, although they were officially outside his province. This explains the remarkable fact that all the proposals and grants made by the Syrian Kings in connection with the transfer of Lydda, Haramatha and Apharaema to Judaea are couched in the past tense. If we consider only the final cession made by Demetrius II,[29] which was based on a formal request from the Jewish high priest,[30] we might assume that the past tense was meant to refer back to the proposals made at an earlier date by the reigning King's father, Demetrius I (even if these proposals were rejected by Jonathan at that time). But even the earlier offer, in which the three districts are mentioned for the first time in the Books of the Maccabees, speaks of the cession of the three districts as a thing already done (*apo tēs gēs Iouda kai apo tôn triôn nomôn tôn prostithemenôn autē*).[31] It seems clear therefore, that all these formal grants were only meant to give official sanction to a state of things already existing.

The final approval of this enlargement of Judaean territory is given in a declaration of Antiochus VI, the son of Alexander Balas. In this document the King confirms Jonathan in the high priesthood and the *four* nomes (*kai kathistēmi se epi tôn tessarôn nomôn*).[32] The identity of the fourth *nome*, which appears here for the first time, has been much discussed. Judaea itself can hardly have been called a *nome,*[33] for rule over Judaea was implied in the confirmation of Jonathan as high priest. Moreover, Judaea itself was composed of districts or *nomes* and would not be put on a level with its component parts. Josephus[34] expressly states in his parallel account that the four districts were attached to the "land of the Jews." Accaron was not considered a toparchy in those

[29] 1 Macc. 11:34.
[30] Ib., 28.
[31] Ib., 10:30.
[32] Ib., 11:57.
[33] G. Holscner: *Palästina in der persischen u.hellenistischen Zeit,* p. 74.
[34] *Ant.* 13:5:4-145.

days.[35] Acraba, which ultimately became a Jewish district, was as yet beyond the scope of their ambition.[36] The most likely assumption seems to be that by the fourth district our sources mean the district formerly ruled by the Tobiads, henceforward known as Jewish Peraea, the land "beyond" the Jordan eastwards.[37] In the days of Judas Maccabaeus and in the earlier years of Jonathan the Hasmonaeans had already defended the Jews settled there from their various enemies, viz. some Arab tribes and the Seleucid governors of the province.[38] Another proof of the early attachment of this territory to Judaea is the fact that in the time of John Hyrcanus I the very first conquest of that prince was the capture of Madaba and Samaga.[39] These two cities were situated beyond the Jordan at a considerable distance from the river. Yet our sources do not mention any fighting in the area between them and the Jordan. It seems clear, therefore, that at the beginning of Hyrcanus' reign the Hasmonaeans already had a bridge-head across the Jordan. This they could use as a base for further conquests. Jonathan's rule over Peraea must have been established *de facto* for some time before it was formally confirmed.

In the course of their expansion, the Jews did not only acquire extensive tracts inhabited by their own people. These annexations made possible further conquests as well as the protection of the area already in their possession. By the cession of Lydda and its territory they acquired a part of the coastal plain and a position straddling the important coastal highway, the *via maris.* This furnished a base for a further advance towards the sea. The districts of Haramatha and Apharaema added control of the north-western and northern approaches to the Judaean highland. By acquiring Peraea they crossed the Jordan and gained a bridgehead which could be widened if the occasion offered.

In 147 B.C. Jonathan and Simeon decisively defeated near Jamnia

---

35 U. Kahrstedt: *Syrische Territorien in hellenist. Zeit.*, p. 66.

36 Cf. Abel, *Géographie,* II, p. 135; id., *Les livres des Maccabées,* p. 216.

37 *War* 3:3:3-44/47 and many other passages.

38 1 Macc. 5:4-6; 9:36-42.

39 *Ant.* 13:9:1-255; *War.* 1:2:6-63.

the Syrian army led by Apollonius, the governor of Coele-Syria.[40] It was their first victory over a regular force trained in the Greek manner, and was won in the open plain. Hitherto the Jewish successes had been gained in the mountains, mostly by ambush or other sudden attack. Now at Jamnia the Syrian phalanx broke up, while Jewish troops stood firm under harassing cavalry charges. The Hasmonaean army thus became the strongest military factor in Palestine, and the feeling of superior strength henceforth inspired all of Jonathan's acts. He began to regard the whole of the Promised Land as his rightful inheritance. Enemies coming from outside should not by right be allowed to tread on it.[41] When the army of Demetrius threatened to invade Palestine, Jonathan fought them at Hamath in the Valley of the Orontes.

At the end of Jonathan's reign and at the beginning of the reign of Simeon occurred the first enlargements of Judaean territory which were not only made without asking the Syrian king's approval but were carried out directly against his will. The earlier of these territorial expansions were clearly meant to safeguard the borders of Judaea and to provide it with an outlet to the sea. The first occupation of Joppa was provisional.[42] The definite annexation of this harbour city, the possession of which was vital to Judaea, was carried out by Simeon at a time of threatening danger. Tryphon, the Syrian general, having taken Jonathan captive, was advancing against Judaea. It was important to secure the country from whatever enemies still lived in the territory held by the Jews. Therefore Jonathan, son of Absalom, the Hasmonean commander, expelled the non-Jewish population from Joppe and replaced them with his own people.[43] Thus Simeon "took Joppa for a harbour and made an outlet to the isles of the sea."[44]

The second conquest of the same period was the capture of Gezer, which dominated the road from the coast to Jerusalem.[45] Here too, the

---

[40] 1 Macc. 10:77-85.
[41] Ib., 12:25.
[42] Ib., 10:76.
[43] Ib., 13:11.
[44] Ib., 14:5.
[45] Ib., 13:43; 47-8.

Gentiles were expelled and the Seleucid fortress became Jewish, a military centre second only to the capital itself.[46]

The Kings of Syria naturally refused to acknowledge such encroachments upon their territory. At an opportune moment Antiochus VII Sidetes succeeded in forcing John Hyrcanus to pay tribute for Joppa and the other cities bordering Judaea.[47] The independence of Judaea, granted officially in 141 B.C., was however left untouched;[48] apparently it could not be undone.[49] Soon afterwards Hyrcanus tried to obtain from the Roman senate an acknowledgment of his rights to Joppa and Gezer, but in vain.[50]

The death of Antiochus VII Sidetes in 129 B.C. removed the last Seleucid King who was capable and energetic, and the agony of the Kingdom began. The kings and peoples who had formerly been subject to the Seleucids now declared their independence as a matter of course. The process even extended to single cities. The usual ways of marking such a declaration were the adoption of a new era (the "era of the people"), the abolition of the count by regnal years, the striking of silver coins and the cessation of minting with the royal image. By these means we can follow the separation from the Seleucid Monarchy of one city after another: Tyre in 125 B.C.[51] and Sidon in 111 (the beginning of a new era).[52] In the same year Ptolemais (Acre) dropped the title: 'The Antiochenes in Ptolemais.'[53] In Gaza the parallel title: 'the Seleucid demos in Gaza' disappeared between the years 112 and 103 B.C.[54] Ascalon began to mint silver coins in 111 B.C.[55] and adopted a new era in 104 B.C.[56] Small local rulers (tyrants in the Greek political terminology)

---

[46] Ib., 13:53; 16:19; for Simen's fortress there cf. R.A.S. Macalister: *Excavation of Gezer,* I, p. 217, Fig. 104.

[47] *Ant.* 73:8:3-246-47.

[48] 1 Macc. 13:41-2.

[49] In spite of the advice proffered to King Antiochus at the time, cf. Diodorus, xxxiv, 1.

[50] *Ant.* 13:9:2-261.

[51] Hill, *BMC Phoenicia,* pp. CXXXIII-V, 233ff.

[52] *Ib.,* pp. CV, 157f.

[53] *Ib.,* pp. LXXIX, 129.

[54] *Ib.,* p. 105.

[55] *Ib.*

[56] *Ib.,* pp. LXI-LXX, 143.

seized power in various other cities at the same time. Zenon Cotylas already ruled in Philadelphia in 134 B.C.;[57] he was succeeded by his son Theodorus.[58] A certain Zoilus governed before 104 B.C. the coastal cities of Dora and the adjacent Tower of Straton.[59]

Simultaneously two Arab nations began to expand and to encircle Palestine from the north and the south. In the north the *Ituraeans* occupied the slopes of Mount Hermon, the valley between the Hermon and the Lebanon and even part of the latter mountain. In this way they opened for themselves an outlet to the Mediterranean. Driving southwest, they occupied large areas south of Damascus and finally penetrated into the upper Jordan Valley and Galilee.[60] The *Nabataeans,* who had remained independent in their mountain fastnesses in Mount Seir, now spread northwards and westwards. Aretas II, King of the Arabs, ruled in the vicinity of Gaza.[61] Obodas, his successor, fought Alexander Jannaeus in the Gaulan or the Gilead.[62] Aretas III occupied Coele-Syria (in the reduced sense, cf. p. 45 above) together with its capital Damascus. Its inhabitants called for his help against the Ituraeans[63] and he only just anticipated a similar move by the Hasmonaeans.

All these developments were but part of a vast movement which was going on at that period in all Hither Asia. The Oriental peoples were attempting to counteract the forces of the west, as represented by the Seleucids and the Greek cities in their midst. This counteraction began in fact immediately after the death of Alexander the Great, the leader of the western attempt to conquer the east. Step by step the area of Greek domination was reduced. India, Bactria, Persia and Babylonia were lost to their Hellenic rulers. At the beginning of the first century B.C. this movement reached its apogee. It seemed for a moment as if the whole work of Alexander and his successors would be rendered null

[57] *Ant.* 13:8:1-235; *War* 1:2:4-60.
[58] *Ant.* 13:13:3-356; *War* 1:14:2-86.
[59] *Ant.* 13:12:2-324-335.
[60] A.H.M. Jones: *Cities of the Eastern Roman Provinces,* p. 256.
[61] *Ant.* 13:13:3-360.
[62] *Ib.,* 13:13:5-375; *War* 1:4:4-90.
[63] *Ant.* 13:15:2-392; 13:16:3-418; *War,* I 1:4:8-103; 1:5:3-115.

and void and that the Greek rulers (if not the Hellenistic culture) would be driven back beyond the sea.

In this time of general confusion the Hasmonaeans had to safeguard the interests of the Jewish nation in Palestine. They therefore undertook a policy of territorial expansion, combined with the conversion to Judaism of the inhabitants of the conquered territories. In this way they hoped to augment the numbers of their people and to secure for them sufficient living space. In the pursuit of this general aim they adopted various tactics. They tried to attach to the Jewish nation the small and weak tribes (the Idumaeans and the Samaritans) who adjoined it territorially. The only way to carry out this union irrevocably was to make them adopt the Jewish faith. At the same time the Hasmonaeans tried to break the chain of Greek cities which bound Judaea on the sea-coast, in the north and in the south. While pursuing these offensive aims, they had also to curb the expansionist tendencies of their Arab competitors. These too tried to fill the vacuum left by the decline of the Seleucid Kingdom. Where the Arab tribes had succeeded in occupying parts of Palestine, the Hasmonaeans felt obliged to dislodge them from what they regarded as a Jewish national heritage. Although a large and growing part of the Jewish nation opposed these policies, they seem to have been supported by a majority of the people.[64] The biblical promise of Canaan to the descendants of Abraham was still regarded as valid and was taken to justify a policy of expansion. The success of the Maccabean revolt against seemingly impossible odds was taken as a sign of divine favour and of the imminent fulfilment of other prophecies.

The Hasmonaeans thus imposed upon themselves three tasks: the annexation of the small nations adjoining Judaea, the conquest of the Greek cities and the driving-back of the Arabs. The first of these was by far the easiest. The Jews were now superior in power to the two small neighbouring nations, the Samaritans and the Idumaeans. The Samaritans were a sect of uncertain allegiance, vacillating between Judaism and Hellenism.[65] The Idumaeans had effectively separated themselves from

---

[64] *Ant.* 13:15:3-394.

[65] *Ib.*, 9:14:3-291; 11:4:3-84; 12:5:5-257.

their Arab brethren.[66] These two peoples were therefore isolated. They could not hope for help from the outside, such as was given to the Greek cities by the Hellenistic Kings within the limits of their power. The Samaritans and the Idumaeans thus formed a kind of soft core within Palestine, a core surrounded by the hard shell of the Greek cities. The Greeks held the whole coast and competed with Joppa, the only port in Jewish hands. They also ruled wide areas beyond the Jordan in the north-east and the east, areas which were cultivable, but which were as yet undeveloped.

The greatest obstacle to Judaean expansion was the barrier formed by the three Hellenistic cities: Tower of Straton—Samaria—Scythopolis. Their areas were adjoining and ran from the coast to the Jordan. They effectively barred the Judaean expansion northwards and the junction of Judaea with Galilee. The three cities also formed a connecting link between the two big blocks of Greek cities—the one on the coast and the other in northern Transjordania. The geopolitical position of the Greek cities was thus particularly strong. They could, moreover, count on external aid. But as against these favourable factors, there were various disadvantages in their situation. The Greek cities in Palestine were as disunited as the cities of classical Greece. They did not succeed in overcoming this fatal weakness of the Greek polis by their own will. In consequence, they did not unite in the face of a common danger, but let themselves be taken one by one. Each city held but a small territory and its strength was limited; it could hardly resist alone a determined onslaught. Moreover, the Greek cities were handicapped by the contrasts in their régimes; some were free cities, while others were ruled by "tyrants." Moreover, their own strength was insufficient to defend them, yet help from abroad was problematic and haphazard. The Ptolemaic kings of Egypt and Cyprus could aid only the towns situated on the coast. The Seleucid rulers were quite helpless most of the time. A determined and persistent assault of a superior power, directed now against one city and now against another, was bound to break down their resistance in the

---

[66] Strabo, XVI, 2, 34.

end. In these circumstances, we need not wonder that only three cities finally succeeded in warding off the Hasmonaean attack. Two of these (Ptolemais and Ascalon) were coastal cities. Even so Ascalon seems to have been left unmolested deliberately. The third city to stay outside the Hasmonaean orbit was Philadelphia beyond the Jordan. There the friendly desert possibly fulfilled the role of the sea in the case of the other two. All the other Greek cities in Palestine were captured in succession.

The beginning of Hasmonaean expansion began under Hyrcanus even before 132 B.C. We can reconstruct its stages from three sources: (a) the decision of the Roman senate of that year as quoted by Josephus;[67] (b) the Book of Judith[68] and (c) the areas described by Josephus as held by Judaea at the accession of Jannaeus.[69] From the first source it appears that in 132 B.C. Hyrcanus had lost to Antiochus VII Sidetes: "Joppa and the harbours and Gazara and Pegae"—i.e. Gezer and Tell Aphek (Ras el 'Ain). The *harbours* in the plural, which are mentioned together with Jaffa, seem to show that in that year the Hasmonaeans already possessed a stretch of the coast in addition to Jaffa itself. The extent of the coastal area in their possession is not clear, however. It might have just included the two anchorages next to Jaffa on the north and south. These are at the mouth of the Yarqon River to the north[70] and an ancient harbour near Bat Yam to the south.[71] It seems more likely, however, that the area conquered included Apollonia in the north and the harbour of Jamnia in the south. As regards the former, we find it included in Judaea in 104 B.C.[72] There is no previous mention of its conquest, so we might assign it to this early date. As regards the latter, Josephus actually attributes the conquest of Jamnia to Simeon, John Hyrcanus' father,[73] but his evidence is not valid, in face of the silence of the

[67] *Ant.* 13:9:2-260-1 and Marcus' note in the Loeb ed. *ad loc.*

[68] Septuaginta ed. A. Rahlfs, Stuttgart, 1949; especially 2:28; 3:9-1.

[69] *Ant.* 13:12:2-324.

[70] Tell Qudadi, cf. the excavation report *QDAP,* VIII, 1939, p. 167f.

[71] Greek and Hellenistic pottery has been found on this site.

[72] *Ant.* 13:12:2-324.

[73] *Ib.,* 13:6:7-215; *War* 1:2:2-50.

First Book of Maccabees. Josephus might have deduced the conquest of the city from the Hasmonaean victory at the battle of Jamnia.

The Book of Judith seems to describe a territorial situation in which Samaria was already Jewish, while Jamnia and Azotus were not. It is, of course, true that this source is a historical romance; but even in such compositions the historical and geographical background of the story must be based on fact, if it is intended to make the tale verisimilar. The political situation as outlined in the Book of Judith is a very peculiar one; it would be difficult to find a parallel to it. According to it[74] the coastal plain, Tyre, Accho, Jamnia, Azotus and Ascalon are independent, at a time when Holofernes' army is supposed to have camped between Gabaa and Scythopolis facing the Judaean border, from Esdraelon to Dothan.[75] Such boundaries could have existed but once in the Persian or Hellenistic period. They did in fact exist after the fall of Samaria, but before the enlargement of the coastal area in Hasmonaean possession. We should, therefore, assign the fall of Jamnia and Azotus to the end of the reign of Hyrcanus, after 107 B.C., the harbour of Jamnia lying at some distance from the inland city (2 Macc. 12:9). They are, however, included in Judaea at the beginning of Jannaeus' rule.[76]

Beyond the Jordan Hyrcanus captured the cities of Madaba and Samaga immediately after the news of Sidetes' death reached him.[77] The mention of the otherwise unknown Samaga (Kh. Samîk) instead of Heshbon, the metropolis of the area, is noteworthy. It is evident, however, that Heshbon was included in the Hasmonaean domain. The list of cities in Jannaeus' possession, as given by Josephus, includes Essebon;[78] as its conquest is not mentioned among those of Jannaeus it must be attributed to Hyrcanus. By these annexations the Hasmonaeans gained a foothold on the second main thoroughfare of Palestine, the 'King's Way' (as it is called in the Bible)[79] This is the great road traversing the whole

---

[74] Judith 2:28.
[75] *Ib.*, 3:9-10; 4:4, 6.
[76] *Ant.* 13:12:2-324.
[77] *Ib.*, 13:9:1-255-6; *War* 1:2:6-62-63.
[78] *Ant.* 13:15:4-397.
[79] Num. 20:17; 21:22.

of Trans-Jordan from north to south along the desert border, and connecting Damascus with the Gulf of Elath. The occupation of Madaba and Heshbon secured these cities for Judaea and prevented their falling to Hyrcanus' rivals, Zenon of Philadelphia and the Nabataeans, both equally interested in carving for themselves as large a share as possible out of the decaying Kingdom of the Seleucids.

We may presume that Hyrcanus rushed to capture Madaba and Heshbon in order to profit from some occasion in this distant direction.[80] After this first blow Hyrcanus resumed his activities much nearer Jerusalem. He proceeded both north and south along the watershed road and thus occupied first the hilly back-bone of the country. The Samaritans, who lived an isolated life around their sanctuary on Mount Gerizim were apparently subdued easily, and they were followed by the equally isolated Idumaeans.[81] Yet the ultimate fate of these two peoples differed considerably. The Samaritans were profoundly attached to their religious tenets and their national sanctuary. They were indeed subdued, but they kept their religion and their national identity and finally regained their territorial integrity. Even if they seem to have lost the toparchy of Acrabitene to Judaea at that time, they regained it after A.D. 70 (cf. below, p. 112).

The Idumaeans, on the other hand, who had cut themselves off long ago from the main Arab stock, were easily persuaded to adopt Judaism. Although they kept their identity for several generations (possibly even until the First Roman War), they were finally absorbed into the Jewish nation. The adoption of Judaism went deeper in eastern Idumaea (the region of Adoraim) than in the west (the vicinity of Marisa). This difference had important political and geographical results later (cf. p. 80 below). With the annexation of Idumaea the southern border of Judaea again reached Beersheba. In the north, Jewish expansion was for a time halted by the cities of Samaria and Scythopolis, which blocked any further advance in that direction. Hyrcanus in the end overcame this

[80] The Hasmonaeans had old scores to settle with Madaba (1 Macc. 9:36-42). This motive might have impelled them to attack this city.
[81] Strabo XVI, 2, 34.

obstacle. After a siege of one year's duration he took Samaria; the 25th of Marheshvan (probably 107 B.C.), on which the wall of the city was breached, was henceforth listed among the national holidays.[82] While the siege of Samaria was still in progress, Scythopolis (Beth-Shan) came into Jewish possession. Our sources differ as to how. According to one account[83] the city was bought from the local Greek commander Epirates. According to the parallel story[84] it was taken by force by Hyrcanus' sons, who at the same time wasted the whole 'inner' Carmel.[85] The whole ridge of the mountain down the seashore was, however, still untouched.[86]

The fates of both Samaria and Scythopolis were almost identical. Samaria was destroyed; the traces of Hyrcanus' destruction have been noted by the excavators of the site.[87] As regards Beth-Shan, the *Megillath Taanith* notes briefly:[88] "On the 15th and 16th of Sivan the people of Beth-Shan and the people of its valley were exiled."

The conquest of Beth-Shan was the first step in the direction of Galilee. Although Simeon Maccabeus had evacuated most of the Jewish population of this province,[89] some of them must have remained, for we find Bacchides killing the people of Arbel on the Sea of Galilee in his campaign against Judas Maccabeus.[90] Again Jonathan was able to find support among the inhabitants of the Plain of Esdraelon, who were presumably Jews.[91] He was also the first member of the Hasmonaean dynasty to regard Galilee as part and parcel of his heritage.[92] In the time of

---

[82] Megillath Taanith, 22. This is a list of days on which fasting was not allowed because of some joyful event which took place on them; cf. also *Ant.* 13:10:2-275, 281; *War* 1:2:7-64-65. H. Lichtenstein, *Hebr. Union Coll. Annual,* VIII-IX, 1931-2, pp. 289, 328.
[83] *Ant.* 13:10:3-280.
[84] *War* 1:2:7-66.
[85] Ibid.
[86] "Mount Carmel" appears among the areas held by Jannaeus at the time of his death (*Ant.* 13:15:4-396), but not among those he inherited (*ibid.* 13:12:2-324).
[87] G. Reisner, C.S. Fisher, D. Lyon: *Harvard Excavations at Samaria,* I, p. 57.
[88] *Op. cit.* 21 (note 82 above), pp. 288, 328.
[89] 1 Macc. 5:21-23.
[90] Ibid. 9:2.
[91] Ibid. 12:47, 49-50.
[92] Ib. 26; Ant. 13:5:6-154.

Hyrcanus Galilee was indeed occupied by the Ituraeans, but its ties with Judaea remained very close. Alexander Jannaeus, for example, was brought up there, so that he might live outside the area ruled by his father[93] but yet with his friends. The Jewish element must have been fairly strong in Galilee by that time. Only thus can we explain both the rapid conquest of this province and its equally rapid and total Judaization. The brief reign of Judah I Aristobulus, which lasted only one year, sufficed for the occupation of both Galilee and the Esdraelon Plain.[94] At the very beginning of Alexander's reign we find Asochis (Tell Shîhîn, Tell el Bedawiye) already an observant Jewish city, which Ptolemy Lathyrus, King of Cyprus, could hope to surprise defenceless on the Sabbath day.[95]

When Alexander Jannaeus ascended the throne Judaea already covered the whole interior of the country west of the Jordan and most of the coastal plain. It also had acquired a foothold beyond the river to the east. On the coast only Ptolemais, Gaza and the territory of Zoilus (Dora and the Tower of Straton) were counted as free by Josephus.[96] Ascalon is omitted from his list. U. Kahrstedt has concluded from this and from the fact that a new era began at Ascalon in 104-103 B.C. (the accession year of Jannaeus), that Ascalon had been taken by Hyrcanus and had freed itself from Hasmonaean domination at the beginning of Jannaeus' reign.[97] On further consideration, however, this coincidence in dates must appear fortuitous. It is well known that, until compelled to do so by the superior power of Rome, the Hasmonaeans did not give up a single one of their conquests. In fact, they usually took good care (if necessary by changing the local population) to ensure the loyalty of the occupied areas. At his death Jannaeus held Gaza and Azotus, the territories of which encircled Ascalon on three sides. It seems most unlikely that after taking Gaza he would have hesitated to tackle Ascalon. Even if the latter city, lying on the sea-shore, would have defended itself with

---

93 Ib. 13:12:1-322.

94 Ib. 13:11:3-318; *War* 1:3:3-76.

95 *Ant.* 13:12:4-337.

96 Ibid. 13:12:2-324.

97 U. Kahrstedt: *Syr. Territorien in hellenistischer Zeit,* 1926, p. 69.

greater ease, yet it seems to have been practically at his mercy. The more likely explanation of the absence of Ascalon in the list of Jannaeus' conquests is that he deliberately left it untouched. In this way he secured for himself a neutral outlet into the Hellenistic world. Surrounded on all sides by enemies, Jannaeus was probably quite satisfied to have on his borders at least one Greek city, which was traditionally friendly to his cause.[97a] Moreover, by reason of its geographical position, Ascalon was amenable to his ends. We may therefore conclude that Ascalon remained independent of the Hasmonaean Kingdom throughout the reign of Jannaeus.

To unite all the rest of Palestine under his rule, Jannaeus at the time of his accession needed but to add to his Kingdom the four corners of the country:

(1) In the North-West he lacked the coast from the Tower of Straton to Ptolemais;
(2) in the South-West he lacked the coast of Gaza and its dependencies;
(3) in the North-East the Greek cities of the Gilead and the Gaulan;
(4) in the South-East the areas bordering on the Dead Sea.

Relying on his military superiority and his command of the interior lines, Jannaeus proceeded to execute his task. He continued with it for the rest of his life, undeterred by the difficulties which his policy caused among his own people. He was apparently always unsuccessful in the field;[98] but managed to survive each defeat. His political ability, his persistence (especially in siege-warfare) and his alternate campaigns in the east and west were successful in the end. Jannaeus carried out his policy of conquest relentlessly until the day of his death. He died in the midst of yet another campaign, and even then his army carried out the task to the end.[99]

[97a] Cf. Jonathan's reception by the Ascalonites, 1. Macc. 10:86.

[98] He was beaten by Ptolemy Lathyrus at Asophon on the Jordan (*Ant.* 13:12:5-338-344); by Obodas the Nabatean king near Gador (ib. 13:13:5-376; *War* 1:4:4-90); by Demetrius Acaerus at Sichem (*Ant.* 13:14:1-378; *War* 1:4:5-95); by Antiochus XII Callinicus (*Ant.* 13:15:1-390-1; *War* 1:4:7:700) and by Aretas III, king of the Nabataens (*Ant.* 13:15:2-392; *War* 1:4:8-104). No victory of Jannaeus in battle is recorded in our sources.

[99] He died during the siege of Ragaba (Rajib) in the territory of Gerasa (*Ant.* 13:15:5-398); the fortress was captured by his wife and successor Alexandra (*ibid.*, 405).

It is characteristic of Jannaeus' approach that he began his reign by tackling the hardest task of all, the reduction of Ptolemais. The city was protected both by its position on the sea-shore and by its natural strength on the tip of a land-tongue.[100] Jannaeus did indeed fail in this enterprise, owing to the intervention of King Ptolemy Lathyrus of Cyprus. However, he succeeded by adroit maneuvering in dispossessing Zoilus the tyrant of the Tower of Straton and Dora, and in acquiring Mount Carmel and Gabaa into the bargain. He thus extended his hold on the coast line and seized the key to the Valley of Esdraelon.[101] The conquest of the Tower of Straton and Dora is recorded directly by Josephus.[102] Mount Carmel appears among Jannaeus' possessions at the time of his death.[103] In yet another place[104] Josephus mentions that "Mount Carmel once belonged to Galilee, and now (i.e. in Josephus' own time) to the Tyrians" (i.e. to Phoenicia, of which Ptolemais was a part). The mountain area of the Carmel appears to have been largely inhabited by Jews in the following generations,[105] probably as a result of Jannaeus' conquest. The capture of Gabaa has been recorded by Syncellus.[106]

For the subjection of the strongly fortified cities of the Gilead two long campaigns were needed. One occurred at the beginning of Jannaeus' reign, the other towards its end. In the first campaign[107] he took Gadara, the capital of the Gilead and very strong both in position and fortifications; and Amathus in the Jordan Valley, which served the rulers of Philadelphia both as a fortress and a treasure-house. The second campaign up from Gerasa, north of Philadelphia, to Pella in the Jordan Valley, Dium and Abila in the Valley of the Yarmuk, Hippus overlooking the Sea of Galilee in the east, Gamala and Seleucia in the Gaulan, and so up to the 'Valley of Antiochus,' probably the Hûle Valley with its

---

[100] *Ant.* 13:12:2-324.
[101] Strabo XVI, 2, 28.
[102] *Ant.* 13:12:4-335.
[103] Ib. 13:15:4-396.
[104] *War* 3:3:1-35.
[105] *Ant.* 14:13:3-334.
[106] Syncellus, ed. Bonn, I, pp. 558-9.
[107] *Ant.* 13:13:3 356; *War* 1:4:2-86-88.

centre, Antiochia, replacing ancient Dan; thus far Josephus;[108] Syncellus adds Philoteria, situated at the outflow of Jordan from the Lake, on the east side of the river.[109]

In the southern part of the coastal plain Jannaeus began isolating Gaza by taking the minor cities in its vicinity. After the occupation of Raphia, Anthedon and Rhinocorura (el Arish), he succeeded in depriving Gaza of all hope of succour, whether from the sea or from the Nabataeans, although the latter were interested in its independence, for it served them as an outlet to the Mediterranean.[110] The siege was long and hard (even Alexander the Great had spent four months in front of Gaza), but in the end the city surrendered.[111] The whole coast from the Brook of Egypt to the Carmel was now in Jewish hands, with the sole exception of Ascalon (for which see above, p. 67).

The cutting-off of the Nabataean trade route Aila-Gaza was only one of the acts of Jannaeus directed against the economic interests of the neighbouring Kingdom. His next step was to complete the encirclement of the Dead Sea, by which he hoped to secure the complete domination of this valuable economic asset. The control of the bitumen derived from its waters had been the aim of Antigonus Monophthalmus' campaign against the Nabataeans, which ended in failure.[112] Jannaeus was more successful. Owing to the territorial advantages gained by his father Hyrcanus, he already controlled the whole western shore of the sea as well as the northern half of the eastern shore down to the river Arnon. Now he completed the encirclement of the Dead Sea by taking various Moabite cities down to and including Zoar at the southern end of the

---

[108] *Ant.* 13:15:3-393-394 (correcting with Marcus "Essa" to Gerasa); *War* 1:4:8-104-5.

[109] Syncellus, loc. cit. above, n. 107. The excavations of the Oriental Institute, University of Chicago, have unearthed in 1952 a church the pavement of which is dated to A.D. 529 by an inscription. The era used proved to be Pompeian, i.e. the site belonged to one of the cities of the Decapolis east of the Jordan, either to Hippus or to Gadara. It follows that if we identify Philoteria with Beth Yerah, that this site was not situated in Galilee, because in antiquity the Jordan flowed west of it; this course of the river can be traced down to Crusader time, and in part down to 1917. Cf. P. Delougaz and R. C. Haines: *A Byzantine Church at Khirbat al-Karak,* Chicago, 1960 (O.I.P., LXXXV), p. 53-54.

[110] *Ant.* 13:13:4-369; J. H. Iliffe, *QDAP,* III, pp. 132-135; N. Glueck, *AASOR* XV, p. 19.

[111] *Ant.* 13:13:3-357-364; *War* 1:4:2-87.

[112] Diodorus XIX, 95-97.

sea. The precise extent of his conquests is not quite clear, as the two passages in Josephus' *Antiquities,* in which they are listed,[113] are very much corrupted. Some of the names quoted there are certainly identifiable. Such are Medaba, Libba (Kh. Libb) and Zoar. Others are less certain, such as Nabaloth (possibly Dabaloth, modern Kh. Duleilât); some are unidentifiable, such as the "Cilician Valley."[114] However, the greatest difficulty is a chunk of corrupted names appearing in one source as *orônaimagelethôn* and in the other as *orônaidigôbasilissaryddalousa.* This has been dissected into Oronaim, Gobalis, Arydda and Alousa, in the latter case, Oronaim-Agalla in the former. Oronaim and Agalla are indeed well known cities in Moab. They appear already in biblical times.[115] Oronaim has been identified with el Irâq,[116] Gobalos (Gabaloth) with el Jiblîn[117] and Agalla (Eglaim) with Rujm el-Jalame.[118] F. M. Abel has proposed to equate Alousa with Elusa in the Northern Negev, Arydda with Naqb el 'Arud near the Sinai border, and Orybda with 'Abda.[119] This view, which would extend the area conquered by Jannaeus deep into the Negeb, has been disputed by A. Schalit.[120] He has pointed out that the place-names listed by Josephus can be equated by emendations with the cities of Moab, as mentioned in the Septuagint version of the "Burden of Moab" in the prophecy of Isaiah (15:4-9) and Jeremiah (31:3-5, 8, 34, 36). Schalit argues that Josephus derived the version of Jannaeus' conquests in the *Antiquities* from a poem praising his exploits in the language of the Bible. This contention does not, however, invalidate the fact of the conquest itself. It enables us, however, to limit it to the area of ancient Moab plus Zoar at the south end of the Dead Sea. With the undisputed occupation of this southernmost point, the whole coastline of the valuable lake would be in Hasmonaean hands.

---

[113] *Ant.* 13:15:4-397 which lists the cities held by Jannaeus at the time of his death and 14:1:4-18 which gives the names of the towns in Moab ceded to Aretas by Hyrcanus II f.

[114] But cf. M. Dothan, *EI,* 2, 1953, pp. 166-169 (Hebrew).

[115] Isa. 15:5; Jer. 48:3 and 34; Isa 15:8.

[116] Musil, *Moab,* p. 72 f.

[117] Abel: *Géographie,* II, p. 149.

[118] *Ib.,* p. 310.

[119] *Ib.,* p. 148.

[120] *EI* I, 1951, pp. 104-121 (Hebrew).

To sum up: at the time of his death Jannaeus ruled the whole of the coastal plain from the Kishon to the Brook of Egypt (excepting Ascalon), the whole of the mountains west of Jordan from Dan to Beersheba, almost the whole area east of the Jordan from Paneas down to Zoar and the River Zared. He had thus virtually restored the Kingdom of David and Solomon.

As may be seen from the preceding pages, we are fairly well documented as regards the outward expansion of the Hasmonaean State. We know much less about its internal administration, its subdivisions, etc. The various districts seem to have been administered by governors called in our Greek sources sometimes *stratēgos*[121] and sometimes *meridarchēs.* The Hebrew equivalent of this title was perhaps *nazib* on the analogy of Solomon's *nizabîm* (I Kings 4:7). The word *meris* already appears as an administrative term in Ptolemaic papyri of the second century B.C., where it designates part of a *nome.*[122] The author of the First Book of the Maccabees and Josephus use *meridarchēs* as the title of the governor of a Seleucid eparchy.[123] This usage stands isolated, however, in comparison with the Greek sources, whether official or unofficial. In comparison with an Egyptian *meris,* an eparchy was enormous in size. It is therefore improbable that the Seleucids would have used the term for a small Egyptian district to designate one of their provinces and we must assume an anachronistic usage both in the Book of Maccabees and in Josephus. This usage might, however, have had its origin in a Hasmonaean innovation. Hyrcanus and his successors very likely deliberately selected a Ptolemaic title for their districts in order to avoid the use of the administrative terminology of their Seleucid enemies. They also seem to have originated the division of the whole country into the 'lands' of Judaea, Idumaea, Samaria, Galilee and Peraea, as set out in Josephus.[124] This division cannot be earlier than the time of Hyrcanus, for it was he who annexed Idumaea and Samaria to Judaea. Under his rule the rapid

121 1 Macc. 16:11; *Ant.* 14:1:3-10.

122 Preisigke: *Wörterbuch,* III, s.v. p. 134.

123 1 Macc. 10:65 (parallel with strategus); *Ant.* 12:5:5-261, 264.

124 E.g. the locus classicus, *War* 3:3:1/5-35-58.

expansion of the Hasmonaean state might have warranted the creation of a unit larger than the toparchy. The Greek cities taken by Jannaeus and the districts conquered in Moab seem, however, to have remained under military rule outside the normal district administration.

As regards the territorial boundaries within the Kingdom, no fundamental changes seem to have been made under Hasmonaean rule. The only exception was the transfer of the toparchy of Acraba from Samaria to Judaea. As regards the local governors, we know that Antipas, the grandfather of King Herod, was governor of the whole of Idumaea in the time of Jannaeus.[125] The King obviously did not hesitate to entrust an Idumaean with the government of his native country. In most cases even the Greek commanders of the conquered fortresses were allowed to retain their posts. Josephus noted the deposition by Jannaeus of Demetrius the governor of Gamala as something out of the ordinary.[126] The usual practice must, therefore, have been to leave them at their posts; this explains why these governors supported Aristobulus II as against the government of the Pharisees under Queen Alexandra.[127] Military rulers of various areas of Judaea occur even before that: John Hyrcanus was in command at Gezer on behalf of his father Simeon,[128] while the latter's murderer, Ptolemy the son of Abubus, was ruler of Jericho.[129]

The necessity to secure their conquests obliged the Hasmonaeans to build many fortresses. Jannaeus constructed Masada,[130] Alexandrium (Qarn Sartaba) overlooking the Jordan Valley, Hyrcania named in honour of his father (now probably Kh. Mird), and Machaerus.[131]

In his *Antiquities* Josephus mentions that in the time of Alexandra, Jannaeus' successor, his son Aristobulus II occupied twenty-two fortresses. This number, which need not be exhaustive, indicates the military

[125] *Ant.* 14:1:3-10.
[126] *Ant.* 13:15:3-394; *War* 1:4:8-105.
[127] *Ant.* 13:16:2/3-411-418; 13:16:5-424-429; *War* 1:5:3-113-118.
[128] 1 Macc. 16:19.
[129] *Ib.*, 11.
[130] According to Josephus Masada was founded by the 'high priest Jonathan' (*War* 7:8:3-285) which is the Hebrew name and earlier title of Jannaeus; for the view which connects Masada with Jonathan the brother of Judas Maccabaeus see *IEJ*, 7, 1957, p. 1 ff.
[131] *Ant.* 13:16:3-417 f.

preparedness of the kingdom.[132] Most of these strong points must have dated from the time of Jannaeus; a few perhaps went back to the time of the earlier Hasmonaean rulers.

The Hasmonaeans founded few cities, contrary to the usage of the Hellenistic Kings. We can assign to them only a village called Aristobulias in Judaea, situated between Carmel and Zif.[133] Possibly this was a consequence of their general policy, which favoured the countryside at the expense of the cities. The latter must have represented in their eyes the Greek element hostile to the Jewish state.

The captured Greek cities presented a problem of peculiar difficulty to the Hasmonaean state. They had their own way of life, their town-laws and constitutions. They maintained close connections with the outside world, and in particular with the Hellenistic kingdoms of the Orient, against which the Maccabeans had revolted. The very fact of the foundation of the Greek colonies rendered them odious. Their assimilation to the rest of the kingdom was almost out of the question, unless either the Greek cities or the Jewish state could radically change their character. Experience had taught the Hasmonaeans that only a complete change in the character of the population—involving the adoption of Judaism—could ensure the continued loyalty of the conquered areas in times of adversity. The Jewish rulers therefore of necessity placed before the inhabitants of the cities the choice of either adopting the Jewish religion or of emigrating. The majority of the population, even of the Greek cities, seems to have accepted the first alternative, at least outwardly. We know definitely of only two cities, Pella and Scythopolis (Beth-Shan) that their inhabitants chose to leave.[134] In the other cities it was probably only the Greek colonists and their descendants who chose exile. With them went those members of the local aristocracies who had become thoroughly hellenized, and who in consequence were particularly attached to the Greek gods and way of life of the Greek polis. To these we should add the inhabitants of the cities who had offered especially strong re-

---

132 *Ib.,* 13:16:5-427.

133 Cyrillus Scytopolitanus: *Vita Euthymii,* 12 (ed. Schwartz, p. 22).

134 *Ant.* 13:15:4-397; *Megillath Taanith* 22 (n. 82 above).

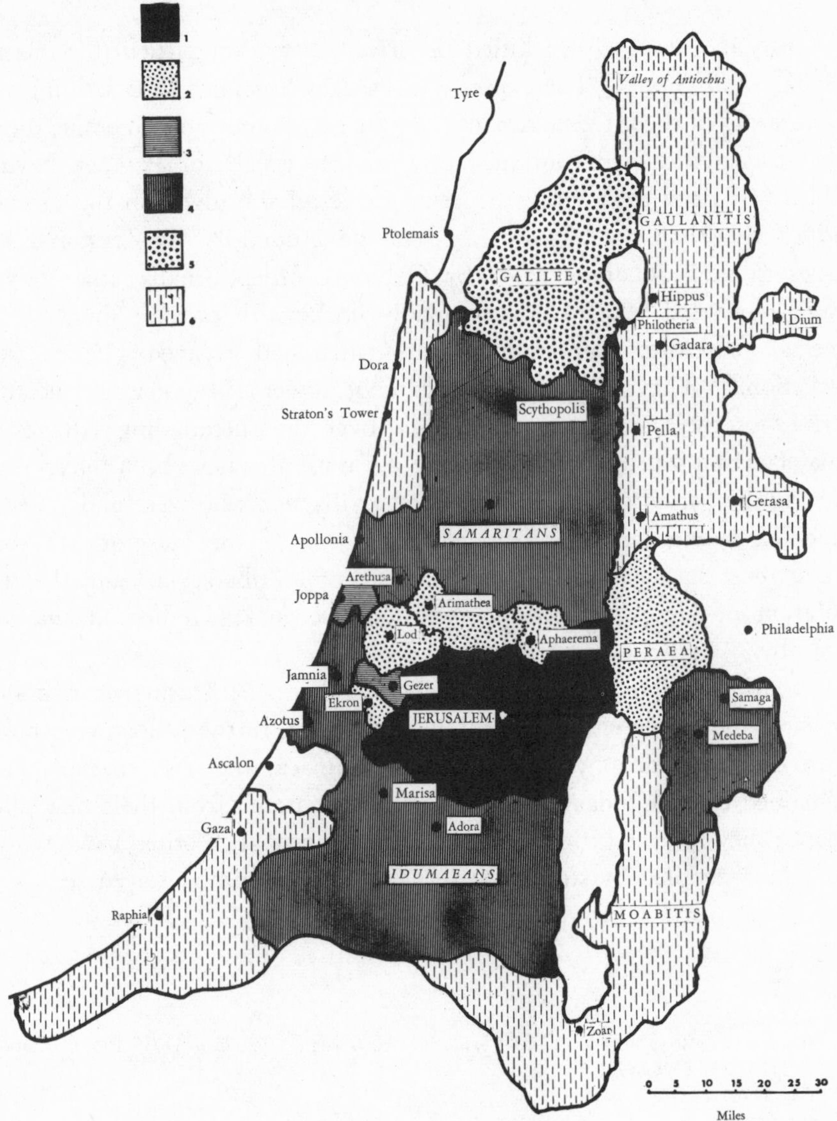

Map 4: THE RISE OF THE HASMONAEAN STATE
1. Judaea at the beginning of the Hasmonaean Revolt
2. Annexations under Jonathan
3. Annexations under Simeon
4. Annexations under John Hyreanus
5. Annexations under Judah Aristobulus I
6. Annexations under Alexander Jannaeus

sistance and were either killed or driven away, in particular Samaria, Gadara and Gaza.[135] The expressions used by Josephus in describing the restoration of the Greek cities in Palestine by Pompey and Gabinius prove that these cities had continued to exist. He speaks of Pompey having "liberated from their (scil. the Jews') rule all the towns in the interior which they had not already razed to the ground;"[136] he "restored the cities to their inhabitants;"[137] by Gabinius' orders "many other towns were repeopled, the inhabitants gladly flocking to each of them."[138] It seems, therefore, that most of the cities had escaped physical destruction.[139] They had continued to exist under Hasmonaean rule, deprived of their autonomy. Their rule over the surrounding villages, a characteristic function of the Greek polis, must also have been interrupted during the period of Jewish rule. To the villagers, who were undoubtedly non-Greek and certainly included many Jews,[140] the Hasmonaean conquest must surely have had the character of a "liberation," and the restoration of Greek "liberties" must have seemed a return to the old tyranny.

From the point of view of the Jewish State the Hasmonaean policy towards the Greek cities certainly justified itself. In the following generation only the neophytes in Galilee, Idumaea and the coastal plain remained true to Judaea. Even if forcibly separated from their new allegiance they returned to it at the first opportunity. The other areas, which remained peopled by strangers, were lost very soon and stayed so.

---

[135] *Ant.* 13:10:3-281; *War* 1:2:7-65 (Samaria); *Ant.* 14:4:4-75; *War* 1:7:7-155 (Gadara); *Ant.* 13:13:3-364 (Gaza).

[136] *War* 1:7:7-156.

[137] *Ant.* 14:4:4-75.

[138] *War* 1:8:4-166. The use of the term oikētōs in both *Ant.* 14:4:4-75 and here, meaning both "inhabitant" and "colonist" indicates the ambiguous character of these cities.

[139] The excavations of Samaria (Crowfoot et al, *Samaria-Sebaste,* III, pp. 5, 284-285) have shown that the town was resettled before the time of Gabinius. According to Josephus (*Ant.* 13:13:2-355) Jannaeus met Cleopatra III in the 'deserted' Scythopolis.

[140] The persistently non-Greek character of the countryside is evident in the Byzantine period; cf. the evidence set out below, Part III, Chapter 2, n. 27.

Chapter V

THE DECLINE OF THE HASMONAEAN STATE

ALEXANDER Jannaeus' successor was his widow, Salome Alexandra (76-67 B.C.). No territorial changes occurred during her reign.[1] The dissensions which began under Hyrcanus and led to civil war and overt treason under Jannaeus, broke out again after her death and took the form of a civil war between her sons Aristobulus II and Hyrcanus II. The first result of this fratricidal struggle was the cession by Hyrcanus of twelve cities in Moab, with their territories, to Aretas III, King of the Nabataeans, in return for his help against Aristobulus. These cities included not only Jannaeus' conquests[2] but even Madaba, which had been taken by Hyrcanus I over sixty years before.[3] While this struggle was still going on, a new power appeared in the Orient,—Rome, destined to rule the East for the next seven hundred years. The Roman army led by Pompey, descended into Syria, after defeating King Mithridates of Pontus. Pompey "invited" the two Hasmonaean brothers to submit their differences to him at Damascus. Following his decision to support Hyrcanus II, he invaded Judaea by way of Coreae in the Jordan Valley. After taking Aristobulus prisoner at Alexandrium, he proceeded to Jerusalem. The city opened its gates but the Temple resisted till it, too, was captured after a siege of four months (64 B.C.). Judaea had lost its independence.

The submission to Rome brought about from its very beginning considerable changes in the territorial set-up of Syria and Palestine. On the one hand Pompey abolished the last vestiges of Seleucid rule in Syria by turning it into a Roman province. Yet, while he put an end to the

---

[1] The expedition to Damascus, undertaken in her reign, either in order to protect the city (*Ant.* 13:16:3-418) or to capture it (*War* 1:5:3-115) led to no results.

[2] See above p. 70 f. and *Ant.* 14:1:4-18.

[3] See p. 64 f.; the position of Heshbon is not clear. It appears among the cities held by Jannaeus at the time of his death (*Ant.* 13:15:4-397), but is not listed among the Moabite cities returned by Hyrcanus II; it appears again as a military colony of Herod (see below, p. 99). It could have remained in Jewish hands throughout, or it could have been ceded by Hyrcanus II and retaken by Herod after his victory over the Arabs.

existence of this Hellenistic kingdom, he nevertheless considered it Rome's duty to protect Greek civilization in the East. The struggle between the Greek cities and the Oriental nations (*polis* vs. *ethnē*), had by then been going on for nearly a century. It was now decided temporarily in favour of the cities. They were recognized as the bearers of Hellenic culture, which had taken root in Rome as well.

At the time of Pompey's conquest almost the entire southern part of what was once the Seleucid dominion was divided between three nations: the Ituraeans, the Nabataeans and the Jews. Pompey reduced the territory and status of each of the three, but in unequal measure. His judgment was moderate as regards the Nabataeans, fair to the Ituraeans, but very harsh to the Jews. The relative geographical position and the military power (both actual and potential) were naturally taken into account by Pompey in effecting his settlement. Obviously, he acted also with a view to securing Roman suzerainty. The Nabataeans were geographically the most difficult to subdue, as Scaurus, Pompey's lieutenant, and Demetrius Poliorcetes had both found out in their time. On the other hand, their offensive power was small; they had been soundly beaten at Papyron by Aristobulus II.[4] The Ituraeans were somewhat more exposed by reason of their Lebanese possessions. They had, however, a convenient place of retreat in the desert, the lava fields of the Trachonitis and the mountains of the Hauran. Their forces were not very strong, even if their bowmen were famous. The Jews were the easiest to subdue, having no place to retreat to and being surrounded by hostile neighbours. They were also the most grievious offenders against the Greek cities, which Pompey intended to take under his wing. Moreover, they were the only one of the three Oriental peoples aforementioned who had seized a considerable length of the sea-coast. They had used it to practise from their ports what they undoubtedly regarded as sea-warfare, but what appeared to their victims as piracy.[5] The Judaean army was, at least potentially, the

[4] Cf. Avi-Yonah, *JPOS,* 1937, pp. 253-254.

[5] Strabo (XVI, 2, 41) roundly calls the Hasmonaean strongholds "repairs of robbers and tyrants." The tomb cave dating to the Hasmonaean period, recently discovered in Jerusalem (*IEJ,* 6, 1956, pp. 127-8; Atiqot IV (H.) has on its walls representations of a war-galley attacking a merchant ship and another galley. Probably some of those buried in the cave

strongest and most troublesome of the local forces. Pompey therefore took good care to render the Jews as powerless as possible. He may have been influenced in his policy by the Greeks in his entourage. In particular, his favourite Demetrius of Gadara, the native of one of the cities subdued by Jannaeus, seems to have played an important role in this respect.[6]

The arrangements of Pompey and his successor and deputy Gabinius in Palestine are set out in two parallel lists in the *Antiquities* and the *Jewish War,* making four lists in all.[7] To these we may add the stray remarks of certain Greek authors.[8] The evidence of inscriptions and coins attests in the case of many cities the adoption of titles such as "Pompeian" or "Gabinian"[9] or of a Pompeian or Gabinian era; the former beginning in 64-61 B.C., the latter in 57 B.C.[10]

Both as a Roman and a practical statesman, Pompey did not attempt to restore the *status-quo-ante* as it had existed under Seleucid rule. He based his arrangements on the existing situation and refused to set up cities which were ruined beyond repair or had no justification for their existence. Thus Philoteria, Antioch in the Huleh, Seleucia or the "city" of Gaulan were not restored. Some of them disappeared entirely, others lived on as mere villages.[11] Pompey also recognized the Judaization of Galilee and of Idumaea as accomplished facts. These concessions to reality apart, his aim was to efface as far as possible all traces of the work of the Hasmonaeans. He split up the country they had united, separated the areas inhabited by Jews into two, cut Judaea off from access to the sea and encircled it with a belt of Greek cities.

(of the family of one Jason) were proud of their part in attacking the Greek sea-trade. One should also keep in mind the possibility of a connection between the Hasmonaeans and the pirates of Cilicia, against whom Pompey was empowered to act simultaneously with his mission to the Orient.

[6] *Ant.* 14:4:4-75; *War* 1:7:7-155.

[7] Pompey: *Ant.* 14:4:4-74-6; *War* 1:7:7-155-7; Gabinius: *Ant.* 14:5:3-88; *War* 1:8:4-166. Cf. E. Bammel, *ZDPV,* 1959, p. 76; Bietenhard, *ibid.,* 1963, p. 24 ff.

[8] E.g. Strabo, XVI, 2, 40; 76.

[9] Head: *Historia numorum,* pp. 786-7; A. H. M. Jones: *Cities of the E. Roman Provinces,* p. 259.

[10] H. Ginzel: *Hdb. d. math.-techn. Chronologie,* III, p. 47 ff.

[11] *War* 2:20:6-574; *ib.,* 4:1:1-1; *Life* 13-71; Eusebius: *Onomasticon,* ed. Klostermann 64, 7; Georgius Cyprius, 1041.

In the coastal area Pompey "restored" the cities of Dora,[12] Strato's Tower, Apollonia, Arethusa (possibly Pegae?),[13] Joppe, Jamnia, Azotus, Gaza and its dependencies;[14] he also returned Mount Carmel to Ptolemais-Accho.[15] In the interior he separated from Judaea the cities of Samaria, Scythopolis (Beth-Shan)[15a] and Marisa (i.e. all western Idumaea). In the list of the cities re-established by Gabinius we find the name of Adoraim and this could imply the separation of Eastern Idumaea as well. As, however, the name of Dora is lacking there (whereas it appears in the list of Pompey's cities) it seems better to read Dora for Adora and to assume that at least Eastern Idumaea—including Hebron with the tombs of the Patriarchs—remained with Judaea.[16] Another city to be made "independent" at that time was Gabaa, which commanded the pass leading from the coastal plain to the Valley of Jezreel. This must have happened during the proconsulate in Syria of Marcus Philippus, who preceded Gabinius in this office (61-60 B.C.). Its inhabitants call their city on coins "Claudia Philippia of the people of Gabaa."[17] As regards the country of the Samaritans the situation is disputed. A. H. M. Jones has argued[18] in favour of its continuation with Judaea, mainly because the sources mention their Council which seems to parallel Gabinius' synedria.[19] However, the omission of this council from the list of the Jewish Synedria (see below p. 84) proves to our mind that the Samaritan people and its territory were detached from Judaea and remained so until 40/39 B.C.[20]

[12] See above, p. 76 as to the terms used by Josephus in this connexion.
[13] For this identification cf. Avi-Yonah, *BJPES,* 10, 1942, pp. 18-19 (Hebrew) and below, p. 145.
[14] The restoration of Raphia and Anthedon is listed only among the works of Gabinius (see n. 7 above) but it seems evidently connected with the restoration of Gaza; the same seems to have applied to Rhinocorura (el 'Arish) which is mentioned only among Jannaeus' conquests, but was certainly separated from Judaea by Pompey.
[15] *War* III, 35 and p. 130 below.
[15a] Avi-Yonah, *IEJ* 12, 1962, p. 131.
[16] *Ant.* 14:14:9-364; *ib.,* 15:3-411.
[17] Head: *Historia numorum,* p. 786.
[18] A. H. M. Jones, *op. cit.,* (n. 9 above), p. 259.
[19] *Ant.* 18:4:2-88. The reference is to the time of Pilate, eighty-nine years after Pompey.
[20] See p. 86 f. below.

Next to the coastal plain, the greatest change was wrought by Pompey in northern Trans-Jordan. Pompey understood that the isolation of the Greek cities had been the most important single factor in their defeat by the Hasmonaeans. He therefore decided to remedy the situation by uniting them into a strong league. The overwhelming power of Rome easily overcame the separatist tendencies of each city. Besides, the inhabitants reinstated by Pompey had just received a very hard lesson in the dangers of separatism. The league was called that of the Ten Cities, the *Decapolis*. We know practically nothing of its constitution and little enough of its membership. Originally it must have been composed of ten cities, as its name shows. Pliny[21] lists them as follows: Damascus, Philadelphia, Raphana, Scythopolis (Beth-Shan), Gadara, Hippus, Dium, Pella, Gerasa[22] and Canatha. In the time of Josephus Damascus seems to have left the league, for by then Scythopolis was its chief city.[23] Ptolemaeus gives another list, excluding Raphana, but adding Abila.[24] This variant is supported by two additional facts: the coins of Abila use the Pompeian era;[25] an inscription dated to the A.D. 134 calls the city "one of the Decapolis."[26] The number of members of the league must in any case have varied from time to time. Stephanus Byzantinus mentions fourteen members in place of the original ten.[27] All the cities of the Decapolis were detached from the Hasmonaean state, except Damascus, Philadelphia and Canatha, which had been formerly Nabataean. The cities re-established by Pompey, whether on the coast or inland, were placed under the direct supervision of the proconsul of Syria.

The area which remained Jewish consisted, after Pompey's surgery, of

---

[21] *Hist. nat.* V, 74.

[22] Gerasa is omitted from the list of cities restored by Pompey; we should note however: (a) it was taken by Jannaeus (see p. 69 above); (b) it appears subsequently as a free city; (c) its inhabitants used a Pompeian era; (d) it is included in the Decapolis. There can be little doubt in view of these four facts that it was rebuilt by Pompey, although Josephus does not mention the fact.

[23] *War* 3:9:7-446.

[24] *Geogr.* V, 14, 8.

[25] Ginzel, *op. cit.* (n. 10 above), III, p. 47.

[26] *OGIS* II, p. 341, No. 631.

[27] Steph. Byz. *s.v.* Gerasa.

the following territories: Judaea itself with the four toparchies attached to it (Lydda, Haramatha, Apharaema and Acraba), and the territory of Gezer, Eastern Idumaea, Galilee (excluding the valley of Jezreel), Peraea with the addition of the regions of Amathus in the North and of Machaerus in the South.

The reduction of the Jewish State, when compared with the area held by Jannaeus at the time of his death, was therefore quite considerable. Yet we should not ignore the fact that, as compared with the area of Judaea at the beginning of the Hasmonaean revolt, a very great expansion had taken place. All the conquest of Jonathan—Lydda, Haramatha, Apharaema and most of Peraea—-had remained to the Jews; so had Gezer, captured by Simeon; half of Idumaea and the toparchy of Acraba from the time of Hyrcanus; and Galilee from the time of Aristobulus I. Of the conquests of Jannaeus, however, nothing remained except the two small areas north and south of the original Peraea. The loss of Joppe and of the access to the sea was especially grievous. Yet Joppe and some others of the lost regions kept their Jewish population and were thus predestined to return to the fold.

As we have said, Pompey treated the Ituraeans with greater leniency than he did the Jews. He left to their ruler Ptolemy, the son of Mennaeus, their original country plus the districts of Batanaea, Trachonitis and Auranitis. Ptolemy did indeed lose part of the Phoenician coast and of the Lebanon, but he obtained the Gaulan and the Ulatha (Huleh region). The Nabataeans handed over Damascus, Philadelphia and Canatha, and kept the rest.

The period between the conquest of Pompey (63 B.C.) and the final pacification of the Roman world under Augustus (30 B.C.) was one long time of war, both foreign and civil, of revolts and other troubles. But, just because of this unsettled state of affairs, there are hardly any permanent territorial changes which can be attributed to this period. One such change was the vain attempt of Gabinius to split up the remaining Jewish territory into five areas, probably on the Macedonian model.[28]

---

[28] In 168 B.C. Macedonia was split up among four provinces, deprived both of the ius comercii and the ius conubii with each other (Livy xix, 17-18; 29. 4-14; 32. 1-2 and 7).

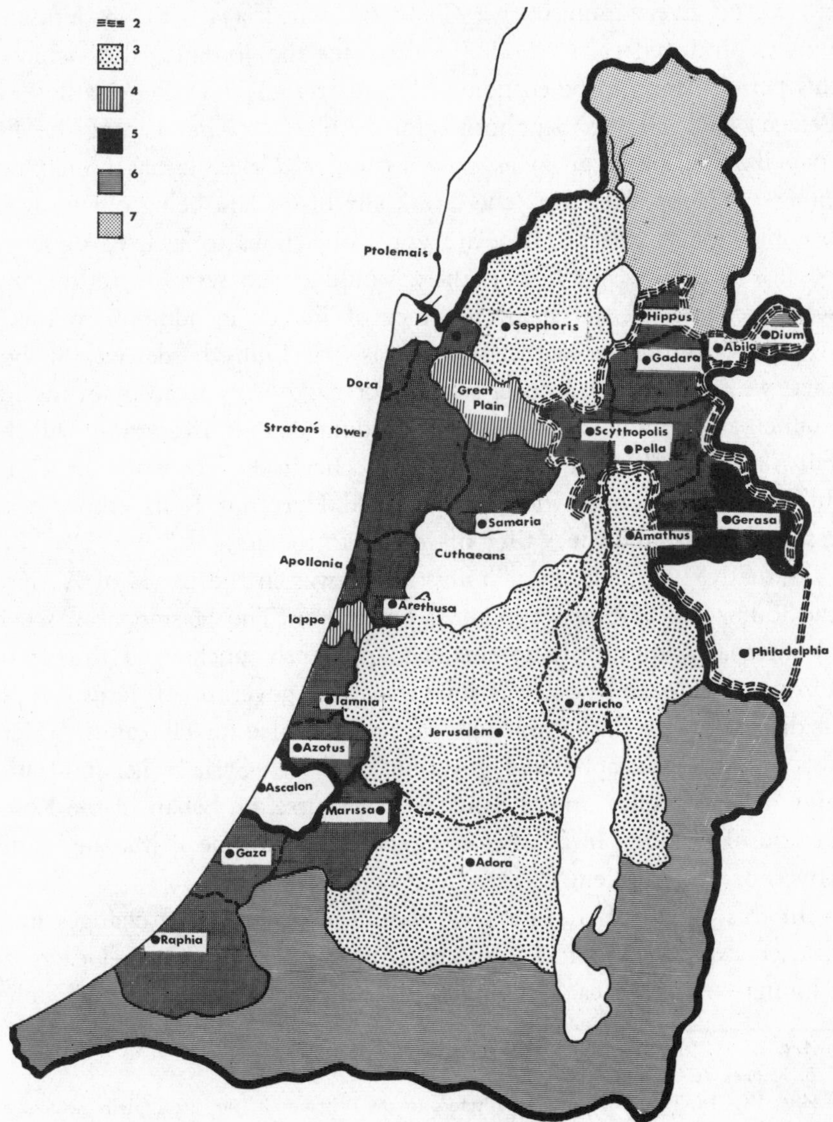

Map 5: POMPEY'S SETTLEMENT

1. Judaea at death of Jannaeus
2. Cities of the Decapolis
3. Area left to the Jews
4. Returned by Julius Caesar
5. Detached Greek Cities
6. To Nabataeans
7. To Ituraeans

He set up five administrative Councils (synedria): (1) in Jerusalem (for Central Judaea); (2) in Jericho (for the Jordan Valley which at this period began to be economically important); (3) in Amathus (for Peraea) and (4) in Sepphoris (for Galilee).[29] The seat of the fifth council is variously given as *gadarois* and *gadôrois*. It has been placed either at Gador in Peraea (the Greek city of Gadara being obviously impossible) or at Gezer. There are grave objections to each of these proposals. In the case of Gador, there would be no sense in setting up a second council in the small province of Peraea in addition to that at Amathus. And Gezer at that period was a declining border city. If, however, we read with B. Kanael *adôrois* for *gadôrois,* we can place the fifth Council at Adoraim and assign Eastern Idumaea to it. Everything will then fall into place.[30] In any case, Gabinius' scheme did not work. In 47 B.C. Julius Caesar reunited Judaea, appointed Hyrcanus II its ethnarch and restored Joppe and the Valley of Jezreel to the Jews.[31]

Actually, of course, the administration was in the hands of Antipater the Idumaean, who was appointed procurator. The Hasmonaean scheme of internal administration remained apparently unchanged throughout. Phasael, Antipater's son, was for some time governor of Jerusalem and its district;[32] Herod, the younger son, ruled Galilee for Hyrcanus.[33] Herod was subsequently appointed governor of "Coele-Syria" (i.e. most probably the Decapolis) and of Samaria,[34] of course, on behalf of the Roman proconsul of Syria. In another context we read of one Peitholaus as vice-governor of Jerusalem.[35]

In this period of transition we should also note some changes in the district capitals. Gophna replaced Apharaema, Emmaus—Gezer, and Thimna—Arimathaea.[36] Josephus indeed already writes of a "Gophan-

---

[29] *Ant.* 14:5:4-91; *War* 1:8:5-170.

[30] B. Kanael, *IEJ,* 7, 1957, pp. 98 ff.

[31] *Ant.* 14:10:6-205, 207; the latter refers to the 'villages in the great plain' which were possessed by Hyrcanus and his forefathers.

[32] *Ant.* 14:9:2-158; *War* 1:10:4-203.

[33] *Ib.*

[34] *War* 1:10:8-213; in the parallel passage *Ant.* 14:9:5-180 only Coelesyria is mentioned.

[35] *Ant.* 14:6:1-93; *War* 1:8:6-172.

[36] *Ant.* 14:11:2-275; cf. *War* 1:11:2-222.

itice" in the time of Bacchides.[37] This, however, is only one of his typical anachronisms, such as the "toparchy" of Accaron in the time of Jonathan[38] etc.

In 40 B.C. Palestine was invaded by the Parthians, who occupied Jerusalem and set up there as King the last of the Hasmonaean rulers, Mathithiah Antigonus. In their campaign they razed the city of Maresha (Marisa) to the ground.[39] Antipater and Phasael perished; Herod fled to Rome, whence he returned in 39 B.C. as King of Judaea on behalf of Rome. In 37 B.C. he captured Jerusalem and put an end to the Hasmonaean Kingdom. With this event begins a new chapter in the territorial history of the country.

---

37 *War* 1:1:5-45.
38 *Ant.* 13:4:4-102.
39 *Ant.* 14:13:9-364; *War* 1:13:9-269.

Chapter VI

HEROD AND HIS KINGDOM

FROM the Roman point of view Herod began to reign in 40 B.C., at the time of his appointment.[1] In fact, however, he had first to conquer his Kingdom, a feat he accomplished after a hard struggle which lasted until 37 B.C. The bounds of his Kingdom were no doubt established either by the basic resolution of the Roman Senate, which turned the private individual Herod into a monarch,[2] or by an edict of Mark Antony who was ruler of the eastern half of the Roman Empire and as such had to carry out the resolution of the senate. The Romans never regarded Antigonus as a legitimate ruler because of the origin of his power. Having accepted his crown from their Parthian foes, he was guilty of contempt of Rome, even if the Romans admitted his rule *de facto.* In appointing Herod to the kingdom they would naturally pass on to him the areas in the possession of Hyrcanus II who was the last legitimate ruler of Judaea from the Roman point of view. Thus Herod must have received the whole of Judaea, including Joppe and Eastern Idumaea, Peraea and Galilee including the Valley of Jezreel.[3] It even seems that he was at the same time granted an important increase of territory. A hint to this effect can be found in Appianus' *Civil War.* According to this source in 39 B.C. Mark Antony settled the affairs of the various kings subject to his rule, including the taxes to be collected from Herod for Idumaea and the people of Samaria.[4] If we take this passage at its face meaning, i.e. as referring to Idumaea and the people of the city of Samaria, we are up

---

[1] This fact influences e.g. the foundation date of Caesarea, which is usually placed in 9 B.C., i.e. the 28th year of Herod, reckoning from 37 B.C.; but Herod undoubtedly regarded his reign as beginning in 40/39 B.C. (*Ant.* 14:14:5-389; *War* 1:14:4-285). His 28th year would, according to the official reckoning, fall into 13/12 B.C. Cf. Avi-Yonah *IEJ,* 1, 1950-1, p. 169.

[2] *Ant.* 14:14:4/5-384-9; *War* 1:14:4-284-5.

[3] See above, pp. 82, 84.

[4] Applianus, *Bell. civ.* V, 75.

against a double contradiction with Josephus. According to the latter, Idumaea was left by Pompey to the Jews[5] and Samaria was given to Herod only in 30 B.C.[6] In the one case there would be no sense in arranging separately for the payment of tribute for something which was only part of the territory Herod had 'inherited' from the Hasmonaeans. In the other he would have to pay for something he did not yet have. In the first case we would expect to find a reference to Judaea (and indeed some authors have emended Appianus' *idoumaian* to *ioudaian*). However, these contradictions can be settled easily if we take the "Idumaea" of Appianus to refer to Western Idumaea (the region of Marisa)[7] and "Samaria" to the territory of the Samaritan people. Marisa had been razed by the Parthians apparently beyond all hope of recovery.[8] Its territory could therefore be reunited with the rest of Idumaea without an infringement of the existing rights of a Greek city. In view of his Idumaean origin Herod was the right person to rule over the whole of this people. The Samaritan lands, on the other hand, had remained a splinter of territory, isolated between Judaea and the Greek cities and connected with neither. They could easily be attached to Herod's kingdom; he was no religious fanatic and had married a Samaritan named Malthace, the mother of Archelaus.[9] Jamnia and Azotus seem to have been handed over to Herod together with Marisa, while Arethusa (Pegae) and possibly also Apollonia went together with the Samaritan territory. This hypothesis is supported by the connection in ancient times between Jamnia and Azotus with Idumaea and of Pegae with Samaria.[10] It seems best therefore to assume that their attachment to Herod's kingdom took place in 40 B.C., for they are not listed in any of the subsequent increases of his territory and yet were of it subsequently. Jamnia and Azotus were left by Herod to his sister Salome in his will. He founded Antipatris

---

[5] See above, p. 80.

[6] *Ant.* 15:7:3-217; *War* 1:20:3-396.

[7] Cf. A. Momigliano: *Ricerche sull'organizzazione della Guidea sotto il dominio romano,* 1934, pp. 348-9.

[8] *Ant.* 14:13:9-364; *War* 1:13:9-269.

[9] *Ant.* 17:10:1-250; *War* 1:28:4-562.

[10] See above, pp. 38, 48.

on the site of Pegae. Apollonia was surrounded by his territories, and yet we do not hear of its remaining independent like Ascalon. The Roman rulers may have hoped to achieve two purposes by this increase of Herod's kingdom. On the one hand the Jews might possibly submit more easily to a ruler who brought with him this handsome gift. On the other hand the addition of non-Jewish subjects would create a better balance within a régime based on a compromise between Jew and Gentile.

In 37 B.C. the Parthians retreated definitely beyond the Euphrates. Thereby ended the generation of unrest in Judaea which followed Pompey's conquest. Roman rule remained unchallenged in the Orient. All the peoples living there were henceforth subject to the Roman administration. Some of them were governed directly, like the Syrians and Phoenicians, others were under native rulers—the fate of the Nabataeans, the Ituraeans and the Jews. Any territorial changes in the future were effected not by conquest but by subtle maneuvering at Rome and were made by an edict from above,

The first ten years of Herod's rule coincide with the last phase of the Roman civil wars, in the course of which the republic turned into a thinly disguised monarchy. The first requirements of a successful vassal during this troubled period were adaptability and time-serving. He had to know when to submit to the strong and how to abandon the fallen in good time. Herod passed this test with flying colours. He succeeded not only in keeping his kingdom intact, but even in increasing it with considerable parts of the lands of his neighbours. The second and longer part of his reign (30 - 4 B.C.) was a period of peace under the sceptre of Augustus Caesar. During this time the required qualities of a ruler were quite different. First of all, he had to show administrative ability, energy combined with moderation, in order to let Roman "law and order" reign unchallenged. Here too, Herod knew how to keep his unruly subjects quiet. Again he prospered and his kingdom continued to grow, at least in extent.

In the early days of Herod's rule (37-30 B.C.) his main danger came from Mark Antony, who ruled the East as one of the Roman triumvirate. Antony was subservient to Cleopatra, Queen of Egypt, to such an extent that he made the Roman power in the Orient serve the ends of Egypt. Cleopatra's aim was to restore Ptolemaic rule in Syria and Palestine. She therefore tried to persuade Antony to hand over to her the Nabataeans and Judaea. Antony resisted her importunities to a certain extent, but in the meantime granted her the whole coast up the river Eleutherus (North of Beirut), excepting only Tyre and Sidon.[11] He also gave her the profitable oasis of Jericho, rich in date groves and balsam plantations.[12] By these transactions Herod lost Arethusa-Pegae, Apollonia, Joppe, Jamnia and Azotus, and his access to the sea. Malichus, the Nabataean King, also lost part of his possessions.[13] At the same time Antony ordered the execution of Lysanias, the son of Ptolemaeus, King of the Ituraeans.[14] Lysanias' territories were divided: Sidon and Damascus received the northern part and had thereafter a common boundary.[15] The southern part went to one Zenodorus who "farmed" from Cleopatra the "House of Lysanias."[16] Herod proved again his adaptability even in the most difficult circumstances. He agreed to hire from Cleopatra the use of his own possessions, as well as the expropriated lands of Malichus. Even so his crown would have been in great danger, if Antony had been victorious at Actium. It was only the victory of his rival Octavianus (Augustus) which saved Herod from the Egyptian danger. Herod succeeded in persuading the victor of his continued loyalty and usefulness. Augustus not only confirmed Herod's rule and returned to him the areas lost to Cleopatra, but granted him rule over several Greek cities: Gadara and Hippus in the Decapolis, Gaza, Anthedon and Strato's Tower on the coast; Samaria and Gabaa in the interior.[17] This increase in territory constituted again an important addition to the Greek, non-Jewish, element under Herod's rule. Herod must have understood by then that all his attempts to obtain the favour of his Jewish subjects would be in vain. A strengthening of the

---

[11] *Ant.* 15:4:1-95; *War* 1:18:5-361; Plutarch: *Antony,* 36, 3.
[12] *Ant.* 15:4:2-96; *War* 1:18:5-361; Dio Cassius XLIX, 32.
[13] See preceding note.
[14] *Ant.* 15:4:1-92; *War* 1:22:3-440; Plutarch, *loc. cit.* (n. 11 above).
[15] *Ant.* 18:6:3-153.
[16] *Ant.* 15:10:1-344; *War* 1:20:4-398.
[17] *Ant.* 15:7:3-217; *War* 1:20:3-396.

Hellenized population in his kingdom would, therefore, strengthen somewhat the foundations of his rule.

Herod's energy found much scope in his new acquisitions. He transformed Strato's Tower into the City of Caesarea and enlarged its harbour Sebastus.[18] The new port served Galilee through the Megiddo Pass and Judaea by way of the Sharon. At the same time it made Herod independent of the harbour of Joppe, a town hostile to him.[19] It also damaged the position of Ptolemais-Accho, which was outside his territory. Herod also rebuilt Samaria, settled there some of his veterans and called it Sebaste.[20]

By 23 B.C. the emperor Augustus was convinced that Herod had indeed shown unusual administrative abilities in his enlarged Kingdom. He therefore entrusted him then with another important task. The inhabitants of Damascus had been complaining for some time of the molestation of their caravans by the people of the Trachonitis. This region included the area of petrified lava (now called the Lejja), which extends north-west of the Hauran mountains. The Trachonitis belonged at the time to the tetrarch Zenodorus who had "inherited" it from Lysanias, the last King of the Ituraeans.[21] Instead of suppressing the robbers, Zenodorus had entered into a profitable partnership with them. The emperor therefore transferred to Herod the Trachonitis, Batanaea and Auranitis.[22] Three years later, Zenodorus died and Herod received the rest of his lands: the Gaulanitis, the city of Paneas and the Ulatha region.[23] In order to pacify the Trachonitis, Herod settled on its borders military colonies of loyal Idumaeans and Babylonian Jews. After one attempt at revolt, the people of the Trachonitis submitted to his energetic rule.

By these successive enlargements of territory, Herod's Judaea finally

---

[18] *Ant.* 15:9:6-331-341; *War* 1:21:5-408-416; for the ruins cf. L. Haefeli: *Caesarea am Meer,* 1923; A. Reifenberg, *IEJ,* 1, 1950-1, pp. 20-32; Hill: *BMC Palestine,* p. 13.

[19] *Ant.* 14:15:1-396; *War* 1:15:3-292.

[20] *Ant.* 15:9:5-296/8; *War* 1:21:2-403; G. A. Reisner, C. S. Fisher and D. G. Lyon: *Excavations at Samaria,* 1924; J. W. Crowfoot et al.: *Samaria-Sebaste* I, 1942.

[21] See above, p. 89.

[22] *Ant.* 15:10:1-343/8; *War* 1:20:4-398.

[23] *Ant.* 15:10:3-359/60; *War* 1:20:4-400.

extended over lands which had never been subject even to Jannaeus. These new additions covered 3500 sq. m., which was over 25% of Herod's former possessions. The real importance of these increases, however, was not in their extent, but in the fact that Herod thus became the master of a new land, largely unsettled and almost without history. Here he was free of the heavy burden of bitter memories which separated him from his subjects in Judaea and in Galilee. Here there was no old-established tradition of government which had been upset by him and no native aristocracy whom he had sent to its death. The wide new lands he had now acquired were sparsely populated. They were easily capable of absorbing some of the surplus population from Judaea, for this surplus no longer had the outlet provided by the Hasmonaean conquests. To the new settlers Herod and his house were patrons and protectors; and they were correspondingly grateful. The many remains of Jewish settlements in this area are a witness to the success of this internal colonization.[24] Some of these settlements continued to flourish even after the expulsion of the Jews from Judaea proper. These areas were therefore to the Herodians the "house royal" of their dynasty. The reverence in which the dynasty was held was not restricted to the Jewish colonists. It is also evidenced by inscriptions in various Gentile temples dedicated to the great King and his successors.[25] Another inscription (from the time of Agrippa I ?) illustrates the amount of civilising labour invested in these areas. It reproduces an address of the King to the inhabitants of the region, in particular, probably the Trachonitis. He tries to persuade them to give up living in caves like wild beasts. They should rather build themselves houses and live like the rest of humanity.[26]

The exceptionally close links between these areas and the house of Herod were known and appreciated by the Roman government. Batanaea, Trachonitis, Auranitis and Gaulanitis formed a kind of school for the

---

[24] H. Kohl and C. Watzinger: *Antike Synagogen in Galiläa,* 1916, s.v. Umm al Qanatir, ed-Dikke, Khirbet Qanaf, er-Rafid; L. A. Mayer and A. Reifenberg, *BJPES,* IV, p. 1 ff. (Hebrew).

[25] H. Butler: *Princeton Expedition to Syria,* II A, pp. 379 ff; *ib.* III, A, pp. 365, 424.

[26] Waddington-Le Bas: *Recueil,* No. 2329; *OGIS,* I, p. 634, No. 424.

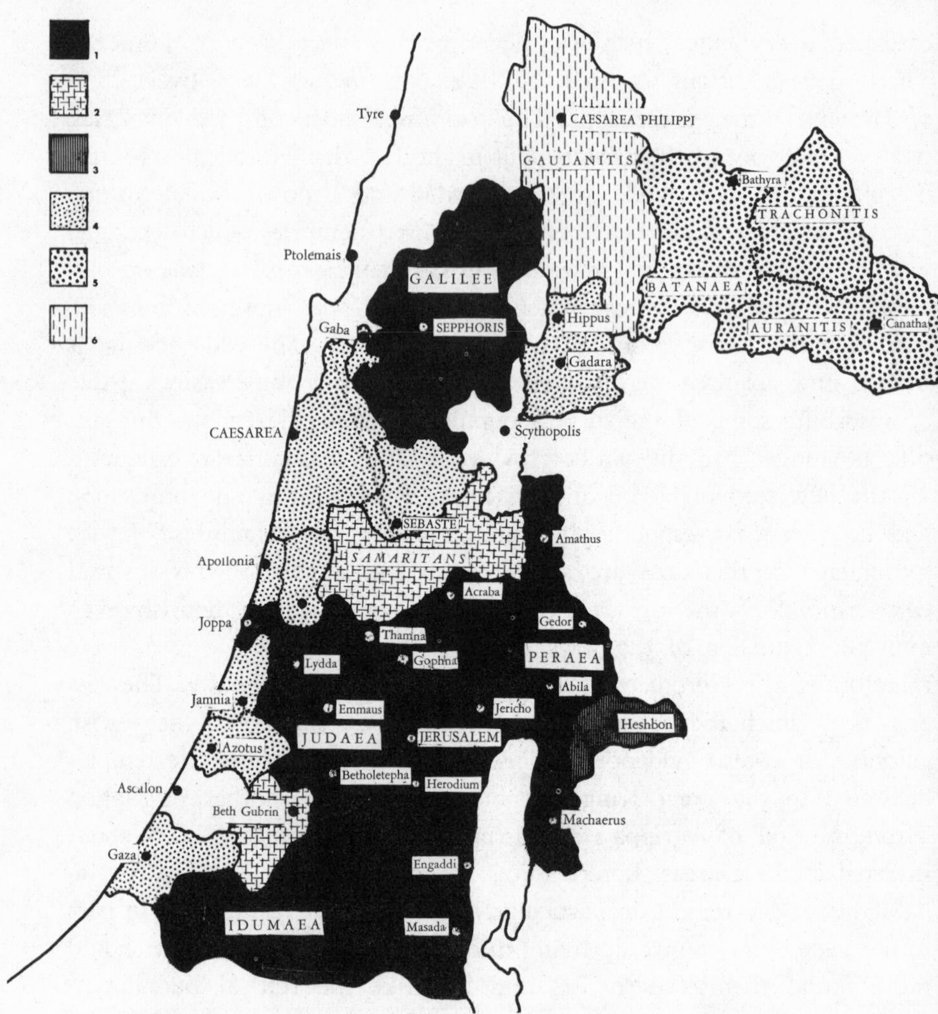

Map 6: THE EXPANSION OF HEROD'S KINGDOM
1 — Transferred to Herod from Hyrcanus II in 40 B.C.
2 — Added in 40 B.C.
3 — Conquered from the Nabataeans?
4 — Granted by Augustus in 30 B.C.
5 — Added in 23 B.C.
6 — Added in 20 B.C.
Jericho — Toparchies in Judaea

princes of the dynasty. They served as a testing ground for the administrative abilities of a new ruler. If he passed the test, he was gradually promoted and his lands enlarged up to the whole of Herod's Kingdom, if possible. Agrippa I completed the whole course. His son Agrippa II was well started on it. He received parts of Galilee and Peraea a few years before the outbreak of the Roman war completely changed the political situation.

With the addition (in 20 B.C.) of the Gaulanitis, Paneas and Ulatha, the Kingdom of Herod reached its greatest territorial extent. If we compare it with the area ruled by Jannaeus, we note that Jannaeus had Dora and the Carmel, most of the cities of the Decapolis and part of Moab—all of which were outside Herod's territory. As against this Herod possessed Batanaea, Trachonitis and Auranitis, areas never reached by the Hasmonaean conquest. A comparison of the areas of the two Kingdoms shows a slight difference in favour of Jannaeus. Herod ruled about 13,000 sq. m., Jannaeus about 14,800 sq. m. We should, however, remember that the political conditions of the times and the security of their respective tenures were quite different.

Chapter VII

THE INTERNAL ORGANIZATION OF HEROD'S KINGDOM

THE peculiar ambivalence of the Herodian monarchy, which oscillated between Judaism and Hellenism, was also expressed in the structure of the state. It was composed of two main divisions: the 'King's country,' most inhabited by Jews, and the Hellenized cities;—and this duality was reflected in the internal organization of each. In the King's country there were parallel organizations of the royal administration and the Jewish courts. In the Gentile area the autonomous cities were supervised by royal officials.

In the Jewish area the lowest administrative unit was the village. Its head was the 'village scribe'[1] who was appointed on behalf of the king. The village inhabitants were represented by their "elders,"[2] the heads of the local families. The royal estates formed, of course, special enclaves, administered by the 'King's man' as is recorded at Cana.[3] The lands of a score or so of villages formed a toparchy. This was the basic district, into which the land was divided from the point of view of the central authorities. The headquarters of a toparchy were in a town, townlet or royal fortress,[4] none of which was autonomous. In the whole Jewish area ruled by Herod there were only two real cities: Jerusalem and Joppa.[5] The municipal rights of the latter appear to have been abolished later on. In the time of Claudius the emperor addressed himself to Jerusalem alone.[6] In Pliny's list Joppa appears only as the headquarters of a top-

---

[1] *Ant.* 16:7:3-203; *War* 1:24:3-479.

[2] Luke 7:3.

[3] John 4:46.

[4] See the list below, p. 95 ff.

[5] *Ant.* 17:11:4-320 (referring to the partition of Herod's kingdom).

[6] *Ant.* 20:1:2-11; cf. Tcherikover, *IEJ*, 14, 1964, pp. 62f., 75f.

archy.[7] The officer administering a toparchy was called a *strategus toparchus* or plain *strategus*.[8]

We possess two lists of toparchies in Judaea. One is the list of Pliny mentioned above. It includes ten toparchies: Hiericuntem, Emmaüm, Lyddam, Iopicam, Acrabitenam, Gophaniticam, Thamniticam, Betholeptephenen, Orinen, Herodium.[9] The second list is that of Josephus.[10] It contains thirteen names, adding to Pliny's list Idumaea, Engeddi and Jamnia. Josephus also has 'Pella' for 'Betholeptephe.' In other places Josephus mentions various other toparchies, from which we can complete his list.

The Jewish half of Herod's Kingdom was accordingly composed of the following toparchies: In JUDAEA[11] the central toparchy was that of Jerusalem, called *Orine* ("the mountainous one"). It corresponds to the Hebrew "Har ha-Melekh," the King's mountain;[12] the former toparchy of Beth-Zur was now administered from the fortress of *Herodium* (Jebel el-Fureidis, south-east of Bethlehem, in the desert of Tekoa);[13] *Jericho* remained as before the capital of its rich district;[14] *Betholeptephe* (Pliny) or Pella (Josephus),[15] modern Beth Nattif, replaced Keila; *Emmaus*[16] took the place of Gezer; *Lydda* (Lod) remained the headquarters of its district; *Thamma*[17] (Kh. Tibneh) was substituted for Arimathaea in the

[7] Pliny, *Hist. Nat.* V, 70.

[8] Cf. 1 Macc. 15:11, the Nabatean strategoi in the provincial towns on the borders of Pereaea (*Ant.* 18:5:1-112) and the Nabataean inscriptions published by Clermont-Ganneau, *RAO*, II, pp. 188, 199.

[9] Plin. *loc. cit.* (n. 7 above).

[10] *War* 3:3:5-54-55. Jamnia is also mentioned *Ant.* 18:2:2-31; *War* 2:9:1-167.

[11] Cf. the division of Judaea in the Persian period, pp. 20 ff. above.

[12] Mishna *Shebiith* 9:23; Tos. *ib.* 7:10/11-71, 20 ff. etc.

[13] *Ant.* 14:13:9-360; 15:9:4-323-325; 17:8:3-199; *War* 1:13:8-265; 21:10-419-420; 33:9-673; Schick *ZDPV*, 1880, p. 88 ff.; Alt *PJb*, 1928, p. 18.

[14] Herodian Jericho was situated at Tulul Abu 'Aleiq, cf. Kelso and D. C. Baramki, *AASOR*, XXIX/XXX, 1955; Pritchard, *ib.* XXXII/III, 1958.

[15] Plin. *N. h.* V, 14; *War* 4:8:1-445. Both sources mention Bethleptepha; *War* 3:3:5, 55 has instead 'Pella' a version supported by an inscription published by Savignac, *RB*, 1904, p. 83.

[16] *War* 1:11:2-222 etc.; Mishnah *Arakhin* 2:4. L. H. Vincent-F. M. Abel: *Emmaüs*, 1932.

[17] Plin. *n.h.* V, 15, 70; *War* 2:20:4-567 etc.; Abel: *RB*, 1925, p. 205 f.; Rad, *PJb*, 1933, p. 32.

north-western district; *Gophna*[18] (Jifna) replaced Aphaerema in the north-east; *Acraba* (Aqraba) extended further to the North. *Joppa* is listed by Pliny, and *Jamnia* by Josephus. These complete the roll of Judaean toparchies.

IDUMAEA (which Josephus considers as part of Judaea) contained two toparchies. One was *Idumaea* in a restricted sense, apparently Western Idumaea, the former region of Marisa. It seems to have been administered from Betogabris[19] (Beth-Guvrin). The second district was *Engeddi*[20] i.e. eastern Idumaea. Its former capital was Adoraim. The transfer of the district headquarters to the inconveniently situated oasis of Engeddi on the shores of the Dead Sea was probably motivated by economic reasons.

In PERAEA, the Jewish region beyond the Jordan, we know for certain of two toparchies only: *Julias* (or *Livias,* formerly Beth-Ramtha, now Tell er-Rame)[21] in the northern part of the Jordan Valley, and *Abila*[22] (Kh. el Kafrein) in the southern. To these we should certainly add *Gadara* (Gedor, Tell Jadur near es-Salt) the capital of all Peraea.[23] The toparchy of Gedor must have included the mountainous parts of Peraea. In later times this region was divided into three parts.[24] For the Herodian period, however, we should assume a fourth toparchy with its headquarters at *Amathus* (Tell 'Amta) in the northern section of the Jordan Valley. A royal palace was situated there in the days of Herod,[25]

[18] *War* 1:1:5-45; 11:2-222 etc.; Plin. *N.h.* V, 14 (15), 70; Tos. *Ohiloth* 18:16; Alt *PJb,* 1926, p. 43.

[19] Corrupted to Betabris in *War* 4:7:1-447; cf. Tos. *Ohiloth* 18:16; Abel, *Géographie* I, p. 443.

[20] *War* 3:3:5-55; 4:7:2-402-4; Tos. *Shebiith,* 7:10; Albright, *BASOR,* 18, p. 14; Mazar et al., *BIES,* 27, 1963, pp. 1 ff.

[21] *Ant.* 18:2:1-27; *War* 2:9:1-168; bab. *Shabbath* 26 a; Glueck, *BASOR,* 91, pp. 20-21; id., *AASOR,* XXV/VIII, pp. 389-91.

[22] *Ant.* 5:1:1-4; *War* 4:7:6-438; jer. *Shebiith* 36 c; Glueck, *BASOR,* 91, p. 15 f.; id., *AASOR,* XXV-VIII, pp. 376-78; Alt, *PJb,* 1936, p. 112, n. 2.

[23] *War* 4:7:3-413; Mishnah *Arakhin* 9:6; Tos. *Shebiith* 7:11; Ptolemaeus V, 14; Haefeli: *Peräa,* pp. 107-110.

[24] The Mishnah (*Shebiith* 9:2) envisages a threefold partition, and the same number of districts follows from the Byzantine sources, for which see below, pp. 112 n. 18, 125.

[25] *Ant.* 13:356; *War* 3:44-47; jer *Shebiith* 38 d; Haefeli: *Peräa,* p. 96; Albright, *AASOR,* VI, p. 44; Glueck, *ib.,* XXV/VIII, pp. 310-1.

probably a heritage from the time of Theodorus the ruler of Philadelphia.[26]

In GALILEE Josephus noticed two toparchies, *Tiberias* and *Taricheae* (Migdal).[27] Together they composed the eastern half of Lower Galilee. The western half of this country we may also divide into two toparchies: *Sepphoris*[28] and probably also *Araba* (Arrabat el-Battuf).[29] This region is certainly too big to have belonged to one toparchy alone. On the other hand *Upper Galilee* could well have formed a toparchy by itself.

To sum up: there were thirteen toparchies in Herodian Judaea, four in Peraea and five in Galilee; twenty-two in all.

The enumeration of the toparchies at once raises the problem of the *ma'amad* and the *mishmar*. The former (literally 'place of standing') represents a provincial district, the members of which assembled in their district capital at set dates and sent a delegation to the Temple. There were twenty-four such districts, corresponding to the twenty-four *mishmaroth* or 'courses of priests.'[30] Various scholars[31] have suggested a link between the two kinds of districts. Indeed, there could hardly have subsisted in the Judaea of that time two separate territorial systems—the one political and the other religious. Such a relation does, however, raise two problems: (a) the time at which this system originated; (b) the discrepancy between the twenty-two toparchies listed above and the twenty-four *ma'amadoth*.

As regards the first problem, the division into twenty-four *ma'amadoth* cannot have originated before the territorial expansion of Judaea. Otherwise there would be no room in it for the Jewish populations of Galilee and Idumaea, the coastal plain and the lands beyond the Jordan. We have thus to assume, with A. Schalit, that the system was built up

---

[26] *Ant.* 13:13:3-356; *War* 1:4:2-86-88.

[27] *War* 2:13:2-252. For the period preceding the foundation of Tiberias we should assume some other centre, such as the fortress of Agrippina; for the location of Taricheae cf. Albright, *AASOR,* II/III, p. 29 ff.

[28] L. Waterman ed.: *Report of excavations at Sepphoris,* 1937.

[29] *War* 2:21:7-629; Mishnah *Shabbath* 17:7.

[30] H. Danby, *The Mishnah,* 1933, p. 794.

[31] S. Klein: *Eretz Yehudah,* pp. 212-213; A. Schalit: *Roman rule in Palestine,* pp. 24-30 (both in Hebrew).

piecemeal during the Hasmonaean period. On the other hand, we have to reject Schalit's view attributing the final form of the system to the time of Jannaeus. A period of dynamic conquests and steady expansion could not be one of rigid systematization. Moreover, the twenty-four districts cannot by any means be fitted into the areas conquered by this King. It seems much more likely that this religious-political system was set up under one of Jannaeus' successors. We should look for a period in which two conditions were fulfilled: the boundaries had become fixed and the influence of the halachic circles (i.e. the Pharisees) had become predominant. The first condition would exclude the rule of Salome Alexandra, the second that of Herod. We are thus bound to assume that the twenty-four *ma'amadoth* were set up under Hyrcanus II.

The second question is how to bring the number of twenty-two toparchies up to that of twenty-four *ma'amadoth.* There were at least two areas outside Judaea (as defined by Pliny and Josephus) which would be suitable for such additional regions. One would be Azotus, which was by then a Jewish city,[32] although formally outside Judaea. The other would be the toparchy of Narbata, a Jewish enclave in the territory of Caesarea.[33]

The existence of toparchies within the areas of the various cities, such as we observe in the case of Caesarea-Narbata, is confirmed by an epigraphical find. It is a boundary-stone, inscribed in Latin, which was found in the neighbourhood of Ptolemais. In it is mentioned a *pagus vicinalis,* i.e. a rural district, as opposed to an urban one. Both together must have formed the city territory.[34]

Herod seems to have continued the convenient Hasmonaean system of grouping various toparchies in a larger unit called a *meris.* In the 'King's land' under his rule there were five such districts: Judaea proper, Idumaea, Samaria, Galilee, Peraea. A *meridarchēs* was placed at the head of each of these regions.[35] Peraea served for a time as a separate te-

[32] *War* 4:3:2-130.
[33] *Ib.* 2:14:5-291.
[34] Avi-Yonah, *QDAP* XII, p. 86 f., No. 3.
[35] *Ant.* 15:7:3-216; cf. *ib.,* 7:9-254.

trarchy administered by Herod's brother Pheroras.[36] Of course, even then it remained under the suzerainty of the King. Herod had moreover to request the permission of the emperor to make this arrangement. We find a possible parallel to this chain of administrative units in a parallel hierarchy of Jewish religious courts: a court of three sat in each village, a court of seven in a toparchy, of twenty-three in a *meris,* and the great Sanhedrin of seventy-one was at the head of the whole system.

The settlements of veterans at Heshbon[37] and Gabaa,[38] and possibly also at Azotus[38a] apparently had a status somewhere between that of the 'King's land' and that of the Greek cities. The areas which were added to Herod's kingdom beyond the Jordan (the Auranitis, Trachonitis, Batanaea and Gaulanitis) were administered as military districts.[39] We know nothing of their sub-divisions, save that the Gaulanitis was divided into an Upper and a Lower district,[40] and the territory of the fortress of Gamala.[41]

The Greek cities, even those 'founded' by Herod himself, seem to have enjoyed the usual rights of a *polis* in a Hellenistic monarchy. They were administered by officials elected by a select city-council. A popular assembly existed at least in theory. The cities formed a separate entity within the Kingdom. Some of those included in Herod's Kingdom were of ancient origin such as Gaza and its dependencies, Anhedon, Appollonia, Gadara, Hippus and Paneas. Others were new or re-founded by the King, such as Caesarea, Sebaste and Antipatris. The autonomy of the cities in both categories was restricted by the supervision of a royal official, the *strategus.* This function was sometimes exercised by the governor of a neighboring province. Thus Cosgabar, the governor of Idumaea, was also in charge of the affairs of Gaza.[42] Josephus indeed relates

---

[36] *Ant.* 16:11:2-362; *War* 1:24:4-483.
[37] *Ant.* 15:8:5-294.
[38] *Ib.,* and *War* 3:3:1-36.
[38a] See p. 149 below.
[39] *Ant.* 16:4:6-130; 17:10:6-274; R. Savignac, *RB,* 1957, p. 200.
[40] *War* 4:1:1-2.
[41] *War* 3:3:5-56.
[42] *Ant.* 15:7:9-254.

this fact of a period when Gaza was not in Jewish possession at all. We may assume, however, yet another of his anachronisms. In other cases the supervising official was specially assigned to the city. We know this for certain as regards Caesarea Philippi at a somewhat later period.[43] The first duty of the royal representative was to see to it that order and public security were preserved in the city and its territory. For this purpose there was also a royal *strategus* in Jerusalem, although the city was not, strictly speaking, fully autonomous.[44]

Herod followed the general line of the Hellenistic kings in multiplying city foundations. These were meant to form positions of strength and foci for the spread of the cosmopolitan Greek culture. The future of the Herodian dynasty was obviously bound up with achieving a blend of Hellenic and Jewish elements. The dynasty's ultimate failure in this respect opened a chasm by which their house was finally engulfed. The foundation of cities was one of the most efficacious ways of bridging this dangerous gap.

Herod called his major foundations in honour of the emperor (Caesarea, Sebaste).[45] Only the smaller towns and fortresses were named after members of his family (Antipatris, Cyprus, Phasaelis). Antipatris was built in the well-watered plain of Capharsaba,[46] on the site of Hellenistic Pegae (Arethusa? now Tell Aphek-Ras el 'Ain). Phasaelis (Kh. Fasayil)[47] was situated in the Jordan Valley, north of Jericho. It was a centre of plantations, with long aqueducts bringing water from the mountains. Neither seems to have had full municipal rights. Herod also took care of Anthedon (Kh. Teda on the coast northwest of Gaza). He called it Agrippias or Agrippeium[48] in honour of Marcus Vipsanius Agrippa, Augustus' general and son-in-law.

Apart from the foundation of cities, one of Herod's main occupations

---

[43] *Life* 13-74.

[44] *Ant.* 17:6:3-156; *ib.,* 8:7/2-209/210; *War* 1:33:3-652; 2:1:3-8; on the status of Jerusalem cf. V. Tcherikover, *IEJ,* 14, 1964, pp. 61 ff.

[45] Cf. also above, p. 90.

[46] *Ant.* 16:5:2-142-143; *War* 1:21:9-417; Mishnah *Gittin* 7:7.

[47] *Ant.* 16:5:2-145; *War* 1:21:9-418; Abel, *RB,* 1913, p. 235.

[48] *Ant.* 13:13:3-357; *War* 1:4:2-87; *ib.,* 21:8-416; Gatt, *ZDPV*, 1884, p. 5 ff.; Pythian-Adams, *QSt.,* 1923, p. 14 ff.

was the construction and strengthening of fortresses. He was all his life suspicious of his own subjects, and rightly so. His fortifications (including those of Jerusalem) were thus like a two-edged sword. They were intended as a protection against his enemies from abroad, but they served in equal measure to secure the king against an internal enemy, his own people. The colony of veterans at Heshbon and the fortress of Machaerus[49] may have served to protect his frontiers with the Nabataeans. Hyrcania (Kh. Mird ? in the Judaean desert) was, however, a state-prison, a place of execution and of secret burial.[50] The fortress of Cyprus,[51] so called in honour of Herod's mother, protected the new palace at Herodian Jericho (Tulul Abu 'Aleiq). The veteran colony of Gabaa, settled by cavalry soldiers, guarded the entry of the Valley of Jezreel and the royal estates there. It was called Gabaa of the Cavalrymen (Hippenus).[52] Another colony of the same character may have existed at inland Azotus. Here was another centre of royal estates, and the appellation Hippenus was added here too to the city name.[53] The newly erected fortress of Herodium was also intended as a royal mausoleum.[54] Masada in a remote corner of the Judaean desert on the shores of the Dead Sea was intended as a last place of refuge, a function it fulfilled in 40 B.C. and again in A.D. 73.[55]

The Kingdom of Herod, studded with cities and fortresses, thus presented a brave face to the world. All this external splendour, however, could not hide its internal weaknesses. It was based on an attempt to make a bridge between two incompatible ways of life and points of view, and it was bound to perish in the open conflict of the two.

---

[49] *Ant.* 13:16:3-417; *War* 7:6:1/2-164/177; Tos. *Shebiith* 7:11; Tos *Rosh ha-Shanah* 2 (1); 2; Strabo XVI, 2, 40; Pliny, *N.h.* V, 72; Haefeli: *Samaria u. Peräa,* pp. 114-20; Glueck, *AASOR* XVIII-XIX, pp. 131-135.

[50] *Ant.* 16:2:1-13; 17:7:1-187; *War* 1:8:2-161; *ib.,* 8:4-167; *ib.,* 19:1-364; *ib.,* 33:7-664; Rhetoré, *RB,* 1897, p. 462.

[51] *Ant.* 16:5:2-143 *War* 1:21:4-407; *ib.,* 21:9-417; 2:18-6-484; Alt, *PJb,* 1925, p. 24.

[52] See above n. 38 and Dalman, *PJb,* 1923, p. 38; Alt, *ib.,* 1925, p. 41; Maisler, *BJPES* VI, p. 37; *ib.,* IX, p. 39 f. (Hebrew). The identification of the site is not certain; it should be somewhere in the vicinity of Canaanite Geba (Tell 'Amr east of Haifa).

[53] Georgius Cyprius 1021; Hierocles: *Synecdemus,* 718, 6.

[54] Cf. n. 13 above.

[55] Avi-Yonah et al., *IEJ,* 7, 1957, p. 1 ff; Yadin, *ibid.,* 15, 196, pp. 1 ff.

Chapter VIII

THE DIVISION OF HEROD'S KINGDOM

WELL before his death in 4 B.C., King Herod realized that none of his three surviving sons was capable of governing all his kingdom. In his will, therefore, he recommended to Caesar Augustus that his lands be divided between them. After much hesitation the emperor decided to risk the experiment. He gave Archelaus, the eldest, Judaea with Idumaea, Samaria, the two great cities founded by Herod (Caesarea and Sebaste), and the distinguishing title of ethnarch. Archelaus' share provided a revenue of six hundred talents a year. The other Greek cities formerly under Herod (Gaza and its dependencies, Gadara and Hippus) were placed directly under the proconsul of Syria. The second son, Herod Antipas, received Galilee, Peraea and the title of tetrarch; his annual revenue was two hundred talents. The third, Philip, also nominated tetrarch, received Batanaea, Trachonitis, Auranitis, Gaulanitis, Panaeas and the Ulatha; his revenue was one hundred talents. Herod's sister Salome was endowed with the cities Jamnia and Azotus in the coastal plain, together with Phasaelis in the Jordan Valley. Her share yielded sixty talents; it was placed under the general supervision of Archelaus as the senior member of the family.[1]

This partition reflects a well-defined political line. The areas inhabited by the Jews (who were feared for their turbulence) was split up between two authorities, the one administering Judaea and the other Galilee and Peraea. Archelaus received two predominantly Gentile cities and the Samaritans, so as to counter-balance Judaea. Idumaea, from which his family originated, could presumably be accounted loyal to the Herodian dynasty. Archelaus himself was the son of Malthace, Herod's Samaritan wife, and as such acceptable to this nation.[2] The areas beyond the Jordan, which were a kind of royal apanage of the dynasty, were set aside and

[1] *Ant.* 17:11:4-317-321; *War* 2:7:6:3-93-98.
[2] *Ant.* 17:1:3-20; *War* 1:28:4-562.

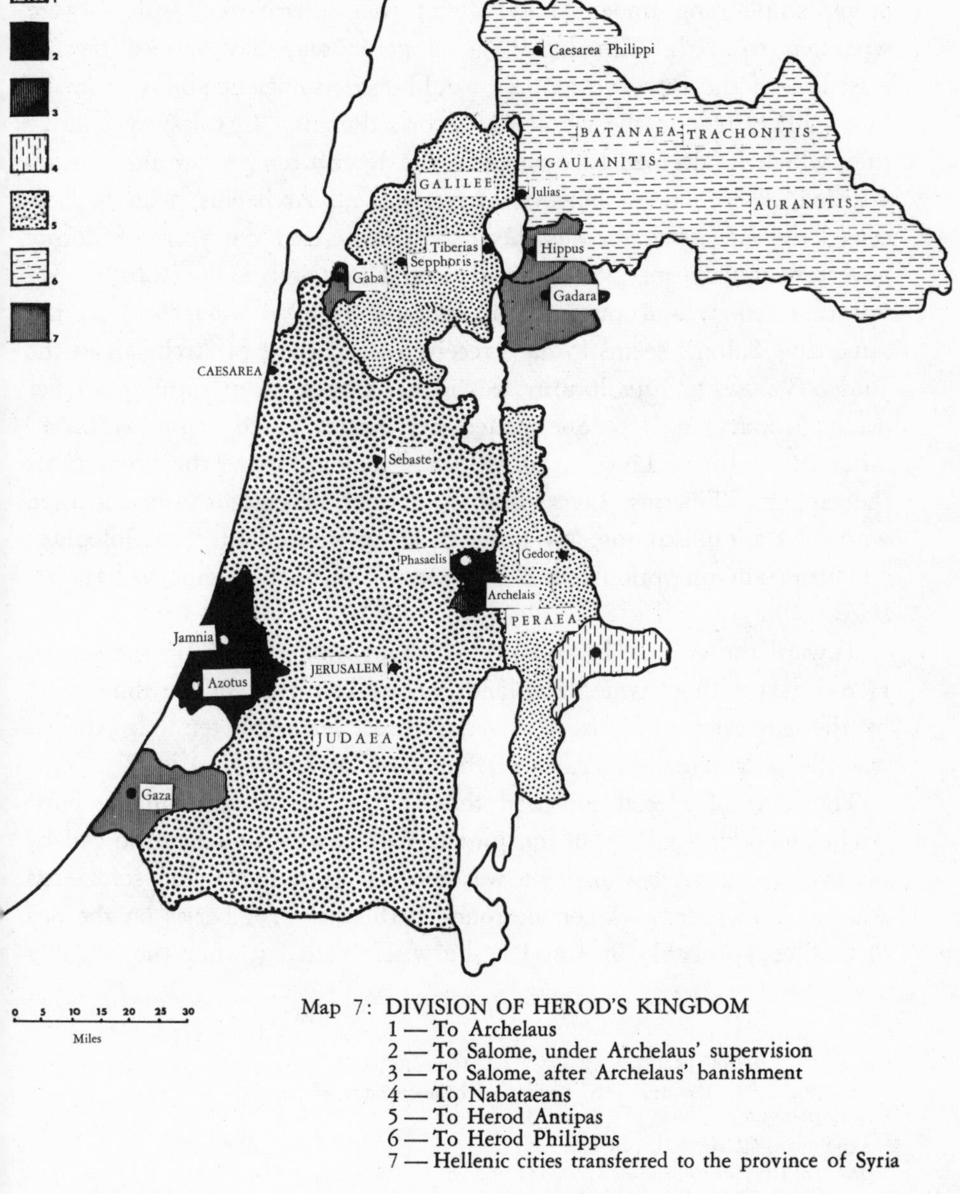

Map 7: DIVISION OF HEROD'S KINGDOM
1 — To Archelaus
2 — To Salome, under Archelaus' supervision
3 — To Salome, after Archelaus' banishment
4 — To Nabataeans
5 — To Herod Antipas
6 — To Herod Philippus
7 — Hellenic cities transferred to the province of Syria

handed over to a third ruler. The Hellenized cities, which had already been complaining under Herod about their "barbarian" ruler,[3] were separated from the Kingdom. The emperor may have hoped that at least one of the three new rulers would show sufficient ability to make him a likely heir to the whole of Herod's domains. In this way indirect rule, which he deemed best suited to the Jewish temper, would be safeguarded. These hopes, however, were dashed. Archelaus, who had received the largest share, was the first to fail. After ten years of stormy government Augustus was obliged to send him into exile (A.D. 6). He was replaced by a Roman official with the title of *praefectus.*[4] At the same time Salome seems to have received the village of Archelais in the Jordan Valley, for this locality was in her possession at the time of her death (about A.D. 10) She willed her estates to the empress Livia.[5] After the death of Livia (A.D. 29) these lands became the property of the emperor Tiberius, Livia's son. A special procurator was entrusted with their administration. We know of his existence both from Josephus[6] and from an inscription found at Jamnia,[7] where he seems to have resided.

Toward the end of Tiberius' rule (about A.D. 34) Philip the son of Herod died without issue.[8] His lands were taken over for the time being by the governor of Syria. For about three years the tetrarch Antipas was the only remaining ruler of the house of Herod.

The sons of Herod followed their father in his founding activity. Archelaus built a village in the Jordan Valley, which he dared to call by his own name: Archelais.[9] He was the last Herodian to do so. Herod Antipas knew better. When he founded the city of Tiberias on the Sea of Galilee (probably in A.D. 18) he wisely called it after the reigning

---

[3] *Ant.* 15:10:3-354.

[4] *Ant.* 17:13:2-344; 18:1:1-2; *War* 2:7:3-111; *ib.,* 8:1-117.

[5] *Ant.* 18:2:2-31; *War* 2:9:1-167 (where Archelais is not mentioned).

[6] *Ant.* 18:6:3-158.

[7] Avi-Yonah, *QDAP* XII, p. 84 f., No. 1.

[8] *Ant.* 18:4:6-106-108; *War* 2:9:6-181.

[9] *Ant.* 17:13:1-340; Pliny *N.h.* XIII, 44. It is identified with Kh. 'Auja et Tahtal Dalman, *PJb,* 1913, p. 74; Alt, *ib.,* 1927, p. 31; 1931, p. 46.

emperor.[10] Tiberias was a proper *polis,* with an archon,[11] a Council of Ten[12] and a Senate of Six Hundred.[13] The city soon replaced Taricheae as the principal locality on the shores of the Sea of Galilee. It has kept this position ever since. Antipas also re-named Beth ha-Ramtha in Peraea Julias, in honor of Livia the mother of Tiberius, who was an adopted member of the Julian family;[14] the place is called Livias in some sources.[15] Philip embellished Paneas and called it Caesarea;[16] to distinguish it from the other Caesarea, the foundation of Herod, it is usually called in our sources Caesarea Philippi.[17] In the Talmud it is referred to as *Qîsarîyôn,*[18] i.e. Little Caesarea. He also turned the fishing village of Bethsaida[19] into a town and called it Julias too in honour of Augustus' daughter.[20] After Julia's disgrace the name was kept with reference to Livia.[21]

Soon after the accession of Caius Caesar (Caligula) in A.D. 37 began the rise of Agrippa, whose father was Aristobulus, the son of Herod and Mariamme the Hasmonaean. The new emperor, who was a personal friend of Agrippa's gave him first the lands of Philippus, together with a principality in the northern slopes of the Hermon and the title of King.[22] Agrippa showed such ability, both as a ruler and a politician, that his domain grew continuously. When Antipas was exiled in 39, Agrippa inherited his tetrarchy.[23] After the crisis which resulted in the accession of Claudius in 41, during which he was very active, he also

---

[10] *Ant.* 18:2:3-36-38; *War* 2:9:1-168; cf Avi-Yonah, *IEJ,* 1, 1950-1, pp. 160-169.
[11] *Life* 27-134; 54-278.
[12] *Ib.,* 13-69; 57-294, 296.
[13] *War* 2:21:9-641.
[14] *Ant.* 18:2:1-27; *War* 2:9:1-168; for this site see above, p. 96.
[15] Ptolemaeus V, 15, 6; Eusebius, *On.,* 48, 13.
[16] *Ant.* 18:2:1-28; *War* 2:9:1-168.
[17] Matthew 16:13; Mark 8:27; *Ant.* 20:9:4-211; *Life,* 13-74.
[18] Tos. *Sukkah* 1:9.
[19] *Ant.* 18:2:1-28; *War* 2:9:1-168.
[20] Now probably Tell el Araj; Schumacher: *Dscholan,* p. 155; Dalman, *PJb,* 1912, pp. 45-48; Proksch, *PJb,* 1918, pp. 18-19.
[21] Cf. above n. 14.
[22] *Ant.* 18:6:10-237; *War* 2:9:6-181; Dio Cassius LIX, 8, 2.
[23] *Ant.* 18:7:2-252; *War* 2:9:6-183.

received the former share of Archelaus.[24] He thus united under his sceptre all the three parts which his uncles had inherited from his grandfather Herod. In comparison with Herod's Kingdom the realm of Agrippa lacked the Greek cities (Gaza, Gadara and Hippus), but he kept Caesarea and Sebaste, although these cities were unwilling subjects of a Jewish King.[25] His Kingdom also seems to have included the territories of Azotus and Jamnia. The imperial estate once formed by these territories (see above, p. 104) must have long ago merged with the procuratorship of Judaea. Agrippa most likely held Apollonia and Antipatris too which were surrounded by his lands.

After Agrippa's sudden death in 44, his lands returned to the administration of a Roman prefect residing in Caesarea. Thus all Judaea was united under Roman rule, for the procurator administered all the lands of Herod save Gadara, Hippus and Gaza.[26]

In the meantime Agrippa II, the son of Agrippa I, began to climb the ladder of a Herodian prince. In 48 he received the lands of his uncle Herod, who ruled the principality of Chalcis on the western slope of Mount Hermon.[27] When Agrippa the younger had proved his abilities there, Claudius gave him in 53 (in exchange for Chalcis) the Herodian lands in Northern Trans-Jordan (i.e. the former territory first of Philippus and then of his father Agrippa I), as well as another principality in the Hermon.[28] In 54, after Nero's accession, Agrippa II ascended yet another step. He was granted two-thirds of Peraea (i.e. the toparchies of Abila and Livias) and about half of Lower Galilee (Tiberias and Taricheae).[29] He was thus well on his way to the kingdom of his father and great-grandfather. The outbreak of the First War with Rome, however, put an end to all such hopes. With the destruction of the Jewish Commonwealth there was no place for a revival of the Herodian monarchy. Agrippa II continued to rule his lands quietly till the end of the

---

[24] *Ant.* 19:5:1-274-5; *ib.*, 8:2-351; *War* 2:11:5-215; Dio Cassius LX, 8, 2.
[25] *Ant.* 19:9:1-356.
[26] *Ib.*, and *War* 2:11:6-220.
[27] *Ant.* 20:5:2-104; *War* 2:12:1-223.
[28] *Ant.* 20:7:1-138; *War* 2:12:8-247.
[29] *Ant.* 20:8:4-159; *War* 2:13:2-252.

first century A.D., embellishing his capital Caesarea (Philippi) which for some time he called also Neronias.[30] He left no heirs.[31] After his death his lands were divided between the Roman provinces of Judaea and Syria. This end to the Herodian dynasty was the common fate of Roman vassal dynasties. Sooner or later, their lands and treasures became the property of the emperor. In some cases the local rulers were exiled, as happened to Archelaus and Antipas. Other dependent princes left their lands to the emperor in their wills, as Salome did with her estates, and sometimes there were no direct heirs, as happened with Philip the tetrarch and Agrippa II. In one way or another, all these kingdoms (except distant Armenia) came under direct Roman rule and became provinces of the empire.

While Agrippa II held his lands on Roman sufferance, part of his Kingdom and most of the procuratorial province of Judaea rose in revolt. The period of the First War with Rome was too stormy to make a reorganization of the political structure either possible or desirable. The only territorial arrangement of which we learn concerned the creation of military commands on various fronts.[32] In the South these military districts were five: Judaea, Idumaea, the coastal plain (the toparchies of Joppa, Lydda, Thimna and Emmaus), Jericho, the northern toparchies (Gophna and Acraba). Peraea in the east and the whole of Galilee in the west formed two separate commands. The revolutionary government continued in this form, but the area under its rule was gradually restricted as one district after another was lost. With the destruction of Jerusalem and the end of the Jewish state another chapter in the territorial history of Palestine was concluded.

[30] *Ant.* 20:9:4-211.

[31] As to the date of his death cf. A. H. M. Jones, *Cities of the E. Roman Provinces,* p. 273 and Rosenberg in Pauly-Wissowa: *Realenc.,* X, col. 149-150.

[32] *War* 2:20:4-566-568.

Chapter IX

FROM VESPASIAN TO DIOCLETIAN (A.D. 70-284)

AFTER the suppression of the Jewish revolt, the Roman authorities naturally began to look for ways of preventing another outbreak. The territorial arrangements made in A.D. 70 were part of the means adopted to that end. However, sixty years later, the Second Roman War broke out (usually called the War of Bar-Kokhba from the name of its leader).[1] It was followed by another administrative reform, and this time the Roman measures proved efficacious. The administrative and territorial arrangements decided in 135 proved capable of peaceful development. They lasted for over five hundred years without any fundamental change.

The First War lasted for over four years and required three to four legions to suppress it. The Romans thus learned to their cost several useful lessons. One was that although Judaea was small in size, it was of much importance owing to its geographical position. It was also a great potential source of trouble because of the unruly character of its inhabitants. The victorious empire now tried to learn from its past mistakes. The Romans noted that the uprising of 66 had turned into a revolt, which had spread over the whole country for several reasons. One was that the official in charge of Judaea (the prefect) was of too low a rank. His authority to act was restricted and he was dependent on the legate of Syria, his official superior. The latter, however, resided several days' distance away, and could not decide on the spot what was to be done. Secondly, there were almost no troops in Judaea, and even those present were mostly stationed away from Jerusalem, the main trouble-spot. The legions stationed at Antioch were too far away; their intervention was in the nature of a full-dress campaign, and in the meantime

[1] The recent discoveries at Magharat Muraba'at and in the Nahal Hever in the Judaean desert have shown that his real name was Simeon ben Kosibâ (T. J. Milik, *RB,* 1953, pp. 276-294; Yadin, *IEJ,* 11, 1961, pp. 40 ff.

the revolt could spread and organize itself. Thus, Roman power was either weak or distant. On the other hand, the Jews were settled close together in two compact territories. They were to a large extent autonomous, while they acknowledged one central authority—that of their Sanhedrin. They had access to the sea and held a stretch of the coast as well. They could thus interfere with Roman maritime traffic to and from Egypt, including the corn-fleets which fed Rome. On land the Jews could easily cut the communications between the great centres of Roman military power in the Orient—between Antioch in Syria and Alexandria in Egypt. Furthermore, they had a line of communications stretching from Gamala beyond the Jordan through the desert to Babylonia. Along this line passed both news and supplies.[2] The country beyond the Euphrates was in Parthia, outside the Roman empire; it had a large Jewish population.[3] This rendered the Palestinian Jews potentially still more dangerous. They might hope for the help of the Parthians, whose feud with Rome was of long standing. On the other hand, the Romans must have noticed that the Greek cities surrounding the Jewish territory had a most beneficial effect (from their point of view) by restricting the area of the conflagration. This was especially true of the barrier formed by the three cities Caesarea-Sebaste-Scythopolis, whose territories adjoined each other. Reaching from the sea to the Jordan, they effectively separated Judaea from Galilee. Messengers and even small bodies of men could pass across these territories, but strategically they cut the Jewish area into two. East of the Jordan the areas held by the Herodian dynasty contained a large Jewish population. They, however, kept almost entirely out of the fighting; their King Agrippa II remained loyal to Rome.[4] His rule in the Batanaea, Trachonitis and Auranitis,

[2] The line of communications is outlined in the list of signal stations from Jerusalem to Babylonia, as given in Mishnah *Rosh ha-Shanah*, 2:4.

[3] The importance of the connection with Babylonia is stressed by Josephus in his preface to the *Jewish War* (1:1:2-5) which gives a concise summary of the expectations of the Jewish leaders at the time of its outbreak.

[4] The exception to this was Western Gaulanitis, where Josephus was able to fortify Sogane Seleucia and Gamala (*War* 2:20:6-574; *Life* 37-187 -without Gamala). According to the later source the region of Gaulanitis as far as the (unknown) village of Solyma revolted from Agrippa II.

moreover, rendered communications with Babylonia much more difficult. To some extent city life had proved incompatible with rebellion. The two Galilean cities, Sepphoris and Tiberias were either lukewarm in their uprising, or openly hostile to the rebels.

The measures adopted by the Roman authorities after the war were clearly intended to reform the defects in the organization of the province. They tried to encourage the factors which had worked in favour of Roman rule, and at the same time to weaken the elements that were opposed to it.

Judaea was made into an independent province, the governor of which (*legatus Augusti pro praetore*) was of senatorial rank and a former praetor. A whole legion, the X (Decima) Fretensis, was placed under his orders. The legion was posted on the ruins of Jerusalem,[5] although the legate himself resided at Caesarea, an unusual arrangement required by the circumstances. The Provincia Judaea included all the cities of the coast, from Caesarea to Raphia, all of Idumaea, Judaea, Samaria, parts of Peraea and Galilee, which were not under Agrippa II, and some of the cities of the Decapolis.[6] After the death of Agrippa II, the last ruler of the Herodian dynasty, most of his lands were added to the province. This addition included Agrippa's share of Lower Galilee (Tiberias, Taricheae and their territories), his part of Peraea, and the Gaulanitis.[7] Caesarea-Philippi (Paneas), the Ulatha, Batanea, Trachonitis and Auranitis were attached to Syria.[8]

The new province was composed, like the Kingdom of Herod, of two balanced entities: the Jews and the Gentiles. From the administrative point of view it was also divided into two parts: the city territories on the one hand, and on the other the areas not organized in municipalities.

---

[5] *War* 7:1:3-17; Avi-Yonah, *QDAP* VIII, p. 56, no. 8.

[6] Pliny places Damascus first in the list of the cities of the Decapolis (*N.h.* V, 74), while Josephus calls Scythopolis 'the largest city of the Decapolis' (*War* 3:9:7-447). This difference in the two sources reflects the change which occurred when the Decapolis was divided between Judaea and Syria after the First Revolt.

[7] Hierocles: *Synecdemus,* 720, 1-6 reflects this situation by listing these territories with Palaestina Prima and Secunda respectively.

[8] *Ib.*, 715.9; part of these areas passed later on to the province of Arabia, see below p. 113.

In the first group the city ruled the villages attached to it. In the second, local affairs were managed by the central authority or its representative.

As we have seen, the Romans had been favourably impressed by the pacifying role of the cities during the Jewish War. They therefore tried to extend the municipal system over as wide an area as possible. Both Jewish and Gentile localities were declared cities as soon as they were thought ripe for municipal life. This urbanization is the fundamental process of the period under discussion.[9] It went on until almost the whole country was parcelled out into city territories. Judaea was thus approaching the status of most of the other provinces of the Empire, that 'Confederation of Municipalities.' Vespasian restored autonomous municipal status to some cities which had possessed it under Pompey and his successors, but had subsequently become part of Herod's domain. Now they were rendered fully autonomous once again. These cities were Jamnia, Azotus, Antipatris (once the Hellenistic city of Pegae-Arethusa),[10] Apollonia and Gabaa. Joppa was made into an autonomous city and was called Flavia Joppe.[11] By this means the Jewish territory was again cut off from the sea, although the town remained Jewish, as is evidenced by its third century cemetery.[12] Vespasian also gave full municipal rights to Sepphoris, which in the time of Hadrian changed its name to Diocaesarea.[13] Tiberias too became fully autonomous (with the right to strike coins) as soon as it was attached to the Provincia Judaea.[14] Both Sepphoris and Tiberias had their territories enlarged, probably at the time of Hadrian. Sepphoris received the toparchy of Araba, and Tiberias that of Taricheae. Together these two city-areas now covered the whole of Lower Galilee. The territory of the Samar-

---

[9] A. Alt, *PJb*, 1933, pp. 67-68; A. H. M. Jones, *Journ. Rom. Studies*, 1931, pp. 78 ff.

[10] This we can learn from the fact that these cities struck coins under the later empire, cf. G. Hill, *BMC, Palestine*, passim.

[11] *Ib.*, p. XXV.

[12] Frey: *Corpus inscriptionum iudaicarum*, II, Nos. 892-960; *Sefer ha-Yishuv*, 1939, pp. 80-88 (Hebrew).

[13] In the case of Diocaesarea the new name appears only on coins of Antoninus Pius; we can hardly doubt, however, that the change occurred under Hadrian, as part of his anti-Jewish policy following the Second Revolt.

[14] For Tiberias we have the evidence of coins, cf. Hill, *BMC Palestine*, p. XIV.

itans was turned into a city called Flavia Neapolis (hence the modern Nablus).[15] It was founded in the heart of Mount Ephraim, between Ebal and Gerizim, in the vicinity of ancient Sichem. The site had previously been occupied by a village called Ma'abartha ('the pass').[16] Vespasian also seems to have added the toparchy of Acraba to the territory of Neapolis. Acraba was, as we have seen, a toparchy of Judaea. In the fourth century, however, it belonged to Neapolis. This transfer can best be related to Vespasian's arrangements after the war.[17] The area of Neapolis together with that of Sebaste now covered the whole of ancient Samaria.

The territories left temporarily or permanently outside the urban organisation included the *campus legionis* around Jerusalem. It consisted of nine toparchies: Orine, Bethletepha, Emmaus, Lydda, Thamma, Gophna, Herodium, and Bethogabris. Jericho and the three districts of Peraea were set aside as imperial estates.[18] Upper Galilee and the Gaulan also remained outside the city areas. In these regions the villages were grouped into administrative districts ruled by representatives of the governor of the province; the Roman government, however, regarded this form of administration as transitional. As a result of the policy of urbanisation most of the non-urban territories were transformed into cities in the course of the second and third centuries. One exception was made in areas of exceptional economic importance (such as the Jordan valley estates), which the imperial treasury wanted to keep for itself. Also excepted were the regions whose inhabitants refused to conform to the prevailing pattern of Greco-Roman culture, which was regarded as a pre-condition of urban life. West of the Jordan only Upper Galilee remained in this latter category, because of the strength of its Jewish population there. In the lands beyond the river the non-urban areas included, for the time being, most of Herod's former possessions in the Gaulan, Batanaea, Trachonitis and Auranitis.

---

[15] *Ib.*, pp. XXVI ff.; Pliny *N.h.* V, 69.

[16] *War* 4:8:1-449 and Pliny, *loc. cit.*

[17] Alt, *PJb*, 1931, p. 110, comparing Josephus, and Eusebius' *Onomasticon.*

[17a] Engeddi was attached to this toparchy under Trajan, witness one of the Nahal Hever documents.

[18] In the city lists of Hierocles and Georgius Cyprius these territories appear as *regiones.*

The arrangements of Vespasian remained in force until after the War of Bar-Kokhba (132-135). In the period between the two wars a new city, Capitolias (Talmudic *Beth Resha,* Arabic Beit Ras), was founded in 97-98.[19] In 106 Trajan annexed the Nabataean Kingdom and created the province of Arabia. Its capital was first at Petra, but its garrison, the Legio III Cyrenaica, was stationed at Bostra. In the time of Hadrian the legate followed suit, and Petra was compensated with the empty title of "Hadriana Petra Metropolis."[20] The cities of Philadelphia and Dium were taken from Syria and transferred to the new province. This is shown by their use of the provincial era beginning in 106.[21] In the later sources Gerasa also appears among the cities of Arabia[22] but the date of its transfer is not clear.[23] The new province was endowed with a magnificent road, the *via nova* joining Bostra with the Red Sea.[24]

The decision of Hadrian to build a Roman colony in Jerusalem was one of the causes of the War of Bar-Kokhba. The war lasted from 132 to 135 and required for its termination the deployment of at least five legions, one of which (the 22 Deioteriana) was lost. The extent of the area controlled by Bar-Kokhba is disputed, some authors assuming the outbreak to cover also Galilee; others, including the author, believing that the absence of any marks of uprooting of the Jewish population in that area precludes its inclusion in the fighting. Even on the minimal assumption, Bar Kokhba controlled the whole of Judaea, including Engeddi (but excluding Zoar) and possibly about half of Samaria (up to Tûr Sime'ôn). For nearly two years in any case Jerusalem was the headquarters of an orderly administration, and so were the district headquarters. How orderly were the procedures of the revolutionary authorities we can learn from the documents found at Murabba'at and in the

[19] Wroth: *BMC Galatia, Cappadocia, Syria,* p. 278.

[20] Hill: *BMC Arabia,* pp. 34-36; Head: *Historia numorum,* p. 812; S. Ben-Dor, *Berytus,* IX, 1948, pp. 41-43; in the time of Heliogabalus it was called colonia Antoniniana. The documents from the Judaean desert cave show Petra was still the provincial capital in 130 (Polotsky, *IEJ,* 12, 1962, p. 259).

[21] Hill, *op. cit.,* pp. 31-2. 37-41.

[22] Hierocles: *Synecdemus,* 721, 7; 721, 9; Georgius Cyprius 1064, 1066.

[23] Stinespring ap. C. Kraeling ed.: *Gerasa,* p. 47.

[24] Thomsen, *ZDPV,* 1917, pp. 34-57.

Nahal Hever.[24a] We find leases of property of the State (represented by the *parnassim* "administrators" of "Simeon Bar Kosiba, Prince [*nassi*] of Israel" to private persons issued at the district headquarters of Herodium and Engeddi well into the third year of the war. The correspondence of Bar-Kokhba with the district officers of Engeddi is less formal in character, but shows a vigorous administration caring for minor details in the Roman style. (cf. the Letters of Trajan to Pliny the Younger).

After the defeat of the Jews, the foundation of the city of Aelia Capitolina was carried out according to plan.[25] Its territory included in the beginning the toparchies of Orine, Gophna, Herodium and Bethletepha. The Idumaean toparchies, as well as those of Emmaus, Lydda and Thamna seem to have been left out. The remnant of the Jewish population of Judaea was uprooted.[26] The sojourn or entry of Jews into the municipal area of Aelia Capitolina was forbidden by edict under pain of death.[27]

Another result of the War of Bar-Kokhba was the addition of a second legion to the garrison of the province. The Legio VI Ferrata (the 'Ironsides') made its camp at Ceparcotnei (Hebrew Kefar 'Otnay)[28] situated at the issue of the 'Irun pass into the Jezreel Valley near ancient Megiddo. This camp ultimately gave rise to another city, called Legio (Arabic: Lejjûn). The Valley of Jezreel was handed over to the legion as its estate. It was henceforward known as Campus maximus Legionis.[29] With the addition of a second legion Judaea was raised to the rank of a consular province. In order to efface the memory of the rebellious people who inhabited it, the name of the province was changed to Syria Palaestina. This revival of the ancient term used by Herodotus has had a lasting effect.[30]

[24a] *DJD* II, pp. 155-166; Yadin, *IEJ,* 11, 1961, pp. 40-52; 12, 1962, pp. 249-257.

[25] L. H. Vincent-F. M. Abel: *Jérusalem nouvelle,* I, pp. 1-88; Pl. I.

[26] Eusebius: *Hist. eccl.* IV, 6, 3 (*Gr. christl. Schriftst.* 9, p. 308); Tertullianus: *Adv. Iudaeos,* 13 (*PL.* II, c. 673). There is archaeological evidence for this e.g. in the third century finds at Beit Nattif cf. D. C. Baramki, *QDAP,* V, p. 1-11.

[27] J. Rendel Harris, *Harvard Theological Review,* 19, 1926, pp. 199-206.

[28] Heron de Villefosse, *RB,* 1897, pp. 598-604; Ramsay, *Journ. Hell. Stud.* VI, p. 219.

[29] *On.* 110, 21; Smith: *Hist. Geography* p. 381 ff.; Alt, *PJb,* 1937, pp. 80-83.

[30] Herodotus, I, 105; II, 104, 106; III, 5, 91; IV, 39; VII, 89.

The next steps in the urbanization of Palestine were taken under the energetic rule of Septimius Severus (193-211). In 200 he transformed Bethogabris in Idumaea into Eleutheropolis, the 'City of the Free.'[31] The new town was endowed with very extensive lands, comprising the two toparchies of Idumaea proper and Engeddi. At the same time the toparchy of Betholetepha seems to have been transferred from Aelia Capitolina to Eleutheropolis. This we may conclude from the evidence of milestones found in the area. Those dating from the time of Hadrian indicate the distances from Jerusalem, those of later date count it from Eleutheropolis.[32] Moreover, in the *Onomasticon* of Eusebius the Valley of Sorek and its villages appear in the area of Eleutheropolis.[33]

Septimius Severus also founded the city of Diospolis[34] in what was formerly Lydda. The new city obtained the toparchies of Lydda and Thamna. Another administrative measure of this emperor which affected the historical geography of the region was the transfer of the Auranitis from Syria to Arabia.[35] Trachonitis and Batanaea were left in Syria; Syria itself was divided into two provinces: Syria proper and Phoenicia. Ptolemais, Caesarea Philippi and Dora were included in the latter.

In the time of Heliogabalus the townlet of Emmaus became the city of Nicopolis, in the year 220-221.[36] This foundation practically completed the urbanization of the whole area west of the Jordan. Apart from the imperial estates in the Jordan Valley and Upper Galilee (now called officially Tetracomia),[37] all the settled area of the province now consisted of city areas.

In Trans-Jordan the area of the Decapolis had long ago been divided into cities. The process of urbanization continued, however, in the lands formerly Herodian. In the Auranitis there had formerly existed only

[31] Hill: *BMC Palestine,* p. LXV; Beyer, *ZDPV,* 1931, p. 209 ff. The Midrash (Gen. R. 41-42, ed. Theodor p. 412) ironically calls it "City of Dwellers in Holes" by a play of words on "free" and "holes."

[32] Alt, *PJb,* 1929, pp. 19 ff., 124 ff.

[33] *On.* 88, 12; 106, 9; 156, 15; 160, 3.

[34] Hill, *BMC Palestine,* p. XXIII; Beyer, *ZDPV,* 1933, p. 218 ff.

[35] Brünnow-Domaszewski: *Provincia Arabia,* III, p. 263 ff.

[36] Hill, *BMC Palestine,* p. LXXXI.

[37] Georgius Cyprius, 1040.

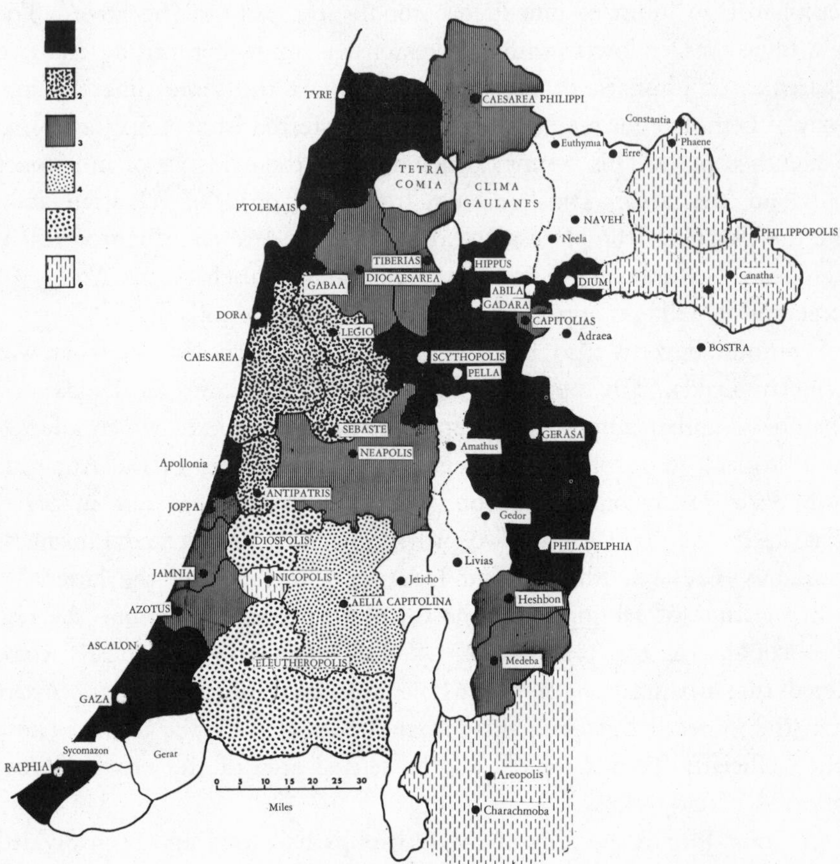

Map 8: THE URBANIZATION UNDER ROMAN RULE
1 — Cities refounded by Pompey or Gabinius
2 — Foundations of Herod
3 — Cities founded from Vespasian to Trajan
4 — Cities founded by Hadrian
5 — Cities founded by Septimus Severus
6 — Later foundations
Non-municipal areas left white

one city Canatha, once a member of the Decapolis.[38] In 242, however, the emperor Philippus Arabs endowed his native village (modern Shuhba) with the rights of a city, calling it Philippopolis.[39] In the province of Arabia the emperor Trajan raised to municipal status the town of Rabbath-Moab (later on called Areopolis, now er-Rabba).[40] Heliogabalus did the same for Characmoba (Kerak)[41] and Heshbon (now officially Aurelia Esbus).[42] From the time of Valerianus (253-260), at the latest Edrei (Adraene, now Dera'a) was accounted a city.[43] We learn of the existence of these cities almost exclusively from the coins struck by them in the exercise of their municipal rights.

[38] Pliny *n.h.* V, 74; It became a colony under Septimius Severus under the title *Septimia kanôtha;* cf. L. Robert, *Hellenica,* II, p. 43 ff.

[39] Sex. Aurelius Victor: *Liber de Caesaribus,* 28; Hill: *BMC Arabia,* pp. 42-43; Hierocles: *Synecdemus,* 722, 12; Georgius Cyprius, 1069; Waddington Le Bas: *Recueil,* 2019.

[40] Polotsky *IEJ* 12(1962), p. 260; Hierocles: *Synecdemus,* 721, 6; Georgius Cyprius, 1048.

[41] Hill, *op cit.,* pp. xxx f., 27

[42] *Ib.,* pp. xxxxiii, 29.

[43] *Ib.,* p. 15.

Chapter X

FROM DIOCLETIAN TO THE ARAB CONQUEST (284-640)

The pacification of the country after the War of Bar-Kokhba was not affected by the occasional struggles between the pretenders to the throne, although these were frequent during the crisis of the empire in the third century.[1] With the accession of Diocletian (284) the crisis came to an end. The reforms of this emperor affected Palestine in the same measure as the rest of the empire. His general policy was to split up the existing provinces into smaller units, to separate the military command from the civil administration and to divide the Roman army into field forces (*praesentiales*) and frontier guards (*limitanei*).

The Diocletian policy was carried out in Palestine partly in the emperor's own reign and partly in the reigns following. The military command was entrusted to a *dux Palaestinae*; his colleague in the east was called *dux Arabiae*. The *Notitia dignitatum* (about 400)[2] gives a list of the units under the command of each of these generals. At the same time some territorial changes were effected. Dora was transferred from Phoenicia to Palestine; we may assign this change to Diocletian, although the earliest source to refer to a provincial border at Cartha (near 'Athlit, north of Dora) dates from 333. It is the *Itinerarium burdigalense,* the itinerary of a Christian pilgrim from Bordeaux.[3] The southern part of Arabia, up to the Arnon River (Wâdi Mojîb) and including Petra was transferred to Palestine. Arabia received in compensation the Trachonitis and Batanaea.[4] Of the Herodian lands beyond the Jordan, only the Gaulan remained hereafter in Palestine. The boundaries

---

[1] The only military campaigns recorded in the civil wars of the third century which might have affected Palestine were (a) Pescennius Niger's defeat by Septimius Severus in 194; (b) the revolt of Aurelius Uranius against Philippus Arabs in 244 and his defeat in 253; (c) Aurelianus' campaign against the Palmyrenes in 272.

[2] Ed. O. Seeck, Berlin, 1876; for the date see J. B. Bury, *Journ. Rom. Stud.* 1920, pp. 131 ff.

[3] *Itinera hierosolymitana,* ed. Geyer, 19, 10

[4] Brünnow & Domaszewski: *Die Provincia Arabia,* III, p. 276 ff.

of the military districts followed in general those of the civil provinces. The *dux Arabiae* seems to have commanded as far as the Zered (Wâdi el Hesâ). His district extended along the Arabian *limes* from Bostra to about the South end of the Dead Sea.[5] The limes between that Sea and the Gulf of Elath (Aila) was the charge of the dux Palaestinae. The pivot of the whole system was Aila (Elath). There the Tenth Legion was posted sometime at the end of the third century.[6] From Aila a fortified line followed the road up Wadi 'Itm and the Mount Seir highlands. The road going north from Aila was protected by two lines of forts, one following the eastern and the other the western borders of the Araba Valley.[7] Other forts were built along the roads leading from it across the Negev deserts towards the settled lands in the north. Owing to the necessity of protecting these areas from the Saracens of the Sinai desert, another fortified line was created—the *Limes Palaestinae.* This *Limes* consisted of large areas along the southern border of Idumaea, which were made into a belt of territory intended to remain under military control. They formed a line consisting of a series of forts linked by a road, and stretched from the Mediterranean to the Dead Sea. The lands of the *limes* were let out to military settlers who were subject to a special fiscal régime.[8] The rear of the *limes* was protected by the garrisons at Chermela[9] and the Terebinth.[10] The need for a *limes* was the greater because apart from troops at Aelia Capitolina, the Jericho region and Diocaesarea, there were no garrisons in Palestine.[11]

---

[5] Alt, *PJb,* 1935, p. 25 ff.; Abel: *Géographie* II, pp. 179-184; 187-191.

[6] *On.* 8, 1; *ND* 73, 30.

[7] Alt, *ZDPV,* 1935, p. 25 ff.

[8] The Beersheba tax edict (A. Alt: *Die Inschriften d. Palaestina Tertia* p. 1 ff.) reflects this régime cf, id., *PJb,* 1930, p. 33 ff.; 1931, pp. 65 ff.; *JPOS,* XVIII, pp. 149-60; *ZDPV,* 1940, pp. 129-140; B. Mazar, *Sefer Epstein* (Hebrew) has suggested the identification of the limes with the *hagar* of Mishnah, *Gittin,* 2:1-2 but this seems to date it too early; cf. Avi-Yonah, *EI,* 5, 1958, pp. 135-137.

[9] *On.* 22, 20; *ND* 73, 20; now el Kurmil, Sejourné, *RB,* 1895, p. 259 f.; Mader: *Altchristl. Basiliken in Südjudäa,* 1918, p. 178 ff.; Alt, *PJb,* 1930, p. 48; 1931, p. 75 f.

[10] The *Botnah* of Jewish sources, Mishnah *Maasar sheni* 5:2; Sifre *Deut.* 306; jer. *Abodah zarah* 39 d; Gen. R. 477, 4. The garrison is mentioned *On.* 6, 12; 24, 16; Hieronymus: In Jerem 31:15 (*PL* XXIV, c. 911).

[11] *ND* 73, 21; 74, 47-48: Beersheba edict, n. 8 above.

The forts of the *limes* included Menois,[12] Birsama,[13] Beersheba (Birosaba),[14] Malatha[15] and Masada.[16]

The date of the creation of this *limes* is disputed. A. Alt, who first drew attention to its existence and traced its line,[17] attributed it to the time following the creation of the Provincia Judaea, when the new province bordered on the Nabataean Kingdom. However, one should note that this state of affairs also existed before A.D. 70 and indeed the recent finds at Arad support a Herodian date for this fort. The praetorian province of Judaea with its legion was later on much better able to defend itself than the old prefectorial province, which was almost without troops. Moreover, the Nabataeans were then as now Roman vassals. It would have been an arrangement unparalleled elsewhere in the Roman Empire to have a *limes* inside the imperial borders. After the annexation of the Nabataean Kingdom by Trajan there was still less need for such a fortified line between two provinces. We are therefore obliged perforce to refer the foundation of the *limes* to the time of Diocletian. In his reign the army was divided into a field army and the *limitanei,* and the Tenth Legion was transferred from Jerusalem to Aila.[18] We should also consider that the late Roman fort near Masada has been dated to the Diocletian period.[19] Moreover, the epigraphic evidence for the *limes* and its special land tenure belongs to the sixth century,[20] while the evidence for the garrisons along its line begins in the fourth and continues in the fifth century.[21] There are also the Syrian parallels such as the *Strata Dio-*

---

[12] Khirbet Ma'in (Maon) *ND* 73, 19; *Cod. Theod.* VII, 4, 30; cf. *On.* 130, 7; Musil, *Edom* I, p. 224; Abel, *RB,* 1940, pp. 70-2.

[13] *ND* 73, 22; *Cod. Theod.* VII, 4, 30 now Kh. el Far (?) Alt, *PJb,* 1931, p. 82 f.

[14] *On.* 50, 1; *ND* 73, 18; in the Madaba map (No. 105, Pl. 9) the town still has the square shape of a typical camp.

[15] Tell el Milh, Malhathah, *ND*, 74, 45; *On.* 14, 3; Alt, *PJb,* 1930, p. 80.

[16] Schulten, *ZDPV,* 1933, pp. 158-161.

[17] See n. 8 above.

[18] See above n. 6 and A. Reifenberg, *JPOS,* 11, 1931, pp. 157-158.

[19] See n. 16 above.

[20] Alt, *PJb,* 1930, p. 62.

[21] Eusebius: *Onomasticon;* the *Notitia dignitatum* and Hieronymus' translation of the Onomasticon into Latin.

cletiana and the *limes* of Chalcis.[22] We should therefore finally assign the creation of the *limes* as such to Diocletian.

Another result of the policy adopted by Diocletian and his successors was the splitting up of the province of Palestine, although it was one of the smallest in the empire. About 358 it was divided into a northern and southern half along the line of the *limes Palaestinae.* The southern province was called in the high-flowing fashion of the period *Palaestina Salutaris;* its capital was at Petra. We learn of this division from a letter of Libanius.[23] About 400 the remainder of Palestine was again divided into two provinces: *Palaestina prima,* which retained Judaea, Idumaea, Samaria and Peraea, and *Palaestina secunda,* to which were assigned Galilee, the cities of the Decapolis which had remained in Palestine, and the Gaulan. Its capital was set up at Scythopolis (Beth Shean). The capital of the First Palestine was Caesarea, formerly the capital of the united province.

In consequence of these changes the province of Palaestina salutaris was now renamed *Palaestina tertia.* The earliest document referring to this second partition besides the *Notitia dignitatum,* pp. 48-49, is an edict of Theodosius II addressed to the Jewish Sanhedrins of the *two* Palestines.[24] As there were practically no Jews living in Palaestina salutaris, we may take this to refer to the division into Palaestina prima and secunda.

Later sources confirm and elaborate this threefold division; in particular it forms the basis of the city lists of Hierocles[25] (sixth century) and Georgius Cyprius[26] (seventh century). The Conciliar lists also conform to it, in particular those of Ephesus (431), Chalcedon (451) and the two provincial synods of Jerusalem (held in 518 and 536).[27]

The mention of the Councils brings us to another most important change, which occurred shortly after the abdication of Diocletian. In

---

[22] Poidebard: *Le limes de Chalcis,* 1945; *La trace de Rome dans le desert de Syrie,* 1934.

[23] Libanius, ep. 337 (ed. Teubner, 334).

[24] *Cod. Theod.* VII, 4, 304; XVI, 8, 29; at the Council of Chalcedon of 451 the three Palestines are already an established fact (Schwartz, *Acta conc. oecum.* II, p. 364;

[25] Hierocles: *Synecdemus,* ed. Burckhardt (Teubner) 1893, 717, 8; 719, 12; 721.

[26] Georgius Cyprius: *Descriptio orbis romani* ed. Gelzer (Teubner) 1890.

[27] *Acta conciliorum oecum.,* ed. E. Schwartz.

324 Constantine the Great defeated Licinius and added the eastern provinces of the empire to his realm. Henceforward the empire and the church entered into a close union. The ecclesiastical divisions were now closely matched to the civil ones. The archbishop took up his seat in the capital of the province; each city had a bishop. In consequence, we may assume conversely that each episcopal see had municipal rights.[28] This general rule underwent however some modifications in the course of time. In 451 the see of Jerusalem was raised by way of exception to the dignity of a patriarchate. Jerusalem was thus placed ecclesiastically above Caesarea, to which it remained subordinated in civil affairs. The needs of the Saracen tribes converted to Christianity required the appointment of bishops of an "itinerant" diocese (P*arembolae*) or of "the Tents" (*Scenae*),[29] without the resulting civic rights.

We learn from the ecclesiastical sources that the process of urbanization went on in the Byzantine period. Most of the territory of the province was, however, already divided among city territories. The urbanization now took usually the form of a splitting up the existing territories. Thus we find in the area of Ascalon a Maiumas Ascalon[30] and probably also a Diocletianupolis.[31] In the region of Gaza, the Christian harbour-city of Neapolis (also named Constantia in honour of Constantine II's sister) was made independent of its mother city, which remained predominantly pagan.[32] Another Constantia was founded in the Auranitis.[33] There we find also a Neapolis[34] and a Hierapolis,[35] the sites of which are unknown. Maximianus, Diocletian's partner in the empire, was honoured by two cities named after him—Maximianupolis.

[28] Alt, *PJb,* 1933, p. 67 ff.

[29] Gerland and Laurent: *Les listes conciliaires,* p. 80 (Ephesus, Chalcedon, Jerusalem 518 and 536).

[30] Antoninus Placentinus, ed. Geyer, 33; Smith: *Historical Geography,* p. 190, n. 1.

[31] Hierocles: *Synecdemus,* 719, 2; Georg. Cyprius, 1912; (Schwartz, ed. *Acta,* III, p. 188) possibly identical with Serifeiâ of the Talmud (B Abodah zarah 11 b).

[32] Eusebius: *Vita Constantini* IV, 38 (*GCS* VII, p. 132); Hieronymus: *Vita Hilarionis,* 3 (*PL* XXIII c. 31) now el Minah.

[33] Hierocles, 723, 2; Georg. Cypr. 1071.

[34] Hierocles 722, 10; Georg. Cypr. 1061-2.

[35] Hierocles 722, 11; Georg. Cypr. 1068.

The one was Legio in the Valley of Jezreel[36] the other was situated in the Trachonitis.[37] The city of Helenopolis in Palaestina secunda[38] can only have been named after Constantine's mother. F. M. Abel has suggested that in view of Helena's well-known interest in the holy cities, the area of this 'town' might have included Mount Tabor and its vicinity.[39] If we accept this view, we should add Nazareth. This townlet would thus be removed from the jurisdiction of Sepphoris, then and a century later a purely Jewish city.[40] Another reduction of its territory was caused by the creation of an independent area at Nais,[41] with its ecclesiastical centre at Exaloth.[42] In the coastal plain Ono was already separated from Diospolis in the time of Diocletian.[43] The localities of Sycomazon[44] and Bitolium[45] extended towards the Egyptian border, adjoining the imperial estates of Gerara (Saltus Geraiticus)[46] and the Constantinian estate,[47] at least the former had a bishop of its own.[48] Both estates were carved out of the lands of Eleutheropolis, and another subdivision of the large territory of this city is probably evidenced by the city of Tricomias appearing in the list of Georgius Cyprius.[49] In the province of Palaestina tertia we find episcopal sees at Augustopolis,[50] Elusa,[51] Mampsis,[52]

---

[36] Hieronymus, *PL* XXV, c. 1515; Hierocles, 720, 10; Georg. Cypr. 1034.

[37] A. H. M. Jones: *Cities of the E. Roman Provinces,* p. 290 considers it identical with Hierapolis.

[38] Sozomenus, *Hist. eccl.* II, 2 (*PG* LXVII, c. 936); Hierocles, 720, 8; Georg. Cypr. 1938.

[39] *Géographie* II, pp. 205; 347 f. cf. Alt, *PJb,* 1932, p. 34 f.

[40] Theodoretus, Hist. eccl. IV, 35, (*GCS* ed. Parmentier, p. 260).

[41] Georg. Cyprius 1042.

[42] Jerusalem Council of 536, ed. Schwartz, III, p. 189.

[43] Pap. Oxyrrhyn. 1205 mentions a bouleutes of Onus in the time of Diocletian.

[44] Hierocles 719, 3; Georg. Cypr. 1022.

[45] Ibid. 719, 10 and 1023.

[46] Theodoret. Quaest. in II Paralip. XIV, 3 (*PG* LXXX, c. 828); jer. *Shebiith* 36 c; *Madaba Map,* Pl. 9, No. 101; Georg. Cypr. 1027; Procop. Gazaeus *PG* LXXXVII, 1212 C.

[47] George. Cypr. 1026; cf. Alt ZDPV 69 (1953), p. 68 f.

[48] Marcianus at Chalcedon (451).

[49] Hierocl. 721, 3; Georg. Cypr. 1024.

[50] Hierocl. 721, 3; Jerusalem (518), Schwartz, ed. Acta, III, p. 188.

[51] Ephesus 431; Chalcedon 451; Jerusalem 518 and 536; Hierocles 721, 10; Georg. Cypr. 1050; Schwartz, *op. cit.,* pp. 79, 188.

[52] Hierocl. 721, 8; Georg. Cypr. 1049.

Zoara,[53] Arindela,[54] Phaenon,[55] Aila[56] and the island of Iotaba,[57] beyond the Jordan at Neela, Erre (Aere), Euthymia and Dionysias.[57a] Apparently all these enjoyed municipal rights and some even a wider autonomy.[58] We cannot, however, in the present state of our knowledge, define the boundaries of their respective territories.

The Byzantine system of administration, as outlined above, received a serious blow during the Persian conquest of Palestine in 614. Laboriously re-established by Heraclius in 627, it went down permanently as the result of the Arab conquest of 636-640.

---

[53] Chalcedon 451; Jerusalem 518; Schwartz, *op. cit.* III, pp. 79, 116, 150, 155; Hierocl. 721, 7; Georg. Cypr. 1031.

[54] Ephesus 431; Jerusalem 536; Schwartz *op. cit.* III, p. 189; Hierocl. 721, 4; Georg. Cypr. 1044.

[55] Ephesus 431; Chalcedon 451; Jerusalem 518 and 536. (Schwartz, *ib.,* III, pp. 80, 189).

[56] Nicaea 325, Chalcedon 451, Jerusalem 536. (*ib.,* p. 189).

[57] Chalcedon 451, Jerusalem 536 (Schwartz, *Acta* II, 1, 2, p. 103).

[57a] All mentioned in the Acts of Chalcedon.

[58] For Iotabe see Malchi Philadelphensis Fragmenta (*FHG* IV, p. 113); Theophanes, *PG* CVIII, c. 340; Procopius *Pers. War* I, XIX, 3; Schwartz, *op. cit.,* III, p. 116).

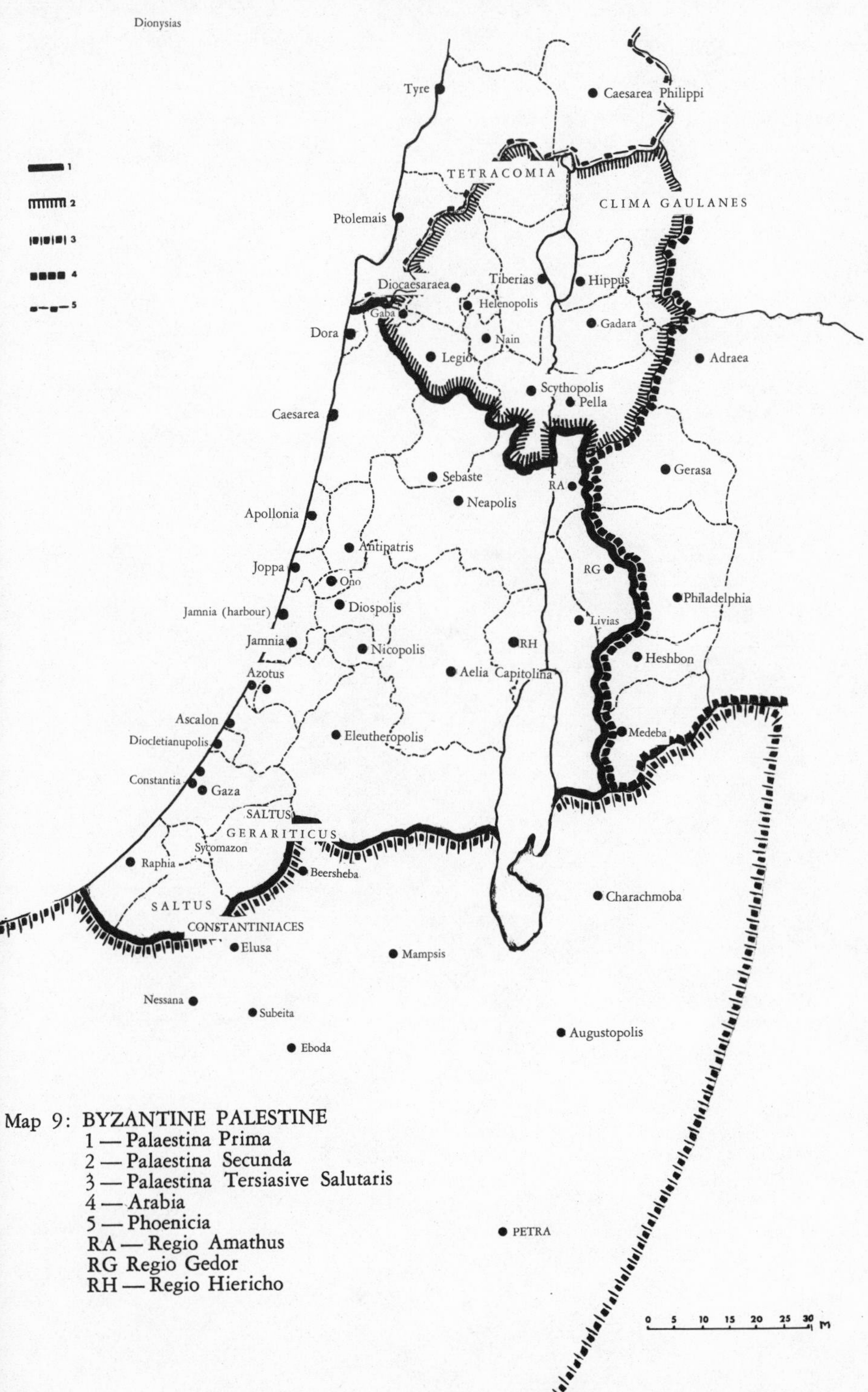

Map 9: BYZANTINE PALESTINE
1 — Palaestina Prima
2 — Palaestina Secunda
3 — Palaestina Tersiasive Salutaris
4 — Arabia
5 — Phoenicia
RA — Regio Amathus
RG Regio Gedor
RH — Regio Hiericho

PART TWO

CITY TERRITORIES

Problems of Method

As we have seen above, by the end of the third century almost the whole area of Palestine had been divided into municipal areas. With the exception of only a few names[1] we are able to identify with certainty the site of these cities. We are, however, on less certain ground when trying to establish the extent of the territories belonging to each city.

In a few cases we are informed directly by a written source that a village or a plain or a mountain belonged to this or that city at a certain period. Such a statement creates a presumption for the preceding and subsequent periods; a presumption which we may regard as valid, unless expressly contradicted. Similarly, if we can reasonably assume that a former province was split up between a certain number of cities, then the border of the city territories should have followed the former provincial boundary. If we know, e.g., that Samaria was divided between the cities of Sebaste and Neapolis, and that its territory extended formerly from Ginae in the North to Anuathu Borcaeus in the South,[2] we are entitled to assume that the territory of Sebaste began at Ginae in the North and that of Neapolis ended a Anuathu in the South. Moreover, if a certain region was attributed to a city as a whole, the villages known to have belonged to it might reasonably be assumed to have passed to that city. Thus, if Daromas was in the lands of Eleutheropolis, Engaddi was also in that territory.

Another important indication of the extent of a city territory is furnished by the Roman road-system. The Romans counted the distances along the road from the cities which were passed by the road. When the

[1] Such as Homonoea (*Life,* 281), Solyma (*Life,* 281), Toxos (Georg. Cypr. 1025), Ariza (Hierocles 719, 10) etc.

[2] *War,* 3:3:4/5-48, 51.

road reached a city boundary and entered another territory, the count began again, with reference to the second city. The distances marked on the milestones are therefore a valuable indication of the extent of city areas. Thus, if we count at one milestone ten miles from Ptolemais and on the next thirteen miles to Diocaesarea, the boundary passed between these two stones. Sometimes we may even be able to learn of transfers of territory from milestones. An earlier milestone might refer to one city, and a later one to another. In this way we learn of the transfer of the toparchy of Betholeptepha from Aelia Capitolina to Eleutheropolis.[3]

This method of marking distances has served us in another way. Eusebius, bishop of Caesarea in the fourth century, has indicated in his topographical dictionary, the *Onomasticon*[4] a considerable number of villages by their distance from a city. We may assume with Beyer and Alt[5] that these indications were taken from a road map, in which the distances were measured from the cities. Therefore, if Eusebius states a certain village to be at such a distance from a city, there is a strong presumption that the village was within the territory of that city.[6] Similarly, when we read of a certain place being between two cities, we may assume that the boundary between them passed near-by.

In Byzantine times the ecclesiastical divisions fitted as a rule to the civil ones. We are able to use the *Notitiae* of the bishoprics as indicating the city limits. Moreover, if we find in an inscription the mention of a church dignitary known to have occupied a certain see, we may be certain that the locality belonged to that diocese and by inference to that city. Thus, the mention of an archbishop of Bostra and the omission of a bishop in some inscriptions from Rihâb in Trans-Jordan raises the presumption that this village and its vicinity was outside the limits of Gerasa.

Another source of information is furnished by archaeological finds. Thus we might reasonably assume that the area passed by a city's aque-

---

3 See above, Chapter IX, n. 32. (p. 115).

4 Ed. Klostermann, 1904 (*GCS,* Eusebius III, 1).

5 *ZDPV,* 1931, pp. 213 ff.

6 There are of course exceptions, as e.g. the case of Jazer (see below, p. 179).

duct belonged to that city. It would be unreasonable for a city to leave its water supply at the mercy of a rival. The roads passing the desert fringe and the forts built along them give an indication of the provincial frontier.

Epigraphy can also be occasionally helpful. The era used in dating inscriptions is often a valuable indication of territorial divisions. Thus we find in Trans-Jordan side by side areas which counted from the Seleucid era (312 B.C.), others which used the Pompeian (63 B.C.), the foundation era of the Provincia Arabia (A.D. 106) or the regnal years of the emperors. These different usages reflect historical developments and geographical boundaries. For example: till A.D. 295 the Batanaea belonged to Syria, but in that year it was transferred to Arabia. Thus, if we find an inscription later than this date using the era of Arabia, we know that the locality of the find was in Batanaea; if the Seleucid era is used, we are in the Gaulan.

By using the methods outlined above, we arrive at a rough outline of boundaries of the various territories. It must be, of course, understood that these delimitations are only tentative unless they follow a well defined natural feature, such as a seashore or a river.[7] We have also assumed that unless there is evidence to the contrary, the boundaries can be assumed as stable. This allows us to use the sources of different periods for defining the same boundary. Experience has shown that the boundaries of even large units, such as a province, were fairly stable in Roman times. The lower we descend in the scale of the territories, the less change there seems likely.

The various regions are discussed below from north to south and from west to east.

The Phoenician Cities

Tyre

Most of the territory of this city is beyond the scope of this work. We should note however, that the southern boundary of ancient Tyre passed well within Palestine. In the time of Josephus the limits of Acre were

[7] And even here there have been changes, as in the case of Beth Yerah (Philoteria?) which was once east of the Jordan and is now west of it; cf. Chapter IV, n. 109 (p. 70 above)

"from the Carmel to the ladder of Tyre" (Ras en Naqura).[8] Later on the boundary of Tyre seems to have been advanced southwards, for an ecclesiastical *Notitia* of the Early Arab period[9] defines the 'great waters of Zip' (Wâdi Qarn) as the boundary. The Talmudic sources too regard *Akhzib* (*Ecdippa*, *ez Zîb*)[10] as the limit of the Holy Land. This is noted already in the Tosephtha.[11] The change must, therefore, have taken place in the third century A.D. In inscriptions of the sixth century found at Mi'ilya and Suhmata the Tyrian era is used and reference is made to the archbishop of Tyre and not the bishop of Acre.[12] Hence the boundary of Tyre seems to have moved inland into the mountains of Galilee. It must have passed north of Mount Meron (Jebel Jermaq) and reached Qadasa (Qadas) a Tyrian city according to Josephus.[13] From here it went straight to the North, as the Hulatha region belonged to Caesarea Philippi (see below, pp. 164-167). The territory of Tyre included quite a number of villages inhabited by Jews.[14]

Ptolemais

According to the Ps.Scylax the territory of Acre extended from south of Ecdippa to north of Haifa.[15] In the time of Josephus this city controlled, however, the whole Mediterranean coast of Galilee, from the ladder of Tyre to the Carmel, including the promontory of the latter.[16] Subsequently its boundary stopped at *Ecdippa* ('Akhzib), which Eusebius fixes 9 miles from Ptolemais "on the road to Tyre," i.e. near the boundary.[17] Further to South the lands of Ptolemais extended eastwards till *Caparasima* (Kefar Sumei'); according to Moschus' *Pratum spirituale*[18] this village belonged to Ptolemais. Here the boundary turned southwards

[8] *War* 2:10:2-188.
[9] *Tacticon* (MS. 326 Patriarchal Library of Jerusalem, ed. Palmer, The Desert of the Exodus, 1871, II, pp. 550 ff.)
[10] *War* 3:3:1-35; Mishnah *Shebiith* 6:1; Pliny, *n.h.* V, 19; *Itinerarium burdigalense* 19, 5.
[11] Tos. *Shebiith* 4:6.
[12] Alt, *ZDPV*, 1949, p. 70-72; *JPOS* XIV, p. 56 f.
[13] *War* 2:18:1-459; cf. *Ant.* 13:5:6-154; Pap. Zenon, 59004.
[14] *War* 2:21:1-588; jer. *Demai* 22 d.
[15] Galling, *ZDPV*, 1938, pp. 66 ff.
[16] *War* 2:10:2-188.
[17] *On.* 30, 13.
[18] *PG* 87, c. 2909.

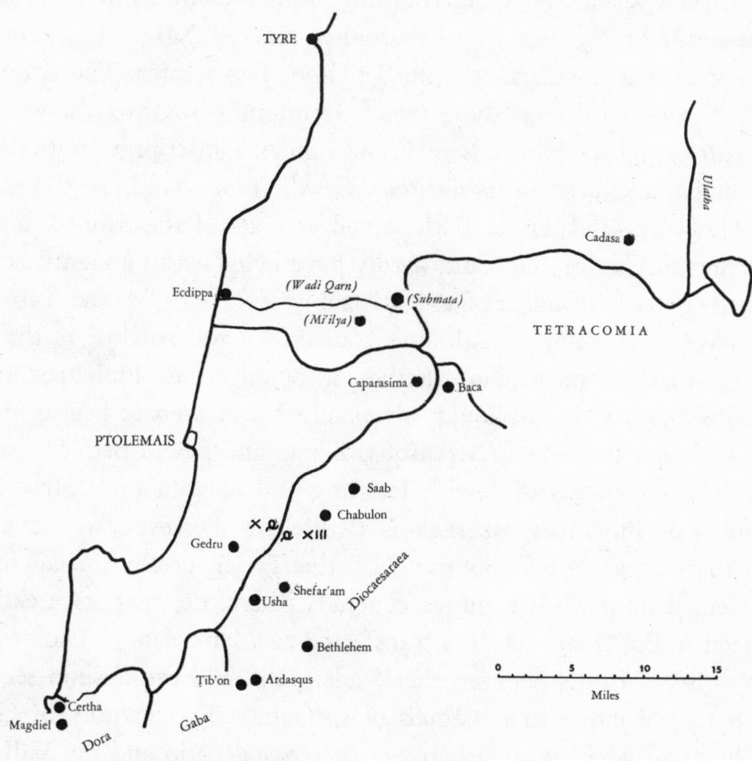

Map 10: TERRITORIES OF TYRE AND PTOLEMAIS
X — Milestones with indication of city name and distance

leaving Baca (Peqi'in) in Galilee.[19] The next fixed points are Saab and Chabulon, both in Galilee,[20] i.e. outside the area of Ptolemais. From the plain of Beth ha-Cerem (Majdal el Kurûm) the border seemed therefore to return to the natural boundary between the Galilee mountains and the coastal plain. At one point we can pinpoint the border with much exactitude: near Bab el Kharûq on the Ptolemais-Sepphoris road a mile-

[19] *War* 3:3:1-39.
[20] See p. 135 below.

stone marked X (i.e. 10 miles counting from Ptolemais) is followed at a distance of barely one mile by another marked XIII. The latter obviously indicated the distance from Sepphoris-Diocaesarea. The boundary passed therefore between these two.[21] Continuing southwards, we note that *Gedru* (Jidru) which is mentioned in one inscription with Ptolemais[22] must have been in its territory. On the other hand, we should exclude Shefar'am and 'Usha. Both served as seats of the Sanhedrin after its transfer to Galilee and could hardly have belonged to a Gentile city.[23] South of 'Usha lies Khirbat S'as'a, probably identical with the Talmudic Kefar Sâsây. According to Talmudic sources,[24] it was so close to the border that there were doubts whether it belonged to Ptolemais or to Sepphoris-Diocaesarea; although ultimately it was seen to belong to the latter. Galilean Bethlehem, 'Ardasqûs, Tib'on and Besara-Beth She'arim[25] were all famous seats of Jewish learning and as such probably outside the limits of Ptolemais. As regards Bethlehem, however, we have evidence that it was called "Sôraiya," i.e. the Tyrian or Phoenician in the Jerusalem Talmud.[26] We might conclude, therefore, that its area once belonged to Ptolemais, but was transferred at a later date to Diocaesarea. In any case, the hills between the Wâdi Mâlik and the Kishon seem to have belonged either to Ptolemais or to Gabaa. The territory of Gabaa must have included the area between the coastal plain and the Valley of Jezreel, as it was presumably built to guard the pass connecting the two. The Carmel promontory belonged certainly to Ptolemais; Josephus calls the mountain "once Galilean now Tyrian."[27] On the coastal road the boundary of Palestine and Phoenicia (i.e. Ptolemais and Dora) in the time of the Bordeaux pilgrim (A.D. 333) was at Certha (Kh. Dustrey).[28] Magdiel, a big village five miles from Dora on the way to

[21] Avi-Yonah, *QDAP* XII, p. 96, No. 12.
[22] *Ib.*, p. 85 f., No. 2.
[23] See below p. 135.
[24] Tos. *Gittin* 2:3; jer. *ib.*, 43 c; bab. *ib.*, 6 b.
[25] See below, p. 107.
[26] Mishnah *Kelim* 2:2; jer. *Megillah* 70 a.
[27] *War* 3:3:1-35.
[28] *IB* 19, 10; John, *QDAP*, III, p. 151; VI, 138.

Ptolemais[29] was, however, in the territory of the former; if the identification with Kh. Mitla is right, the boundary must have curved north of Wâdi Shellâla.[30]

Galilee

Tetracomia (Upper Galilee)

Josephus[31] defined Upper Galilee as extending from Meroth to Thella in a west-east direction, and from Baca to Beersheba (of Galilee) in the north-south one. *Beersheba* is certainly Kh. Abû esh Shîba at the eastern extremity of the Valley of Beth ha-Cerem[32] and *Thella* Tuleil on the Lake Huleh.[33] If we identify *Baca* with Peqi'in then the common identification of Meroth with Meirûn is impossible; the north-south and east-west extensions given could by no means be fitted into the map. It seems much more likely that Meroth should be identified with Marûn er-Râs in the Lebanon. Josephus' description should be amended accordingly to read: Meroth to Beersheba in a north-southern direction, Baca to Thella from west to east. These boundaries do not seem to have changed in Roman and Byzantine times. Beginning from Baca the border followed the Mount Meron massif on the north-west; we might presume that the sites of Sa'sa[34] and Kefar Bar'am,[35] which contain remains of synagogues, should be included in Upper Galilee. The same applies, of course, to *Gischala* (Jîsh),[36] possibly the head-village of the whole area. Going east 'Alma[37] and *Qisyôn*[38] with their synagogue remains should be included in Galilee. As we have seen, Cadasa belonged to Tyre,[39] and so did probably the site of Kh. Harrawi, where there are remains of a temple of Athena.[40]

---

[29] *On.* 130, 21.
[30] Unless we have here another of the exceptions noted above, p. 128, n. 6.
[31] *War* 3:3:1-40.
[32] *War* 3:3:1-39; *OuW* p. 209.
[33] Ib., *OuW,* p. 210.
[34] *SWP* I, p. 256.
[35] *KW,* p. 89.
[36] *War* 2:20:6-575; Mishnah *Arakhin* 9:6; *KW,* p. 107; *SWP* I, p. 225.
[37] Dalman, *PJb,* 1914, p. 47.
[38] jer. *Bezah* 63 b; Renan, *Mission de Phénicie,* p. 774.
[39] See p. 130 above.
[40] Abel, *RB,* 1908, p. 574; Albright, *BASOR,* 19, p. 12.

Map 11: TERRITORIES OF TETRACOMIA, TIBERIAS, DIOCAESAREA, LEGIO, SCYTHOPOLIS, HELENOPOLIS AND NAIN

As we have seen, the border reached Lake Huleh at Thella (Tuleil) and followed the Jordan southwards. The southern border of Upper Galilee was common with Tiberias. Its line is uncertain until we reach the neighbouring sites of *Ḳefar Hananîya* (Kafr 'Inân) and Beersheba. The former marks the limit of Upper Galilee according to the Mishna[41] and the latter according to Josephus. From Beersheba to Baca the boundary is marked by nature in the high mountain wall following the Beth ha-Cerem valley on the north.

Lower Galilee

From the lists of cities of Palaestina Secunda, as given by Hierocles[42] and Georgius Cyprius,[43] it follows that Lower Galilee was originally divided into the region of Sepphoris-Diocaesarea and the region of Tiberias. This division corresponds to what is known of the historical evolution of the area. After the abolition of the Jewish Commonwealth Sepphoris came under the governor of the provincia Judaea, while Tiberias remained under Agrippa II. Only upon the death of this ruler did it become a self-governing city, striking its own coins.[44] The division of Lower Galilee into these two units lasted till the Byzantine times. Then Helenopolis and Exaloth-Nain were separated from Diocaesarea and became independent administrative units or parts of such.

Sepphoris-Diocaesarea

The western boundary of this city has already been described, as it corresponded to the eastern boundary of Ptolemais-Acre.[45] It included the localities which Josephus places 'in Galilee'; *Saab*[46] (adopting the version Σαάβ of some MS instead of the Σαβὰ of Niese's text; it corresponds to the *Shaab* of the Midrash[47] and to modern Sha'ab), *Chabulon* (the *Kabûl* of the Toseftha,[48] modern Kabûl); further the seats of the Sanhedrin; *Shefar'am* (mentioned in the Tosephtha,[49] modern Shefa 'Amr), *'Usha*

[41] Mishnah *Shebiith* 9:2.
[42] Synecdemus, 719, 12.
[43] Georg. Cypr. 1028 ff.
[44] Hill: *BMC Palestine,* p. xiv.
[45] See p. 131 f. above.
[46] *War* 3:7:21-229.
[47] Levit. R. xx.
[48] *War* 3:3:1-38; Tos. *Shabbath* 7(8):16.
[49] Tos. *Mikwaoth* 6:2; bab. *Rosh ha-Shanah* 31 a; bab. *Sanhedrin* 13 b; bab. *Abodah zarah* 8 b.

(Kh. Hôsha)[50] and *Besara—Beth She'arim* (Sheikh Ibreik);[51] to these we might add *'Ardasqûs* (Kh. Qusqus)[52] and *Tib'ôn* (Tab'ûn),[53] important seats of Talmudic learning, and *Kefar Sâsây* which was discussed above.[54] The territory of Sepphoris seems to have been enlarged here by the addition of *Bethlehem Sôraiya* (the 'Tyrian')[55] and of Besara, formerly the storage centre of the estates in the Valley of Jezreel.[56]

From the meeting point of the boundaries of Sepphoris and Gabaa we follow the border in a south-westerly direction. The problem here lies in defining the boundaries of the royal (and later imperial) estates in the Valley of Jezreel. These estates filled the gap between Galilee, which (according to Josephus)[57] ended at Xaloth (Iksal), and Samaria which began at Ginae (Jenin).[58] The only certain indications as to the line of the boundary are the milestones near Sarid[59] which count from Legio, the city which inherited the plain. It has been argued that *Tarbenet*[60] (Kh. Tarbâna) belonged to Sepphoris, because its rabbi was appointed by the Jewish patriarch, but this fact seems to reflect a religious and not a civil dependence. Josephus calls *Simonias* (Talmudic *Sîmôniyah,*[61] modern Kh. Semmûniye) a village on the frontier of Galilee. South-east of it was *Gabatha* (modern Jebâta situated, according to Eusebius,[62] in the territory of Diocaesarea, but near the Great Plain, i.e. near the border with Legio. East of it lies *Mahalôl* (Ma'lûl),[63] which was one of the communities addressed by the patriarch and possibly an administrative centre of a

---

50 *Ib.*
51 *Life* 24-118; Tos. *Sukkah* 2:2; bab. *Sanhedrin* 32 b; bab. *Rosh ha-Shanah* 31 b; bab. *Ketuboth* 113b.
52 Tos. Erubbin 9(6):4.
53 Mishnah *Makhshirin* 1:3.
54 See p. 132 above.
55 *Ib.*
56 *Life* 24-118.
57 *War* 3:3:1-39.
58 3:3:4-48.
59 Avi-Yonah, *QDAP* XII, pp. 96-97 (Nos. 13-16).
60 jer. *Megillah* 75 b.
61 *Life* 24-115; jer. *Megillah* 70 a.
62 *On.* 70, 9.
63 jer. *Megillah* 70 a; *SWP* I, p. 322 f.

lower rank.[64] *Iaphia* (Yâfa) is listed among the villages fortified by Josephus and was thus certainly in Galilee.[65] Exaloth= *'Îksalô* (Iksâl) was another boundary point of this province.

In the time of Eusebius[66] *Dabira* (the Dabaritta of Josephus,[67] modern Dabbûriye) was still within the territory of Diocaesarea; the boundary passed up *Mount Tabor* (the Itabyrium of Hellenistic times[68] and a fortified place of Josephus).[69] This mountain was a prominent landmark and seems to have served as a boundary point in Roman times[70] just as it did in the time of Joshua.[71] From this summary outline of the southern boundary of Sepphoris-Diocaesarea we note that it passed along the hills bordering the Plain of Jezreel to the north, leaving almost all its fertile area to others.

From Mount Tabor the boundary seems to have turned northwards; but we have almost no indication as to the line it followed. A hint in this direction might be contained in the statement found in the Jerusalem Talmud[72] to the effect that *Maskanah* (Kh. Meskene) was a road station between Tiberias and Sepphoris; probably it was situated on or near the boundary. The line seems to have been following a north-south direction till it reached that of Upper Galilee at Beersheba.[73]

Helenopolis appears as the name of a city in the history of Sozomenus (444)[74] in the "Synecdemus" of Hierocles between Tiberias and Diocaesaera (535)[75] and in the synodal list of Jerusalem (536).[76] The actual identification is not certain, but its area appears to have included

---

[64] jer. *Maaser sheni* 56 a.
[65] *War* 2:20:6-573.
[66] *On.* 78, 5.
[67] *War* 2:21:3-595; *Life* 37-188.
[68] Polybius V, 70, 9.
[69] *War* 2:20:6-573; 4:1:8-54-61; *Life* 37-188.
[70] *On.* 98, 23 etc.
[71] Jos. 19:22, 34.
[72] jer. *Sanhedrin* 21 a.
[73] See above, p. 133.
[74] Hist. eccl. II, 2 (*PG* LXVII, c. 936).
[75] 720, 8.
[76] Schwartz, *Acta,* III, p. 188, No. 28.

Mount Tabor and Nazareth,[77] the sacred sites which were the special interest of Helena, the mother of Constantine.

Tiberias

The remainder of Lower Galilee belonged to the territory of Tiberias. It is the only city in this area appearing in later lists. In Josephus we read indeed that Agrippa II received from Nero Tiberias, Taricheae and their toparchies.[78] After the War of 66-73 Taricheae no longer appears as a city and we may presume that its territory was included in that of Tiberias. The area of the latter did, therefore, extend to the Jordan, including *Capernaum;* the fact that there was a custom officer at this village[79] proves its vicinity to a border. The expression used in the Gospel of John 12:21 *Bēthsaida tēs Galilaias,* 'Bethsaida of Galilee' has led some commentators to extend the area of Galilee (and consequently that of Tiberias) beyond the Jordan. There is no reason to rely on this singular verse, which is contradicted by all other sources.[80]

On the south the area of Tiberias certainly extended to the Jordan at its issue from the Sea of Galilee. It inherited here the former boundary which Galilee had in common with Hippus and Gadara.[81] It should be remembered, however, that the Jordan has certainly changed its course since antiquity. The excavation of a church at *Beth-Yerah* (Kh. Kerak) dated 529 according to a Pompeian era, have proved with certainty that this cite belonged to a city of the Decapolis and was, therefore, east of the river.[82] This view is confirmed by the remains of a bridge (the Crusader 'Bridge of Sinnabra')[83] in the former river bed. The boundary followed the Jordan till the Roman bridge at Gesher (Jisr el Majami'). South of this bridge began the territory of Scythopolis (Beth-Shean), as is proved by the milestones in the Jordan Valley along the road leading to the bridge. However, the area of Scythopolis did not in all probability

[77] A Jewish village at the time, *Anton. Placent.* ed. Geyer, pp. 161-2. It would thus be freed from its dependence on Jewish Diocaesarea.

[78] *Ant.* 20:7:4-159; *War* 2:13:2-252.

[79] Matthew, 9:9.

[80] *War* 3:3:1-37 etc.

[81] *Ib.*

[82] Cf. n. 109 to Chapter IV.

[83] L. A. Mayer, *IEJ,* 2, 1952, p. 183 ff.

extend beyond the Jordan Valley itself. For, if the fortress of *Agrippina*[84] is identified with Kaukab el Hawa, it belonged to Galilee. According to the Talmud the signals given by the Sanhedrin at Jerusalem were repeated from that fortress. It must, therefore, have been in Jewish territory. Possibly even the place-name *Gebul* (meaning 'boundary') which occurs in the Jerusalem Talmud[85] and has been identified with modern Jabbûl might have marked the limits of Galilean territory. From this point, the boundary Tiberias turned westwards, following the Wâdi Bire, till it reached Mount Tabor. For the rest of the line it was identical with the eastern boundary of Diocaesarea.

Scythopolis — Beth Shean

The northern limits of this territory correspond to the southern boundary of Tiberias. The milestones counting from Scythopolis continue for eleven miles till el Khân near the Jisr el Majami' bridge. To the west the territory of Scythopolis extended along the Valley of Harod till the tenth milestone found near 'En Harôd; Jezreel (Zîr'în) was excluded, as it belonged to Legio. From this westernmost point, the boundary turned southwards, including *Araba* (*'Arabi* of the Midrash,[86] modern 'Arrabûne) which Eusebius places three (?) miles west of Scythopolis.[87] From here the boundary continued in a south-easterly direction, excluding Bethacath but including *Gelbus* (Jalbûn), six miles from Scythopolis.[87a] For the continuation of the boundary we have a valuable indication in the numbering of the milestones on the Neapolis-Scythopolis road. Till the twentieth mile they were in the territory of Neapolis, which probably reached as far as Conas (Qa'ûn).[88] On the other hand, the seventh milestone at Tell Abû Faraj shows that the territory of Scythopolis extended along the Jordan further south. It included *Aenon* near *Salumias* (Umm el 'Umdân) which was distant eight miles from the city.[89] The furthest

---

[84] Mishnah *Rosh ha-Shanah* 2:4; Dalman, *PJb*, 1923, p. 43 f.
[85] jer. *Hallah* 59 a.
[86] Gen R. 33, 5.
[87] On. 16, 13.
[87a] *On* 72, 10.
[88] Thomsen, *ZDPV*, 1917, pp. 74-5; Vincent, *RB*, 1901, p. 96 f.
[89] *On.* 40, 1.

point reached in this direction were the springs of *Bethmaela*[90] (Tell el Hilu) ten miles from Scythopolis. The boundary seems to have passed between this point and Abelmea which was situated on the road descending from Neapolis (Wâdi el-Mîlh). The eastern boundary of Scythopolis was naturally the River Jordan from Jisr el-Majami' to about Tell Fâtur.

The territory thus defined formed a well-knit unit, composed of the Jordan and the Harod Valleys and the Gilboa mountains. Its limits followed a natural boundary which has been used again and again in medieval and modern times.

Nain—Exaloth

In the list of Georgius Cyprius there appears a *Komē Nais* which has been identified with the *Naim* of Eusebius [91] (Nain of Luke 7:11, *Na'im* of the Midrash,[92] modern Nein). It was situated two miles south of Mount Tabor near Aendor. According to the same source *Endor* (Indûr) was four miles south of Mount Tabor[93] and in the vicinity of Scythopolis. A third village *Sulem* (Sûlem) was situated five miles south of the mountain.[94] The episcopal see of *Exaloth* (Talmudic 'Îksâlô, modern Iksâl) mentioned in the second synod of Jerusalem (536) seems to have belonged to this district.[95] We have here a small estate which seems to have formed originally part of Scythopolis (Endor), part of Sepphoris (Exaloth) and part of Legio.[96] It seems to have extended as far as Mount Tabor, which served as its point of definition and included the fertile *Plain of 'Îksalô* of the Talmud.

Gaba Hippeum

The existence of this city is certain, but its location is doubtful. The topographical data concerning Gaba are as follows: (1) it was in Galilee;[97] (2) it adjoined Mount Carmel;[98] it was 60 stadia distant from

---

90 *On.* 34, 23.

91 Georg. Cypr. 1042; *On.* 140, 3.

92 Gen R. 98(99), 12.

93 *On.* 34, 9.

94 *On.* 158, 11.

95 *Life* 44-227; *War* 3:3-1-39; *Gen* R. 98(99), 12; *On.* 22, 4; Schwartz, *Acta,* III, p. 189.

96 See p. 142.

97 *Ant.* 15:8:5-294.

98 *War* 3:3:1-36.

Simonias, 20 stadia from Besara, which was situated between Gabaa and Simonias, with rocky ground and passes between it and Gabaa.[99] A further help towards an identification is the Kb in the list of Thutmosis III. It is generally identified with Tell 'Amr situated in the pass between the coastal plain and the Valley of Jezreel.[100] This tell is, however, too small for Roman Gaba, and the remains on its surface are too early. The site of the Hellenistic-Roman city must be somewhere in the vicinity. Possibly it was situated at el Harithiye, for the earlier identification with Sheikh Bureik must be abandoned. The area of Gaba cannot have been large. In the west the coastal plain belonged to Ptolemais; in the east Cimona (Yoqne'am) was already in the lands of Legio. Herod allotted to his veterans lands in the Great Plain,[101] but these need not be confused with the territory of Gaba.

Legio-Maximianupolis

After the war of Bar-Kokhba the sixth legion was encamped at *Ceparcotnei*[102] of Ptolemy,[103] *Kefar 'Otnay* of the Mishnah,[104] which was henceforth known as Legio (modern Lejjûn). It received as its estate the Plain of Jezreel (the 'Great Plain' of Josephus),[105] which was therefore called by later sources the *Campus Maximus Legionis.*[106] With the removal of the legion in the time of Diocletian the camp became a city. It was called *Maximianupolis*[107] in honour of Diocletian's colleague Maximianus Herculius. The extent of its territory is defined by the villages which measured their distances from it. In the west there are *Cimona* (Tell Yoqne'am),[108] *Apharaea* (Kh. Fureir?),[109] both six miles distant from Legio. Going further south we find Beth Anath ('Anîn) excluded

---

[99] *Life* 6-24.
[100] No. 41 on the list of Thutmosis III.
[101] See n. 97 above.
[102] W. Ramsay, *Journ. Rom. Stud.* VI, p. 219.
[103] Ptolemaeus V, 15, 3.
[104] Mishnah *Gittin* 2:5; 7:7.
[105] *War* 2:10:2-188 etc.
[106] *On.* 110, 21; in the Midrash the biblical "Valley of Jezreel" is used (*Gen R.*, 98(99)12).
[107] *On.* 14, 21; *Itin. burd.* 19, 19; Hierocles: *Synecd.* 720, 10.
[108] *On.* 116, 21.
[109] *On.* 28, 26.

from this territory; it included however *Thaanach* (Tell Ti'innik) four miles from Legio,[110] and *Janua* (el Yamûn?) three (?) miles to the south.[111] The remotest point of this territory is *Bethacath* (Beit Qâd) fifteen miles from Legio;[112] it is attributed by Eusebius in the same sentence to Samaria and the Great Plain. The reference to Samaria seems, however, derived from a misunderstood passage in the Bible (2 Kings 10:12). The mountains of Gilboa with the villages Gelbus and Araba situated thereon were in the territory of Scythopolis. The boundary of Legio seems in general to have followed very closely the limits of the plain. It thus included *Jezreel* of Eusebius, *Stradela* of the Bordeaux pilgrim (modern Zir'în)[113] which was situated 'between' Scythopolis and Legio, i.e. near the boundary. However, as it was situated in the 'Great Plain,' we should attribute it to the latter. From this point the boundary turned northwards and westwards including *Arbel* (Affulah?) nine miles from Legio, again in the Great Plain.[114]

The area of Legio seems to have included at some time the Plain of Exaloth, if not the village itself. Only thus can we explain the addition (by Hieronymus) to the Greek text of the *Onomasticon* (111, 21). In it Mount Tabor is defined as situated in the Great Plain 'east of Legio.' With the creation of the Come Nais as an independent unit, the plain of Exaloth was apparently transferred to this region.

The northern boundary of Legio corresponds to the southern one of Sepphoris-Diocaesarea, which has already been discussed above.

The Cities of the Coast

The coastal plain was divided between nine cities: Dora, Caesarea, Apollonia, Joppa, Jamnia, Azotus, Ascalon, Gaza and Raphia. We can distinguish two groups in this list. The northern group (from Dora to Joppa, but excepting Caesarea) were typical harbour cities with comparatively small inland areas. The southern group (excepting Ascalon)

---

[110] *On.* 110, 7.
[111] *On.* 108, 5.
[112] *On* 56, 26.
[113] *On.* 108, 13; *Itin. burd.* 19, 20.
[114] *On.* 14, 20.

was composed of twin cities, an *epineion* on the shore itself and the mother-city further inland. Often indeed the port city gradually became the more important of the two. The areas of these southern cities were proportionally larger. It should, of course, be borne in mind that the Palestinian coast becomes broader as we advance southwards. This geographical factor was naturally reflected in the city areas.

Dora

The northern limit of this city has been defined by the Bordeaux pilgrim at *Mutatio Certha* (Kh. Dastri),[115] for he places there the boundary of Phoenicia (Ptolemais) and Palestine. According to the later lists, Dora belonged to the latter, probably since Diocletian.[116] In the south we have to consider the fact that the aqueduct of Caesarea reaches the *Chorseus* river (Nahr ed Difle).[117] Hence the territory of Dora did not reach beyond this watercourse. From the Chorseus the boundary passed northwards to the *Me'arat Telimon* (Cave at Kh. es Suleimaniye) which belonged to Caesarea, according to the Jerusalem Talmud.[118] Further north, the whole of the Carmel range seems to have been outside the area of Dora, including Gaba. This might reflect the conquest of the 'inner Carmel' by John Hyrcanus[119] and its subsequent attribution by Herod to Caesarea.

Caesarea

As has been stated above, Caesarea was the only coastal city in the north which was endowed with a considerable inland area. Herod was naturally interested in securing the inland communications of his principal port and achieved this by adding to it almost the whole of the Megiddo pass, up to and including Beth Anath (*Beth Yânay* of the Tosephtha (?),[120] modern 'Anîn), which Eusebius places fifteen miles

[115] *Itin. burd.* 19, 10; Cf. Johns, *QDAP* III, p. 151; VI, p. 138.
[116] See above, p. 132.
[117] Ptolemaeus V, 14, 3; Abel: *Géographie* I, p. 469 f identifies it with the Nahr ez Zerqa; the latter is however much more suitable for the Crocodilon flumen of Pliny V, 75.
[118] jer. *Demai* 22 c.
[119] *War* 2:5:1-66.
[120] Tos. *Shebiith* 7:14.

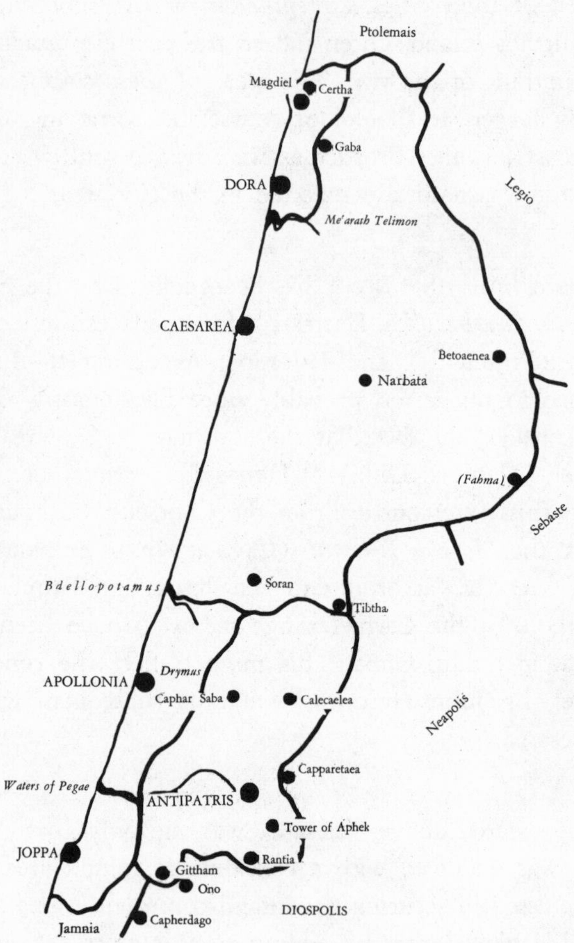

Map 12: TERRITORIES OF DORA, CAESAREA, APOLLONIA, JOPPA AND ANTIPATRIS

from Caesarea to the east.[121] The area of Caesarea was further expanded northwards by the addition of the 'Inner Carmel' including *Geba* (the—[E]g[a]batana of Pliny,[122] modern Jaba') sixteen miles from the

[121] *On.* 30, 5.
[122] *N.h.* V, 18.

city.[123] To the south the toparchy of *Narbata* (Kh. Beidûs)[124] was added, which might have extended as far as modern Fahma, where the remains of a synagogue were discovered.[125] This is a valuable indication, for the Narbattene was predominantly a Jewish district. The southern boundary of Caesarea is defined by the Jerusalem Talmud[126] as passing the caravanserai (*pundeqa*) of *Tibetah* (et Taiyibe)[127] and a locality called *Sôran* (Umm Sûr). To this we should add the information contributed by the episcopal *Notitia* based on that of Nilus Doxopatrius.[128] According to this source the dioecesis of Joppa extended to the *Bdellopotamus* (probably the Nahr Faliq), which thus formed a boundary of the see (and city) of Caesarea.

Apollonia

This town, (the city of Reshef-Apollo, hence modern Arsuf) was also called *Sozousa* ('City of the Saviour' in Christian times).[129] Its area must-have been comparatively small, bordered on the north by the Bdellopotamus, on the south by the 'Waters of Pegae;' the Plain of Capharsaba, which belonged to Antipatris, limited its area on the east. The big forest of the Sharon, the *Drymus* might have formed part of its boundary.

Antipatris

The city of Antipatris was founded anew by Herod. There is hardly another place in Palestine which changed its name so many times. It is identified with Biblical Aphek,[130] a name which was still preserved in the vicinity in the form Pyrgus Aphecu (Tower of Aphek) in the time of the First Roman War.[131] In Hellenistic times it was apparently called

---

[123] *On.* 70, 8.

[124] *War* 2:14:5-291; 2:18:10-509; jer. *Berakhoth* 10 b (variant in the Lehmann ed. 27 a from the Nabrakhta in the usual texts.

[125] *BJPES* XIII, 155-4 (Hebrew).

[126] jer. *Demai* 22 c.

[127] *Ib.* Cf. B. Maisler, *JPOS* 1935, p. 100. The identification assumes that this et Taiyibe represents an ancient name, and did not stand for an ancient place name with the root *'fr* (such as Ephraim or Aphairema or Ophrah) which the Arabs changed to Taiyibet el Ism ("Good-in-Name") out of fear of the *'Ifrit* or demon.

[128] See Palmer: *Desert of the Exodus,* 1871, pp. 550 ff.

[129] Pliny *N.h.* V, 12; Hierocles: *Synecd.* 719, 5.

[130] 1 Samuel 29:1, etc.

[131] *War* 2:19:7-513.

Pegae,[132] this name has also left its trace in the *Waters of Pegae* (*Mê Pîgah*) of the Mishnah, viz. the Yarkon River. Still later, in the time of Pompey, appears the name of *Arethusa* which has also been identified with this site.[133] In later periods it has been called Le Toron aux Fontaines Sourdes, Tell Ras el 'Ain and Tell Aphek. The northern boundary of this city was identical with part of the southern boundary of Caesarea, and the western with those of Apollonia and Ioppe. *Caphar Saba* (Kh. Sâbye) was obviously situated in this area, as Antipatris was founded in its plain.[134] In the south Onus was certainly outside the territory of Antipatris, for it belonged to Lydda-Diospolis.[135] *Rantia* (Arab Rantiye, now Rînatyah) on the other hand belonged to Antipatris, this we may conclude from the episcopal *Notitia* referred to above.[136] According to this source Rantia was included in the Middle Ages in the see of Joppa. As the latter inherited inter alia the territory of Antipatris, but not that of Lydda, we may assume that Rantia belonged to Antipatris. A more difficult problem is that of *Gittham.* According to the "Onomasticon"[137] this big village was situated on the road from Antipatris to Jamnia between the two cities. According to the usual rule of interpretation, as defined above,[138] this should mean that Antipatris and Jamnia had a common boundary and that Gittham was situated near it on the territory of Antipatris, however. The site of Saqiye has been proposed for Gittham as fulfilling this condition. Such a common boundary must have consisted of a strip of the lands of Jamnia passing between Joppa and Beth Dagon (Ceparadagon) which later belonged to Lydda-Diospolis. This is a probable, but by no means a certain solution. It has been suggested recently[139] that Gittham should be identified Ras Abu Hamid near Ramle, at which the biblical Gath-Yam or Gitthaim is supposed

---

[132] Pap. Zeno *PSI* IV, No. 406; *Ant.* 13:9:2-261; Mishnah *Parah* 8:10.
[133] *BJPES* X, p. 18 (Hebrew).
[134] Ant. 16:5:2-142; Tos. *Niddah* 7:5. For the name Antipatris see Mishnah Gittin 7:7; Ant. 13:15:1-390; Hill *BMC Palestine* pp. XV f., 11.
[135] See below, p. 158.
[136] See n. 128 above.
[137] *On.* 68, 15.
[138] See p. 128 above.
[139] B. Mazar, *IEJ,* 4, 1954, p. 227 ff.

to have been placed. If so, we should postulate here one of the exceptions from the rules governing the composition of the "Onomasticon," which is not impossible by itself; the matter should best be left undecided till more evidence is produced. If we follow the boundary of Antipatris from Rantia northwards we should note the following points: the Tower of Aphek (*Pyrgus Aphecu*[140] Majdal Yaba'), to which the Jews of Antipatris retired on the approach of Cestius Gallus and his army in A.D. 66, was certainly in this territory. The villages to the north-east of it Kefar Qesem and Capparetaea were in Samaria, hence presumably outside it. *Galgulis* (Jaljûlye) and *Calecaelea* (Qilqîlye) north of these were, however, (again according to the medieval Notitia)[141] in the lands of Antipatris.

Joppa

In common with most harbour cities, Joppa (Jaffa) seems to have had a very small territory. Its northern boundary ran most likely along the Waters of Pegae (River Yarkon). On the east Beth Dagon was outside its lands. On the south it could hardly have reached beyond the sand dunes extending north of the Sôreq Valley, for near the mouth of this river was the harbour of Jamnia. On the sea coast Joppa was unique among the coastal cities in possessing the small built-over islands of Paria, "insula ante Ioppen tota oppidum' according to Pliny.[142] He probably refers to Andromeda's rocks outside the Jaffa harbour, now largely blasted away.

Jamnia

This city, for some time a toparchy of Judaea and later on an imperial domain, had also a rather small territory, which reached north of the Sôreq Valley to the Lachish Valley (Suqreir); Kîdron-Gedrus (Qatra) was already outside its area. It included on the sea-shore an *epineion*, maritime *Jamnia* (Mînat Rubîn, Yabneh-Yam) which is mentioned in the Second Book of Maccabees[143] and by Ptolemaeus.[144]

---

140 See n. 131 above.

141 See n. 128 above.

142 *N.h.* V, 13.

143 2 Macc. 12:9.

144 Ptol. V, 15, 2.

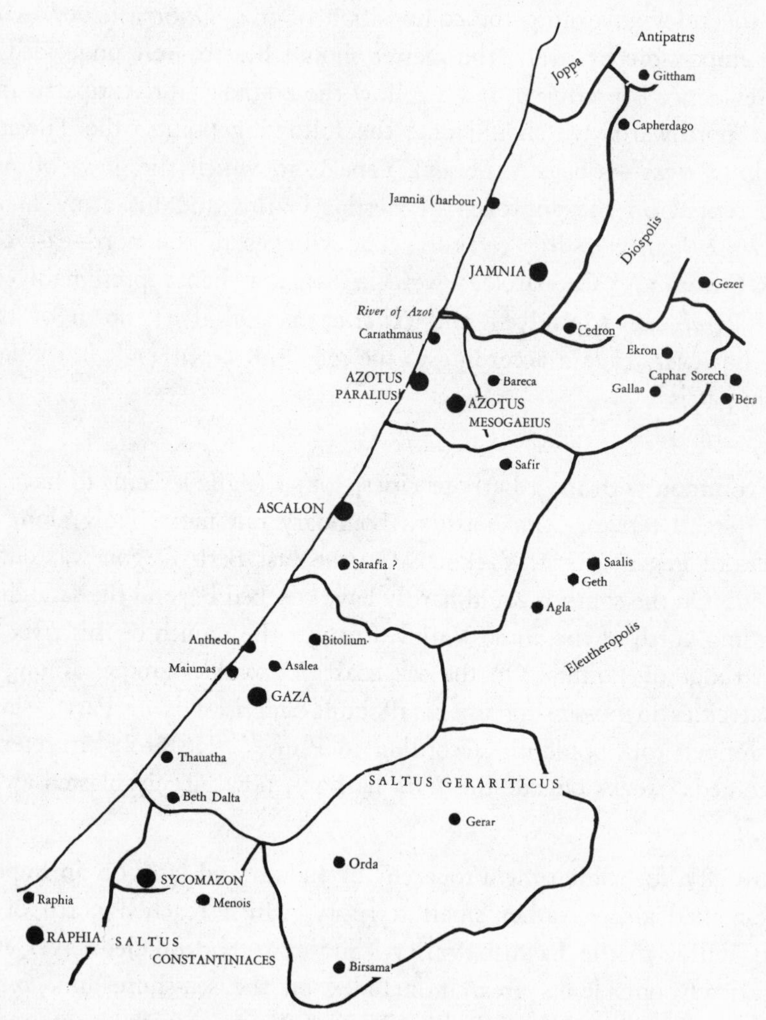

Map 13: TERRITORIES OF JAMNIA, AZOTUS, ASCALON, GAZA, RAPHIA, SYCOMAZON, SALTUS CONSTANTINIACES AND SALTUS GERARITICUS

Azotus

The area of Azotus comprised two cities. The one was called *Azotus Mesogaeus*[145] or *Hippenus*[146] (the 'inland' or 'of the cavalrymen'—hence the supposition that it was, like Gaba, a colony of Herod's veterans. The other was the harbour city of *Azotus Paralius.*[147] If we are to rely on the Madaba Map, the harbour was (in Byzantine times) by far the bigger city,[148] and this has been confirmed by recent excavations. The area of Azotus seems to have extended over a strip some eight miles wide, which included the secondary harbour of *Cariathmaus*[149] (Qiryat Mahôz—Nabi Yûnîs).[150] It reached in the north the *River of Azot* of the medieval Notitia[151] (in this source Azotus is included in the see of Ascalon.) The area of Azotus included to the north *Bareca*[152] (Barqâ) which Eusebius places in the vicinity of Azotus. Cedron-Cedrus was outside it. The territory of Azotus seems however to have received a considerable extension eastwards by the addition of the toparchy of *Accaron* (Biblical Ekron). Here again, as in the case of Gittham,[153] we have to interpret a statement of Eusebius, which is by no means clear. According to the "Onomasticon" Accaron was a very big Jewish village situated "between Azotus and Jamnia to the east." The name has been preserved in the village of Kefar 'Eqron (Arabic 'Aqîr) which is indeed situated west of Jamnia, but which can hardly be placed "between that city and Ashdod." The recent identifications of Biblical Ekron are with Tell Batashi,[154] or, more plausibly, with Kh. el Muqannah.[155] This would place it in a position better in accord with one of the data of Eusebius, and with a presumed dependence on Azotus. It would, however, contradict the other data,

---

145 Hierocles: *Synecd.* 718, 6.
146 Georg. Cypr. 1021.
147 Hierocl.: *Synecd.* 718, 5.
148 *Madaba Map,* Pl. 8, No. 93.
149 *Vitae prophetarum* ed. Schermann p. 18, 19.
150 Abel, *JPOS* 1922, p. 177-8.
151 See n. 128 above.
152 *On.* 54, 3.
153 See p. 146 above, and *On.* 22, 9.
154 B. Mazar, *EI* 2, 1953, p. 17 (Hebrew).
155 J. Naveh, *IEJ,* 8, 1958, pp. 166-170.

for then his Accaron could hardly be "between" (i.e. near the boundary of) Jamnia and Azotus. There would be a strip of the territory of Diospolis with Gedrus in between.[156] Nevertheless, there is no other area to whom we could attribute the former toparchy of Ekron. It should be noted that *Galaa* (Jilya)[157] depended, according to the *"Onomasticon,"* on Accaron and that Beerah (Kh. el Bîr) Sorech and Gezara (Gezer) were outside its area.

Ascalon

Here again, we cannot give any certain boundaries beyond the assumption—on geographical grounds—that *Sapheir* (Sawâfîr), which was situated between Eleutheropolis and Ascalon, was near the border, but in the territory of the latter.[157a] *Maiumas Ascalon*[158] was certainly in this area, but its identification is not certain. If *Diocletianupolis*[159] is to be identified with the *Sarafia* of Antoninus Placentinus[160] it could be placed, as suggested by A. Alt, at Kh. est Sheraf south of Ascalon. On the other hand, Bitolium, Agla, Gath and Sallis were certainly outside this territory.

Gaza

The area administered by this city hardly corresponded to its importance. It reached in the north the Wâdi Hasi (Valley of Shiqmah) as we learn from the medieval Notitia.[161] On the coast it included *Anthedon* (Kh. Teda), a city of some importance in the Roman period,[162] but which does not appear in the later sources. The port of Gaza, *Maiumas*[163] or *Neapolis* (New Gaza)[164] formed from the time of Constantine onwards a separate city called *Constantia*[165] (el Mineh). The territory of Gaza

---

156 See p. 158 below.
157 *On.* 72, 7.
157a *On.* 156, 23.
158 Anton. Placent. 33.
159 Hierocl.: *Synecd.* 719, 2.
160 See n. 158 above, and Alt, *ZDPV*, 1931, p. 178, n. 2.
161 See n. 128 above.
162 Plin. *N.h.* V. 13; *Ant.* 13:13:3-357.
163 Sozom. *Hist. eccl.* V, 3.; Marcus Diaconus: *Vita Porphyrii* 57.
164 Sozom. *loc. cit.;* Anton. Placent. 33.
165 Hieronymus: Vita Hilarionis 3 (*PL* XXIII, c. 31); Eusebius, Vita Constantini IV, 38 (*PG,* XX, 1188).

might have included to the north *Bitolium*[166] (Tell esh Sheikh Hamdân) and *Asalea*[167] (Nazle), both of which are mentioned by Sozomenus (A.D. 445). To the south it extended to *Migdal Thauatha* (the Migdal Tawtah of Petrus Iberus, now Kh. Umm el Tût), and possibly to *Beth Daltha* (ed Damîta?).[168] Orda, Birsama, Gerar and Sycomazon were outside it.

Raphia

This, the southernmost of the cities of Palestine, was also composed of an inland town (ed Rafah) and a harbour (Tell Rafah) on the sea shore. Its area extended southwards along the shore. The Madaba Map shows a locality B(et)ylium[169] beyond which is marked the border of Palestine and Egypt; according to Theodosius[170] this was placed 12 miles beyond Raphia. However, according to the "Onomasticon" it was Beth Tappuah (Bethtaffa) *fifteen* miles to the south which marked the boundary of Palestine and Egypt.[171] The territory of Raphia did not reach far inland; Menois and Sycomazon being both situated outside its boundaries.

Samaria

We are now returning inland. The province of Samaria extended, according to Josephus, from Ginae (Jenîn) to Anuathu Borcaeus on the boundary of Judaea. It was an early date split up into two territories: The Hellenistic city of Samaria, later Sebaste, and the territory of the Samaritans, which formed since Vespasian the territory of Neapolis.

Sebaste

The northern boundary of Sebaste corresponded to the southern one of Legio-Maximianopolis and Scythopolis-Beth Shean. It excluded therefore Janua and Bethacath, but included *Ginae* (Jenîn) situated in "the great

166 Sozomen. Hist. eccl. VII, 28 (*PG* LXVII, c. 1505).
167 *Ib.* III, 14 (*PG* LXVII, c. 1077).
168 Hieronymus: Vita Hilarionis 30 (*PL* XXIII, c. 45); *Petrus d. Iberer,* ed. Raabe, p. 96 f.
169 Pl. 9, No. 120.
170 Ed. Geyer: *Itinera hierosol.*, p. 138.
171 *On.* 50, 18.

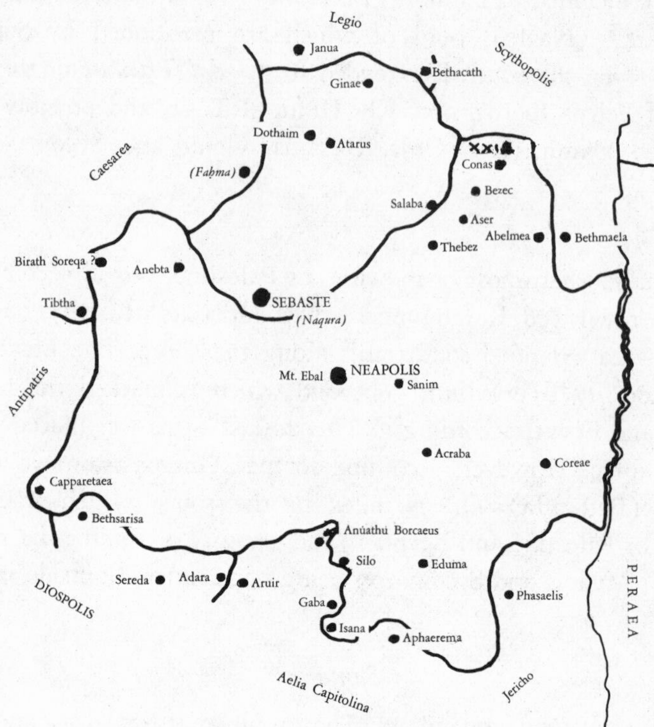

Map 14: TERRITORIES OF SEBASTE AND NEAPOLIS

plain of Samaria,"[172] i.e. where the valley of Jezreel extends southwards into Samaria. On the west it excluded the Narbattene. Fahma might thus have been outside its territory, but *Dothaim* (Tell Dûthân)[173] and *Atarus*[174] (el 'Attâra) were certainly inside it. In the south the boundary must have passed along the valley connecting Tulkarm with Nablus; the Samaritan village of 'Anabta being probably in Neapolis.[175] The dis-

[172] *War* 3:3:4-48.
[173] *On.* 76, 13.
[174] *On.* 26, 19.
[175] It was in any case settled by Samaritans, Ben-Zevie: *Sefer ha-Shomronim,* p. 100 (Hebrew).

tance between Sebaste and Neapolis was small and the boundary must thus have passed close between the two cities. The fact that the aqueduct of Sebaste went as far as en Naqûra[176] allows us to extend its territory as far as this locality. Mount Ebal probably belonged to Neapolis; from there the boundary between the two cities ran in a north-easterly direction, leaving the Neapolis-Scythopolis road in the territory of the former; however, *Salaba*[177] (Kh. Selhab) was in the lands of Sebaste.

Neapolis

This city obtained the whole area left to the Samaritans, as well as the toparchy of Acraba detached from Judaea by Vespasian. Its northern boundary corresponded to the southern one of Sebaste. Included in Neapolis was the road leading to Scythopolis at least as far as the twentieth milestone, and probably till *Conas* (Qa'un),[178] which was in Samaria on the evidence of the Book of Judith. The villages along the road: *Bezek* (Kh. Ibziq) at the 7th mile,[179] *Aser* (Tayâsîr) at the 15th[180] and *Thebez* (Tûbâs) at the 13th[181] all belonged to Neapolis. From Aser branched off a road to *Abelmea* (Wâdi el Milh)[182] which was in the lands of Neapolis but close to the border of Scythopolis, beyond which was near-by Bethmaela. The border of Neapolis seems to have reached the Jordan a short distance south of Bethmaela, and to have followed the river to a point between *Coreae* (Tell Mazar in the Qarâwa) which was formerly a boundary point of Judaea,[183] and Phasaelis (Kh. Fasayîl) belonging to Jericho. With the Accrabittene Neapolis received its capital Acraba[184] (*'Aqrabah* of the Mishna, now 'Aqraba) and *Eduma*[185] (Dûma).

---

176 Crowfoot et al: *Samaria-Sebaste* I. *Buildings,* p. 74 ff.
177 *On.* 158, 22.
178 Judith 4:4.
179 *On.* 56, 4.
180 *On.* 26, 22.
181 *On.* 100, 13.
182 Judith 4:4; *On.* 34, 22.
183 *War* 1:6:5-134.
184 *War* 3:3:5-55; *On.* 14, 8; Mishnah *Maaser sheni* 5:2.
185 *On.* 86, 24.

A quite peculiar case was that of Salem (Sanim[186] Samaritan *Salem* Rabtah, modern Sâlim.) According to the "Onomasticon,"[187] it was situated "in the territory of Sebaste, in the Acrabbittene, now called Sanim." There is an obvious contradiction between the two data: the Acrabbittene was not in the territory of Sebaste. It seems more reasonable to regard the attribution to "Sebaste" as a mistake for "Samaria." The connection with the Samaritans, as known from their sources supports this view. In this case Salem was included in Neapolis.

Apharaēma (et Taiyibe) was outside this area, *Isana*[187a] (Burj el Isâna) on the Jerusalem-Neapolis road was in Samaria, hence it belonged to Neapolis. From here to Anuathu Borcaeus northward the boundary follows the road, leaving Geba (Kh. el Tell) in the lands of Aelia-Jerusalem, while *Selo*[187b] (Biblical and Talmudic *Shiloh,*[188] now Kh. Seilūn) was in Neapolis, 12 miles from that city. From Anuathu Borcaeus the boundary followed the Wâdi Deir Ballut till Sereda, excluding Aruir (ʿArûra) and Addara (Kh. ed. Deir?). Here it turned northwards, leaving Bethsarisa (Ky. Sirîsya) to Diospolis, but including in Neapolis the Samaritan villages of *Capparetaea* (Kh. Kafr Hatta)[189] and *Kefar Qesem*[190] (Kafr Qasim). The western boundary followed from here the eastern limits of Antipatris and Caesarea to *Birath Sôreqah* (Tulkarm?)[191] and ʿAnabta.

Judaea

The first city area to be carved out of this province was that of Aelia Capitolina (Jerusalem); this was followed by Diospolis (Lydda) and Eleutheropolis (Bethogabris) in the time of Septimius Severus, and Nicopolis (Emmaus) under Heliogabalus. The imperial estates (*regiones,*

---

[186] Epiphanius: Adv, haer. I, 55, 2 (*PG* XLI, c. 973).
[187] *On.* 160, 13.
[187a] *Ant.* 14:15:12-458; Albright, *BASOR,* 9, p. 7.
[187b] *On.* 156, 28.
[188] bab. *Sanhedrin* 113 b.
[189] Justinus Mart.: Apol. I, 26 (*PG* VI, c. 368).
[190] Tos. *Abodah zarah* 6(7):8.
[191] jer. *Abodah zarah* 47 b.

saltus) of Jericho, Gerar, Constantinus and Sycomazon remained such till the end of the Byzantine period.

Aelia Capitolina—Jerusalem

The area of this city, which was founded by Hadrian in 132 out of the territory of the Tenth Legion, was originally composed of the four Judaean toparchies: Oreine, Gophanitica, Herodium and Betholetepha. With the foundation of Eleutheropolis Betholetepha was transferred to the new city.

The northern boundary of Aelia corresponded to the southern one of Neapolis. It included *Anuathu Borcaeus* (Kh. Berqît) the ancient boundary point of Judaea and Samaria[192] and *Aruir* ('Arûra). Eusebius places this village at the seventh mile from Jerusalem to north, but St. Jerome corrects this to the twentieth.[192a] From here the boundary inclined southwestwards, leaving Addara and Thamna to Diospolis. *Ganthah* ('Ain Jennâtâ) was an estate of the empress Eudocia in the territory of Aelia.[193] So was *Caphargamala*, the legendary place of the burial of St. Stephen, for the local priest who "discovered" the tomb applied to "the patriarch"[194] of Jerusalem. It should accordingly be placed at Jammâla and not at Beit Jimâl in the lands of Eleutheropolis.[195] Both Upper and Lower *Bethoron* were in the territory of Aelia Capitolina (Beit 'Ur el Fauqa, et Tahta).[196] Betoannaba (Beit Nûba) belonged to Diospolis, Alus (Yâlu) and Apedno (Kh. el Beddadein) to Nicopolis. *Chasalon* (Kesalon, Kasla) was a big village of Aelia,[196a] while Esthaol, Jarimuth and Enadab were all in Eleutheropolis. The boundary passed between these villages and Beth Ther (Kh. el Yahûd near Battir),[197] leaving Gabatha to Eleuthero-

[192] *War* 3:3:5-51.

[192a] *On.* 32, 10; 33, 11.

[193] Joh. Rufus: Plerophora 20 (*PO* VIII, p. 39).

[194] Epist. Luciani (*PL* XLI, cc. 807, 809 sq.) The fact that the report was made to the patriarch of Jerusalem and not the bishop of Eleutheropolis excludes the identification of Caphargammala with Beit Jimal.

[195] A. Sacchetti: *Studi Stephaniani,* 1934.

[196] I Macc. 3:16; *War* 2:19:1-516; *On.* 46, 21; Tos. *Niddah* 7:7.

[196a] *On.* 172, 16.

[197] Eusebius: *Hist. eccl.* IV, 6, 3; Mishnah *Taanith* 4:6.

polis, and *Gedora*[198] (Kh. Ijdûr) to Aelia. The boundary then turned east at *Beth Zur* (Bethsura, et Tubeiqa), the boundary of Judaea in Maccabaean times.[199] *Alulos* (*Alula* of St. Jerome, modern Halhul) was in Aelia.[200] *Sior* (Si'îr) was near the boundary,[201] but probably also in Aelia. So was also *Tekoah* (Kh. et Tuqû),[202] from which the boundary probably followed the Wâdi Mu'allaq to the Dead Sea. The boundary between Aelia and Jericho is rather vague: *Hyrcania* (Kh. el Mird) was apparently in Aelia,[203] *Maledomnei* (*Ma'ale Adummîm* of the Talmud, Tal'at ed Damm) was a fort, 'castra inter Aeliam et Hierichunte,'[204] i.e. near the border. Further north the Judaean mountains belonged to Aelia, the Jordan Valley to Jericho. In the former were included *Machmas* (*Mikhmas* in the Mishnah, modern Mukhmâs),[205] *Rimmon* (er Rammûn) fifteen miles from the city[206] and *Aphaerema*[207] (et Taiyibe, *Ephraim* of Eusebius)[208] which was connected with *Bethel* (Beitin)[209] itself dependent on Aelia, *Geba* (On. 74, 2) in W. Jaba' was dependent on Gophna.

Diospolis—Lydda

The territory of this city[210] included naturally its own toparchy and in addition that of Thamna. According to the "Onomasticon" *Addara* (Kh. ed Deir?) was situated on the boundaries of Diospolis 'round about the Thamnitice';[211] and 'the very big village' of Thamna itself was also situated in this city area. Diospolis extended therefore along the coastal

[198] *On.* 68, 20.
[199] 1 Macc. 4:61.
[200] *War* 4:1:8-522; Hier. *On.* 87, 12.
[201] *On.* 156, 4.
[202] *War* 4:9:5-518; *Life* 75-420; *On.* 98, 17.
[203] *Ant.* 15:10:4-366; 17:7:1-187; *War* 1:19:1-364. Rhetoré, *RB,* 1897, p. 462.
[204] *On.* 24, 10; Hier. 25, 9; Y *Rosh ha-Shanah* 57 d; *ND* 74, 48.
[205] 1 Macc. 9:73; *On.* 132, 2; Mishnah *Menahoth* 8:1.
[206] *On.* 144, 11.
[207] 1 Macc. 11:34.
[208] *On.* 28, 4.
[209] *On.* 40, 20; 1 Macc. 9:50; *War* 4:9:9-551.
[210] Colonia Lucia Septimia Severia Diospolis (Hill, *BMC Palestine,* p. xxiii); Lod (Mishnah *Shebiith* ix, 2). Its district 1 Macc. xi, 34.
[211] *On.* 24, 3.

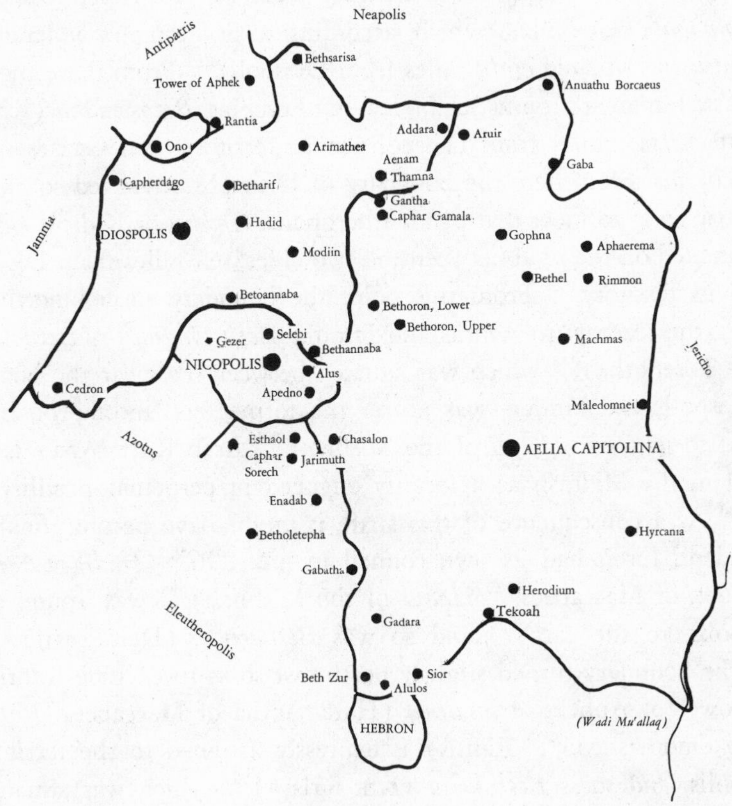

Map 15: TERRITORIES OF AELIA, DIOSPOLIS AND NICOPOLIS

plain and north-westwards into the mountains, between the land of Neapolis and of Aelia.

The eastern boundary of Diospolis corresponded in its northern section with that of Aelia. From Addara onwards it included *Thamna* (Kh. Tibne)[212] and the spring of *Aenam*[213] near-by, but excluded Ganta and Caphargamala. *Modiin* (Midya) the home of the Maccabees is connected

[212] Plin. V, 15; *On.* 96, 24.
[213] *On.* 8, 12.

by Eusebius with Diospolis.[214] Leaving Bethoron to Aelia it included *Betoannaba* (Beit Nûba) which, according to St. Jerome's addendum to Eusebius, was situated *eight* miles from Diospolis.[215] From there the frontier passed in an arc round Selebi, leaving Eusebius' *Betoannaba* (Kh. Beit 'Annaba) *four* miles from Diospolis in its territory, and Gazara in that of Nicopolis. From here the boundary of Diospolis advanced southwards in a strip so as to meet that of Eleutheropolis. *Gedrus* or Kidron (Qatra) was situated on the road between the two cities, ten miles from Diospolis, i.e. in its territory.[216] From this point the boundary turned northwards leaving the seacoast to Azotus and Iamnia. *Beth Dagon*[217] (*Beth Dagôn* of the Tosephtha)[218] which was situated between, i.e. near the boundary of Diospolis and Iamnia, was nearer the former and most probably belonged to it. *Onus* (*'Ônô* of the Mishnah,[219] Arab Kafr 'Ana) is mentioned in the Midrash as a locality engaged in perpetual hostility with Lod.[220] As a consequence of this strife it might have become finally independent, for it had its own council in A.D. 296.[221] *Hadîd* (*Adida* of the Book of Maccabees,[222] *Hadîd* of the Mishnah)[223] was 'round about' Diospolis 'to the east';[224] and so was *Betharif*[225] (Deir Tarif). From here the boundary turned slightly north-east so as to exclude Rantia and the Tower of Aphek; *Arimathea* (Haramantha of Maccabees; *Remfthis* of the Onomasticon,[226] Rantis) is expressly assigned to the territory of Diospolis, and so is *Bethsarisa* (Kh. Sîrîsya)[227] which was situated 15

[214] *On.* 132, 16.
[215] Hier. 21, 19.
[216] *On.* 68, 22.
[217] *On.* 50, 16.
[218] Tos. *Ohiloth* 3:9.
[219] Mishnah *Arakhin* 9:6.
[220] Thr. R. i, 17.
[221] Pap. Oxy. 1205.
[222] 1 Macc. 12:38.
[223] M. *Arakhim* 9:6.
[224] *On.* 24, 24.
[225] *On.* 28, 10.
[226] *On.* 144, 28.
[227] *On.* 56, 21.

miles north of the city, and marks the extreme of its lands in that direction.

Nicopolis—Emmaus[228]

As the latest corner among the cities of Palestine,[229] Nicopolis disposed only of its own toparchy. Its territory was therefore comparatively small. It included in the north *Selebi* (She'albim),[230] in the east *Alus* (Yâlu).[231] In the south Cafarsorech, Saraa and Esthaol were outside its limits; but *Gazara* (Gezer) was included in them to the west.[231a]

Eleutheropolis—Betogabri[232]

Although this city was only founded by Septimius Severus in A.D. 200, it was endowed with a very extensive territory, including practically the whole of Idumaea, with the toparchy of Betholetepha in addition. The latter was transferred to Eleutheropolis from Aelia at its foundation. Thus we find included in the lands of Eleutheropolis the villages of *Sorech* (Kh. es Sureik),[233] Zorah (Sar'ah),[233a] *Eshthaol* (Ishwa')[234] and *Jarimuth* (Kh. el Marmîta)[235] The two latter are distant 10 and 4 miles respectively north of the city, but are said to be near each other. Obviously, we should correct the distance in both cases to 14, in accordance with Procopius' of Gaza "Commentary on the Octateuch".[236] These villages made the northernmost point of the territory of Eleutheropolis. It therefore included the hills on both sides of the Valley of Sorek. From Jarimuth southwards the boundary excluded Chasalon, but included *Enadab* (Beit 'Itab)[237] ten miles from Eleutheropolis on the road to Aelia. Further south it included *Gabatha* (el Jeba')[238] 12 miles from the

---

228 Hill, *BMC Palestine* p. lxxxi; 1 Macc. 3:59. Cf. Beyer, *ZDPV*, 1933, pp. 241 ff.

229 Hill, *loc. cit.*

230 Hier. In Ezech. xlviii, 22 (*PL* XXV, 488).

231 *On.* 30, 27.

231a *On.* 68, 19.

232 Cf. Beyer, *ZDPV*, 1931, p. 209 ff.

233 *On.* 160, 3.

233a *On.* 156, 15.

234 *On.* 88, 12.

235 *On.* 106, 9.

236 *PG* LXXXVII, 1020 C.

237 *On.* 94, 29.

238 *On.* 70, 24.

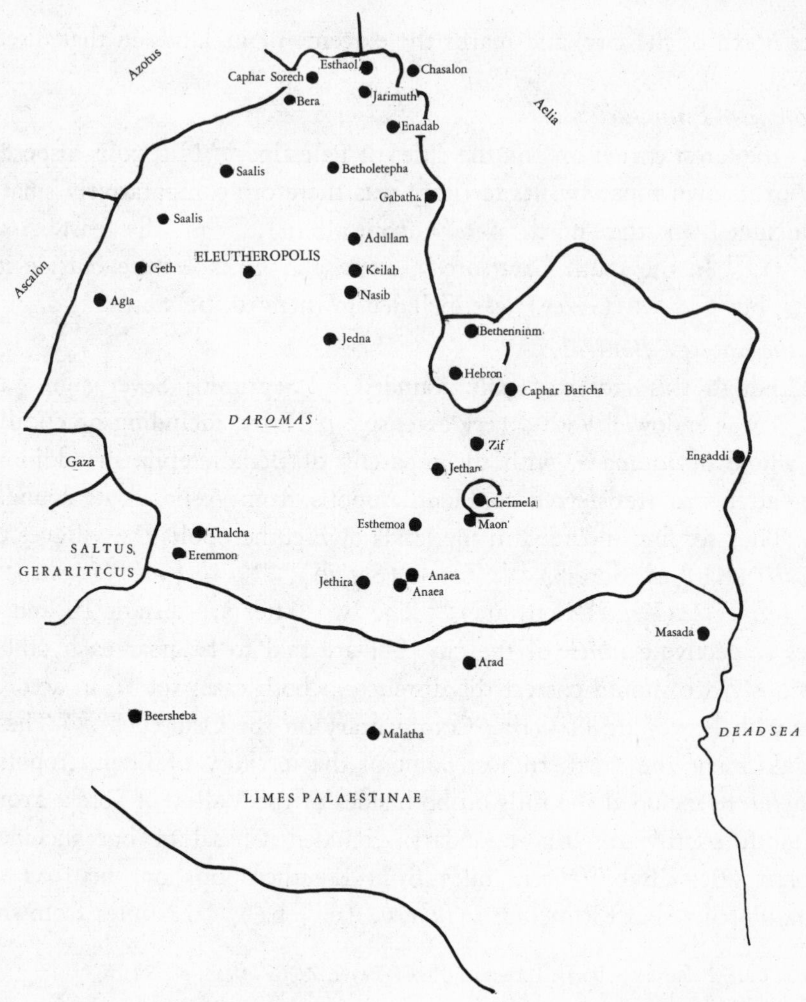

Map 16: TERRITORIES OF ELEUTHEROPOLIS AND THE LIMES

city; *Adullam* (Kh. 'Id el Minya), a very big village, was ten miles east of Eleutheropolis; *Keila* (Cela, Kh.Qeila),[239] eight miles to the east, on the way to Hebron. Hebron itself was apparently outside this area.

An important part of the territory of Eleutheropolis was the area

[239] *On.* 24, 21 (Adollam); 114, 16 (Cela).

known as *Daromas* (from Hebrew *darom,* the South). It seems to have constituted a strip of land extending from Engaddi on the Dead Sea to Lachish. Its distinguishing characteristic was that it contained an unusually high number of Jewish settlements which had apparently survived Bar-Kokhba's War. These include seven out of the eleven Jewish villages listed by Eusebius.[240] Of these two, Esthemoa and Rimmon (Eremmon) are stated to be both in the Daromas *and* in the lands of Eleutheropolis.[241] Two other villages of the same kind, Thella and Jethan were 'in the Daromas,' while their situation is measured from Eleutheropolis.[242] We have therefore here an administrative entity dating from the time of Hadrian, who excluded its Jewish inhabitants from the expulsion decreed for their brethren in the rest of Judaea. Later on this area was handed over to Eleutheropolis and formed the southern half of its lands.

The boundary of Eleutheropolis continued from a point south of Hebron, encircling the Terebinth and Bethennim. It included *Caphar Baricha* (Bani Na 'im), which appeared to have been dependent on its bishop, and followed the southern boundary of Aelia to the Dead Sea.[242a] *Engaddi,* being in the Daromas, was probably included in this area.[243] Masada, which was garrisoned as part of the *limes,*[244] was probably outside it. The boundary left the shore of the Dead Sea north of Masada and turned west, excluding Arad and Malatha, but included: *Maon* (Kh. Ma 'in) 'in the east of the Daromas';[245] *Anaea* the Greater and the Lesser (Ghuwein el Gharbiye and esh Sharqiye) both expressly assigned to Eleutheropolis;[246] *Jethira* 'in inner Daromas' (Kh. 'Attir),[247] *Thella* (Kh. Khuweilife) 'in the Daromas' (17 miles from Eleutheropolis),

[240] See p. 216 below.
[241] *On.* 26, 11; 88, 17; 146, 25.
[242] *On.* 98, 26; 108, 8.
[242a] Hier. Ep. 108, 11 (*PL* XXII, 886).
[243] *On.* 86, 16.
[244] See p. 120 above.
[245] *On.* 130, 12.
[246] *On.* 26, 9; 29, 14.
[247] *On.* 88, 3.

Eremmon, Rimmon ('En Rimmon, Kh. Umm er Rumâmin)[248] with the same indication. From Thella the border turned northwards leaving the Saltus Gerariticus on the outside. The villages which mark the boundaries of Eleutheropolis are *Eglon* (*Agla,* Kh. 'Ajlân) 10 miles from that city on the way to Gaza; *Geth* (On. 68.4) four miles to W., *Biththerebis* (Kh. Deir el Butm?) which Sozomenus assigns to its episcopal see, and finally *Berah* (Kh. el Bir)[249] in the Sôreq Valley, 8 miles distant to the north.

As we shall see below, Chermela, although situated between Maon and *Zif* (Tell Zif),[250] both of which belonged to Eleutheropolis, did not itself belong to this city.

The Limes Palaestinae

According to Josephus[251] Judaea extended southwards to Jorda; this is not to be identified with 'Arad[252] but with Orda;[253] it seems certain that the whole valley of Beersheba was included in it (Malatha e.g. was Idumaean, i.e. belonged to Judaea in the time of Agrippa I).[254] With the establishment of the *limes* (see pp. 119-121), a strip of territory running from the Mediterranean to the Dead Sea was detached from Judaea. With the division of Palestine into the provinces it was split up, the western part remaining in the original province, the eastern one, including Beersheba, passing to Palaestina salutaris.

At its western end the *limes* was later on divided into three areas: the *Saltus Constantiniaces*[255] with its centre probably at *Menois* (Ma'in); the city of *Sycomazon* (*Suq Mazay* of the Aramaic translations of the Old Testament[256]—Kh. Sûq Mâzin) and the *Saltus Gerariticus.* Although

---

[248] See n. 242 above.

[249] *On.* 48, 18 (Agla); Sozom. Hist. eccl. ix, 17 (*PG* LXVII, c. 1392); (Biththerebes); *On.* 54, 26 (Bera).

[250] *On.* 95, 15.

[251] *War* 3:3:5-51.

[252] Thomsen: *Loca Sancta* s. v.

[253] B. Maisler, *BJPES* 1935, pp. 38-41. (Hebrew).

[254] *Ant.* 18:6:2-147.

[255] Georg. Cypr. 1026; *ND* 73, 19; *On.* 130, 7.

[256] Hierocl.: *Synecd.* 719, 3; Georg. Cypr. 1022; Targ. Yer. *Num.* xxxiv, 15.

the name of the latter was derived from Gerara, its centre was probably at *Birsama* (Kh. el Fâr ?).[257] The remainder of the *limes* included *Bersabee* (Beersheba) with one garrison,[257a] and *Malatha* (Tell el Milh) with another. The garrison towns extending northwards along the Malatha-Hebron road were first attributed to the limes by A. Alt.[258] This assumption can be supported by the data of Eusebius concerning Hebron. In the "Onomasticon" we find Hebron mentioned in three different contexts: (1) as the terminus of roads starting from Aelia and Eleutheropolis; villages on this road which are related to these cities obviously were on their territory. Such is the case of Bethlehem and Beth Zur in Aelia,[259] Iedna, Keila and Nasib in Eleutheropolis.[260] (2) Villages whose distance is given from Hebron, but which are said to be 'in the Daromas,' sometimes even with the addition: 'in Eleutheropolis.' These have also to be attributed to Eleutheropolis. Such places are Zif[261] and Anaea;[262] (3) There remains a third group which is related to Hebron only. This includes the *Terebinth* (Ramet el Khalil),[263] *Bethennim* (Kh. Beit 'Anûn)[264] two miles from the Terebinth and four from Hebron; *Chermela* (Kh. el Karmil)[265] ten miles from Hebron to east Beersheba, twenty miles from it, and *Arad,* (Tell 'Arad), twenty miles from Hebron and four from Malatha, and finally *Thamara* on the way from Hebron to Aila.[266] Of these places Chermela, Beersheba, Thamara and Malatha were garrison towns, Hebron and Bethennim have remnants of Roman forts.[267] The conclusion is that these areas formed one unit, administered by the army, and excluded from the city areas of both Gaza and Eleutheropolis.

---

[257] Theodoretus, Quaest. in Paralip. II, XIV, 3 (*PG* LXXX, c. 828); Georg. Cypr. 1027.
[257a] *On.* 50, 1; *ND* 73, 18.
[258] *PJB,* 1930, p. 43 ff.; 1931, p. 75 ff.; *JPOS* XVIII, pp. 149-60.
[259] *On.* 42, 10; 52, 1.
[260] *On.* 106, 15; 114, 16; 136, 21.
[261] *On.* 92, 15.
[262] *On.* 26, 9.
[263] *On.* 6, 12; 24, 16.
[264] *On.* 24, 16.
[265] *On.* 92, 20.
[266] *On.* 14, 2; 8, 8; Aharoni, *IEJ,* 13, 1963, p. 30.
[267] *ND* 73, 20; 73, 18; 74, 46; 74, 45; Mader, *Altchr. Basiliken,* pp. 39, 123.

Further south we know of the names of several cities such as Elusa, Eboda and Mampsis, but we have not enough data to define their boundaries.

Jericho

The *Regio Jericho* appears as a separate unit in the late lists. Its boundaries can be defined as the Dead Sea in the south, the Jordan River on the east; its western boundary coincided with that of Aelia, its northern with that of Neapolis. The villages related to it by the Onomasticon are *Beth Hoglah* (*Bethagla,* Deir Hajla),[268] 3 miles; *Naorath* (Duyûk)[269] a big Jewish village 5 miles; it was traditionally hostile to Jericho; *Magdalsenna* (Kh. Beiyudât),[270] 8 miles to the north. We might consider the villages and palm plantations of *Archelais*[271] ('Auja et Tahta) and *Phasaelis*[272] (Kh. Fasayîl) to be included in this region, which was created for the purpose of administering the groves of date-palms and balsam for the benefit of the fisc.

East of the Jordan

We shall now attempt to set out, as far as seems possible, the limits of the various areas beyond the Jordan, again from north to south:

Caesarea Philippi-Paneas—

This city belonged to Herod, Agrippa I and II. After the death of the latter it was attached to Syria and not to Judaea; on the division of Syria it passed to Phoenicia. Its area included *Lake Phiale* (Birket er-Ran);[273] *Chedar* (Komē Chedaron, Hadar), according to an inscription from the time of Tiberius II (A.D. 578-582), which refers to Phoenicia.[274] The region of el Quneitra, in which was buried the security officer of Phoenicia probably also belonged to it.[275] The *Ulatha* (Huleh region)

---

268 *On.* 8, 19.
269 *On.* 136, 24; Thr R. i.
270 *On.* 154, 16.
271 *Ant.* 17:13:1-340.
272 *Ant.* 16:5:2-145; *War* 1:21:9-418.
273 *War* 2:18:10-509-11; 19:1-513.
274 *Supp epigr. graec.* VII, No. 327.
275 *Ib.* No. 25.

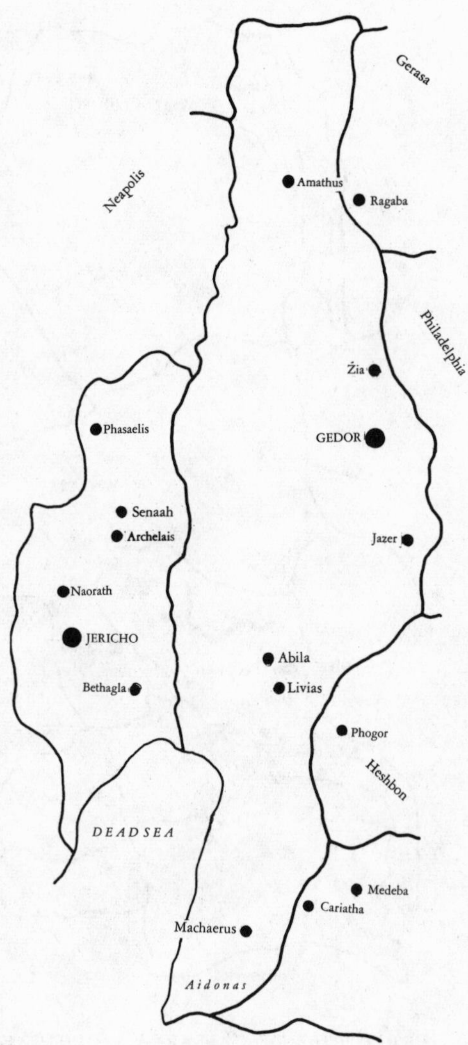

Map 17: REGIO JERICHO AND PERAEA

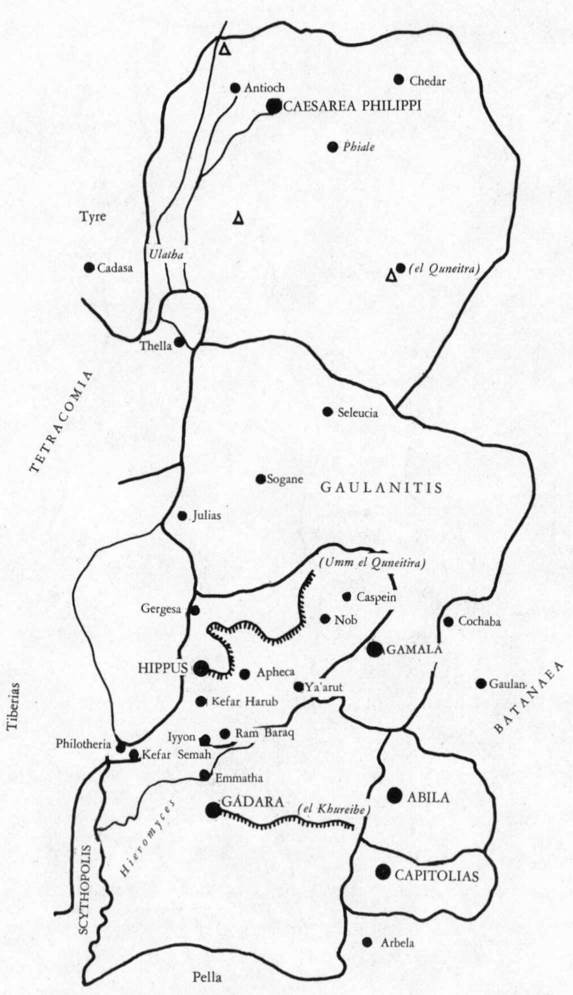

Map 18: TERRITORIES OF CAESAREA PHILIPPI, GAULAN, HIPPUS, ABILA, CAPITOLIAS AND GADARA
△ Boundary stone

usually went with Caesarea Philippi[275a] and probably remained attached to it. The two last-named attributions are supported by the boundary stones set-up by the governor of Phoenicia Aelius Statutus in the time of Diocletian; such stones were found at Shamir in the Huleh, at el Quneitra, and various other sites.[276]

Gaulanitis

This territory appears to have remained a non-municipal area till the end (it appears as Clima Gaulanes in Georgius Cyprius),[277] possibly because of its numerous Jewish population. Its northern boundary corresponds to that of Caesarea Philippi; in the west it was bounded by the Jordan and the Sea of Galilee; in the south it excluded Chorsia, Caspein and Nôb in the lands of Hippus. It included *Gamala* (Tell el Ahdab near Jamle) which was also once in the hands of Agrippa.[278] The fact that in A.D. 295 Diocletian's transfer of Batanaea from Palaestina to Arabia caused inscriptions in that area later than this year to be dated by the era of A.D. 106, while the inhabitants of Gaulanitis continued to use the Seleucid era. This enables us to fix the boundary of the two provinces along the Nahr el ʿAllân[279] and the Nahr er Ruqqâd till its junction with the Yarmuk. It should be noted that the village called Gaulan is placed in Batanaea.

Batanaea

The region called Batanaea in the 'Onomasticon'[280] corresponds to the "Territory of Naveh" i.e. *Naveh*[281] in the Tosephtha and the Jerusalem Talmud. In the lists of Hierocles and Georgius Cyprius it is split-up between many small units, a process which must thus have occurred in the fifth and sixth centuries A.D.[282] In the Jewish sources the names of

---

275a *Ant.* 15:10:3-360.

276 Y. Aharoni, *Atiqoth,* I, pp. 94-98; *ib.,* II, 152 ff; *ib.,* III, p. 186; Alt, *ZDPV,* 71, 1955, p. 178.

277 Georg. Cypr. 1041.

278 *War* 4:1:1/2, 4/8; 4:7; 9-62/83; Plin. *n.h.* V, 14.

279 Brünnow & Domaszewski: *Provincia Arabia* III, p. 270.

280 *On.* 44:11; 52:24 etc.

281 Tos. *Shebiith* 8:3; jer. *Demai* 22 d.

282 *Synecd.* 723, 6, 8; Georg. Cypr. 1080 ff.

the villages included in the lands of Naveh have been much corrupted. It is possible, however, by way of a number of emendations to arrive at the following identifiable names:[283] *Sayyer* (Suraiye), Gasimea *Gashmey* (Jâsim), *Zeizûn* (Zeizûn), *Danab* (Dannaibe) and *Kokhabah* (Kaukab); the latter is identical with the *Cochaba* of Epiphanius.[284] The Onomasticon also suplies us with several names of places related to Nineveh (i.e. Naveh) and therefore apparently in its territory. These are *Ashtaroth* (Tell 'Ashtara),[285] *Karnaim* (esh Sheikh Sa'ad),[286] *Namara* (Namer),[287] *Tharsila* (Tsil),[288] *Neela* (Khirbet en-Nîle)[289] and *Gaulan* (Sahm el Jaulan).[290] From Josephus we learn that *Bathyra* (Basir) was situated in Batanaea.[291] This fact is confirmed by the boundary stones there which were not set up by the governor of Phoenicia, i.e. they were outside his province.[292] Other boundary stones with names of various officials (other than the same Aelius Statutus) allows us to include *Euthymia* ('Aqraba)[293] and Namara (see above) in Batanaea. An inscription referring to *Maaga* of Batanaea (Muhajja) adds yet another place name.[293a] *Aere* (es-Sanamein) used the imperial era, which shows that it once belonged to the House of Herod, and not to Damascus where the Seleucid era was common; it was therefore situated in Batanaea.[293b]

We can accordingly define the limits of Batanaea as follows: in the west the Nahr el 'Allân, Nahr er-Ruqqâd; in the north a line including 'Aqraba, Namer, es Sanamein and Basir; in the east Nahr el Hureir till east of Zeizûn and continuing along this river till the Yarmuk.

---

283 See note 281 above.
284 Epiph. Panarion XXX, 2, 18 (*GCS* 25, pp. 335, 357).
285 *On.* 12:12.
286 *On.* 112:3.
287 *On.* 138:11.
288 *On.* 102:5.
289 *On.* 138:7.
290 *On.* 64:7.
291 *Ant.* 17:2:2-26.
292 See note 276 above, and Jalabert—Mouterde, *MFO* V, 1910, p. 222, Dunand, *RB,* 41 (1932) p. 572, No. 109.
293 *Ib.* and *OGIS* II, No. 769.
293a *Suppl. epigr. gr.* VII, 1099.
293b Waddington-Le Bas: *Recueil* 2413 f-l.

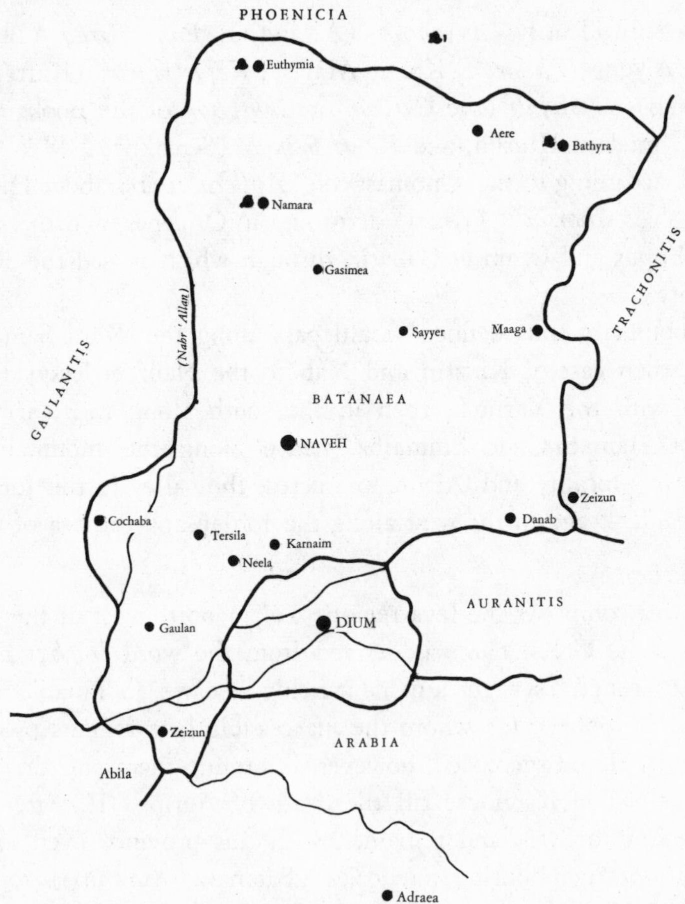

Map 19: TERRITORIES OF BATANAEA AND DIUM

Hippus—Susitha[294]

The area of this city fits in between the Sea of Galilee, the Yarmuk and the Gaulanitis. Its boundaries are referred to (again with many corruptions in the text) in the Tosephtha[295] and the Jerusalem Talmud.[296]

---

[294] Head: *Historia numorum* p. 786.
[295] Tos. *Shebiith,* 4:10.
[296] jer. *Demai* 22 d.

We can still identify *'Ayyanosh* (Awânish), *Ram Baraq* (Bureiqa), *'Iyyôn* ('Aiyûn), *Ya 'arût* (Kh. er Arâyis), *Kefar Harûb* (Kafr Hârib), *Nôb* (Nâb), *Hasfîyah* (the *Caspein* or *Chasphon* of the Books of Maccabees,[297] modern Khisfin, and *Kefar Semah* (Semakh?).[298] To this we may add, according to the 'Onomasticon,' *Apheca* 'round about Hippus'[299] Gergesa[300] or *Chorsia*[301] (Kursi) according to Origenes, and the area between Hippus and Umm el Qanatîr, through which passed the aqueduct of the city.

The boundary thus defined would pass along the Wadi Samakh till Khisfîn, then east of Khisfîn and Nâb to the Nahr er-Ruqqad till its junction with the Yarmuk, then in the south along the Yarmuk till north of Hamath-Gader-Emmatha, hence along the mountain slope between this locality and 'Aiyûn, and across the valley to the Jordan below Semakh,[302] and in the west along the Jordan and the Sea of Galilee.

Trachonitis

This area comprises the lava region (Lejja) north-west of the Hauran mountains. Its Greek name is derived from the word *trachys* meaning 'jagged' or 'rough,' 'savage,' a name it richly deserves. Its inhabitants were notorious as robbers, for whom the inaccessible lava regions provided a safe retreat. Herod succeeded, however, in taming them and the Trachonitis remained in his house till the death of Agrippa II. After that it was attached to Syria and remained with this province even after the transfer of its neighboring territories (Batanaea, Auranitis) to Arabia in A.D. 295. Thus the people of Trachonitis continued to use the imperial era, while the other regions began to use the era of Arabia. This difference, as well as the inscriptions set up after 295 by the governors of Syria, enable us to define the boundary of the Trachonitis as including

---

297 1 Macc. 5:26; 2 Macc. 12:13.

298 This spelling is not certain; the Arabic name of the locality was Samakh; the Hebrew might have been similar, and possibly it was adapted in the middle Ages to the Semah ("flower") or our MSS.

299 *On.* 22:20.

300 Origenes: *In Joan.* VI, 24.

301 Cyrillus Scythopolitanus: *Vita Sabae,* 24.

302 Including Philoteria in Hippus, cf. above, p. 70.

Philippopolis (Shuhba),[303] *Aerite* ('Eire),[304] *Eeitha* (Hit)[305] and Umm ez Zeitûn, while excluding from it Duma and Juneineh. The northern boundary passed north of *Phaene* (Masmiye),[306] the capital of this region, and possibly also north of *Constantia* (Burâq).[307] For a reconstruction of the southern boundary, viz. that separating the Trachonitis and the Auranitis we might use the boundary defining the Land of Israel in the Tannaitic sources.[308] Originally this line was defined in order to separate lands which were subject to certain rules of Jewish law and others excluded from their operation. Nevertheless, it seems to have corresponded in certain sections with political boundaries, possibly because the latter were ethnical ones as well. One such boundary segment passed *Zaraua,*[309] (*Zoro'a,*[310] now Ezra); *Nimrin* (Namir),[311] then 'the Trachonitis of Nimra in the boundaries of Basra,'[312] (the latter being the *Bosor* or *Bosora* in the First Book of Maccabees, now Busr el-Harîri) and *Sakutah,* Greek *Saccaea* (Shaqqa)[313] later on called *Maximianupolis,*[314] in honour of Diocletian's co-emperor. The western boundary of Trachonitis corresponds to the eastern one of Batanaea (in its northern half).

Auranitis

This region included not only the Hauran mountain itself, but a strip of territory running westwards between the Trachonitis and Arabia to the boundaries of Batanaea and Dium. This fertile area is known to-day as the Nuqra. The frontier of Auranitis with the Nabataean Kingdom (and later with Arabia) can be established by using the same criterion of

303 Aurelius Victor: *Liber de Caesaribus* 28, 1; Hierocles: *Synecd.* 723, 3; Georgius Cyprius 1069.
304 Waddington-Le Bas: *Recueil,* No. 2437 f.
305 *Ib.* No. 2113.
306 Hierocles: *Synecd.* 723, 1; Georgius Cypr. 1070; *ND* 80, 11, 23.
307 *Ib.,* 723, 2; 1071; Waddington-Le Bas: *Recueil,* No. 2537 a.
308 Tos. *Shebiith* 4:11; Sifre on Isa. xlix; cf. Alt, *ZDPV* 71 (1955), p. 178.
309 Waddington-Le Bas, Nos. 2479-2504.
310 See n. 308 above.
311 *Ib.*
312 Tos. *Peah* 4:6, and *ib.*
313 Waddington-Le Bas, Nos. 2136-64.
314 *Ib.,* Nos. 2361, 2413.

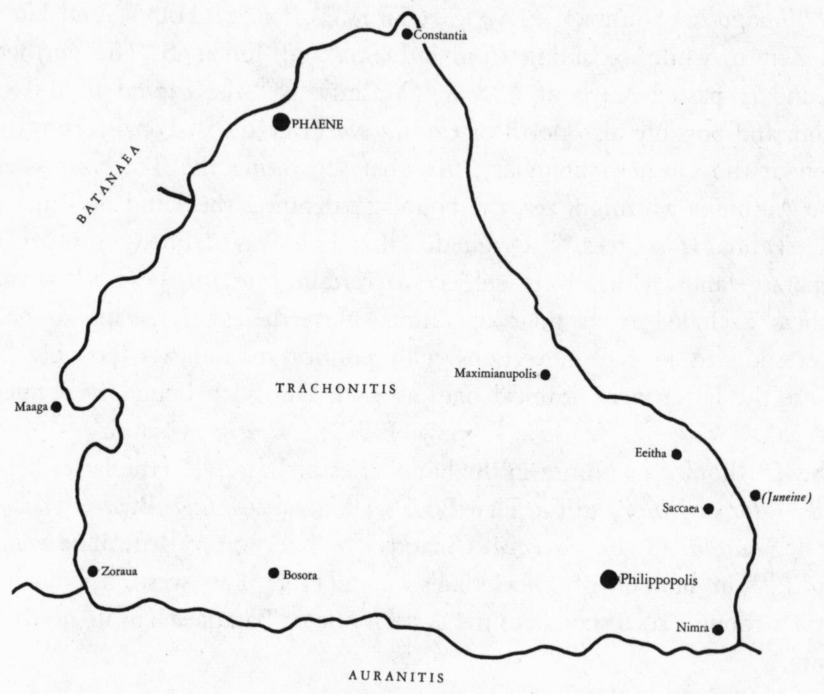

Map 20: TRACHONITIS

eras (imperial or Arabian) which has been referred to above.[315] We can state accordingly that el Mushannaf, *Bosana* (Busan),[316] Habrān, *Dionysias*-Soada (Suweida)[317] and *Charax* (el Kerak)[318] belonged to the Auranitis, while Duma, Sahwet el Kheidar, 'Urman, Salkha, el Quraiye, Bosra and el Musheirifa were in Nabataean territory.[319] Moreover, a series of ten inscriptions, dated A.D. 104-108, which commemorate the construction of an aqueduct of *Canatha*;[320] (*Kenat*, el Qanawât) men-

---

[315] See n. 279 above.

[316] Waddington-Le Bas, No. 2242.

[317] *Ib.* 2299, 2309; Hierocles: *Synecd.* 723, 3; Georg. Cypr. 1072.

[318] 2 Macc. 12:17.

[319] Brünnow-Domaszewski: *Provincia Arabia* III, p. 268 f.

[320] Dunand, *Syria* IX, 1930, pp. 272-9.

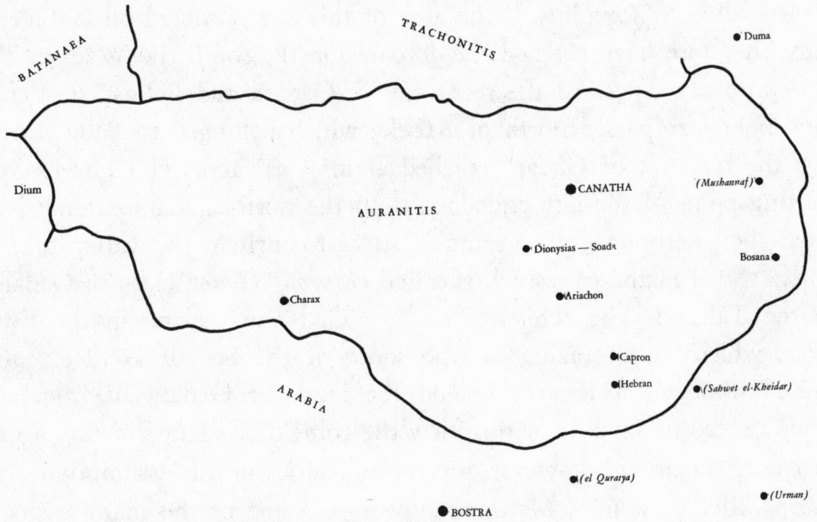

Map 21: AURANITIS

tions the names of the following villages: *Ariachon* (er Raha), *Capron* (Kafr); these, as well as el ʿArije, Rassas and Sahwet el Balāt—through which passed the aqueduct—were thus in the territory of the Auranitis, of which Canatha was the chief city. We can therefore define the boundaries of the Auranitis as follows: in the north the limits of the Trachonitis, in the west—those of Batanaea; in the south the Wadi edh-Dhahab till the Jebel Druze; and in the east the slopes of this mountain in a line passing south of Habran and east of Busân and el-Mushannef.

Dium

We know nothing of the area of this city, which was one of the Decapolis. If it is to be placed at Tell Âshʿari[321] its territory, which was necessarily small, seems to have filled a corner between the lands of the Batanaea, the Auranitis and of Edrei in Arabia.

---

[321] Ptolemaeus V, 15, 8; Pliny *n.h.* V, 18; Alt, *PJb,* 1933, p. 22, n. 3.

Gadara (Umm Qeis)[322]

According to Josephus,[323] the area of this city bordered on Galilee; it must therefore have reached the Jordan. On the south the Wâdi et Taiyibe probably separated the territories of Gadara and Pella. Their common boundary passed north of Arbela, which belonged to Pella. In the east the territory of Gadara reached at least as far as el Khureibe, the starting point of the city aqueduct.[324] In the north Gadara extended beyond the Hieromices[325] (Yarmuk) so as to include the valley of *Emmatha*[326] (el Hamme), which is called *Hammat-Gader* (i.e. "of Gadara) in the Talmud. The reference to the "Gadarene" swine in the Evangiles, which were grazing on the shore of the Sea of Galilee,[327] has caused some authorities to extend the lands of Gadara till the lake, They quoted in support of this view the coins of Gadara showing a naumachy.[328] There are, however, several difficulties in this assumption: (a) the parallel version of Matthew as well as some of the manuscripts of Mark and Luke[329] have "Gergesa" instead of Gadara, and we have the authority of Origenes to support this version;[330] (b) the naumachy in itself proves nothing, for it was arranged occasionally in the amphitheatres of inland cities; (c) if we extend the territory of Gadara to the lake, then Hippus-Susitha ceases to border on Galilee, which would contradict a statement of Josephus';[331] (d) the whole story seems to imply a hilly ground descending steeply into the sea, which suits better the lands around Gergesa (Kursi).

---

322 *Ant.* 13:13:2-356; 14:4:5-75; Pliny *N.h.* V, 18, 74; Origenes, *In Joan.* VI, 24; Polybius V, 71, 2.
323 *War* 3:3:1-37.
324 Schumacher: *N. Ajlun,* pp. 46-80; Steuernagel, *Adschlun,* pp. 492, 497-8.
325 Plinius, *N.h.* V, 18, 74; Mishnah *Parah* 8:10.
326 *On.* 22:26; Anton. Placent. 7; Tos. *Erubbin* 5(6):13.
327 Matthew 8:28.
328 Schürer: *Gesch. d. jüd. Volkes,* II, p. 161.
329 Mark 5:1; Luke 8:26.
330 See above, n. 322.
331 See n. 323 above.

Abila (Tell Âbil)[332]

The territory of this city is not mentioned in any ancient source. It was probably bounded on the north by the Yarmuk, in the east by one of its confluents. On the west it must have stopped short of el Khureibe (see above); on the south it might have included the area of *Capitolias* (*Beth Rêsha* of the Talmud, now Beit Ras) which became a separate city in A.D. 97-98,[333] for it is unlikely that the emperor Nerva would have set up a city in Nabataean territory before its annexation.

Pella (Kh. Tabaqât Fâhil)[334]

This city of the Decapolis was bound on the north by Gadara, i.e. it reached presumably the Wâdi et Taiyibe. It certainly included *Arbela* (Irbid), according to Eusebius;[335] on the west Pella was bordered by the Jordan. In the south it included the village of *Jabesh Gilead,*[336] which lay in its territory six miles distant from the city on the road to Gerasa. The boundary must therefore have reached the Wâdi el Yâbis, where it bordered with the Peraea.[337] Further east it turned south of this valley, including Ba'ûn, where a milestone gives the distance from Pella.

Gerasa (Jerash)[338]

Gerasa was also a city of the Decapolis. Its territory bordered on the north with that of Pella, and included 'Ajlun, on the evidence of the 12th milestone,[339] *Enganna* ('Ain Jinne) and *Erga* ('Arjân) according to Eusebius.[340] It extended in this direction as far as the quarries of Sâmthâ, from which were taken the stones used to build the city.[341] Further east its lands did not, however, reach Rihâb, because the inscrip-

---

[332] Head: *Historia numorum,* p. 786.

[333] *Ib.* 787; Ptolemaeus V, 14, 18; Tabula Peutingeriana; B *Hulin* 80 a.

[334] Polybius V, 70, 9; Ptolemaeus V, 14, 18; *On.* 14, 19; Plin. V, 18, 74; *Ant.* 13:15:4-397; 14:4:4-75; *War* 1:4:8-104; 3:2:3-47; jer. *Shebiith* 36 c.

[335] *On.* 14:19.

[336] *On.* 110:12.

[337] *War* 3:2:3-47.

[338] *War* 1:4:8-104; 2:18:1-458; Plin. *N.h.* V, 18, 74; C. Kraeling, ed.: *Gerasa,* 1938.

[339] Thomsen, *ZDPV,* 1917, p. 66, No. 221.

[340] *On.* 94:25; 16:21.

[341] Steuernagel, *Adschlun,* pp. 253-4.

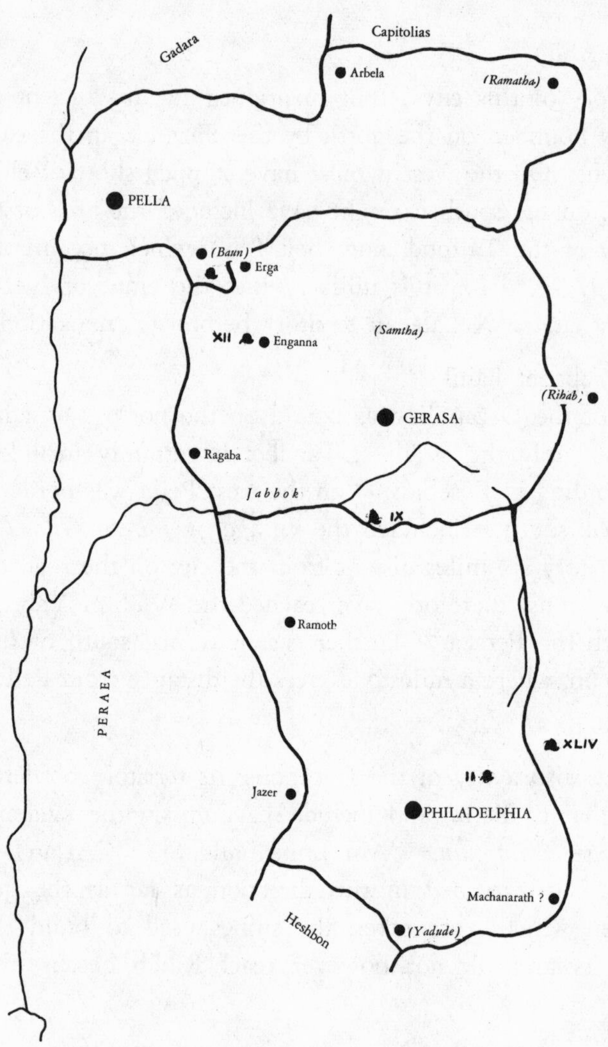

Map 22: TERRITORIES OF PELLA, GERASA AND PHILADELPHIA

tions found there in a church indicate its dependence on the see of Bostra, i.e. its inclusion in Arabia.[342] The *via nova* made by Trajan in Arabia from Aila via Philadelphia to Bostra probably also by-passed this terri-

[342] *QDAP*, XIII, p. 71.

tory. In the south the border between Gerasa and Philadelphia continued along the Jabbok River, according to Eusebius.[343] We have, however, to admit an exception as regards the point at which the Gerasa-Philadelphia road crossed the river. Here the territory of Gerasa extended that south of the river, on the evidence of the 9th milestone.[344] In the west Gerasa bordered on Peraea,[345] including the fortress of *Ragaba* (or Râjib) in its territory.[346]

Philadelphia (Amman).

This was the southernmost of the cities of the Decapolis,[347] and after A.D. 106 one of the cities of Arabia.[348] It bordered with Peraea on the west[349] and with Gerasa on the north. Its territory included *Ramoth* (Kh. Jal ʿad), fifteen miles from the city.[350] In the east the border passed very close to the city; the second milestone on the *via nova* indicates the distance from Philadelphia, but the sixth gives it already from Bostra.[351] In the south this territory included Yadûda (second milestone)[352] and *Machanarath* (if there indeed was such a locality).[353] In the fifth century the areas of *Maiuthus* (Yajûz ?)[354] and *Bacatha*[355] (ʿAin Bakhata) were possibly separated from Philadelphia and made into independent units.

Heshbon (*Esbus,* Hisbân).[356]

This area was bordered on the north by Philadelphia and on the west by the Peraea. According to our sources it included *Elealeh* (el-ʿÂl) one

---

343 *On.* 102:21.
344 Thomsen, *ZDPV,* 1917, p. 63, No. 204.
345 *War* 3:2:3-47.
346 *Ant.* 13:75:4-398.
347 Pliny, *n.h.* V, 74.
348 *On.* 16:15.
349 *War* 3:2:3-47.
350 *On.* 144:5.
351 Thomsen, *ZDPV,* 1917, p. 45, Nos. 106, 110.
352 Alt, *PJb,* 1936, p. 110 ff.
353 *On.* 126, 18. The name represents a version of Deut. 3:17: "from Chinnereth" in Hebrew, misread by Eusebius as a place name.
354 Hierocles: *Synecdemus* 722, 8.
355 Acta Conc. Ephes. ed Schwartz; Jerusalem *ib.,* III, pp. 80, 188. cf. Alt. *ZDPV,* 1944, p. 99, n.l.
356 *On.* 84:4; Hill: *BMC Arabia,* pp. xxxiii, 29.

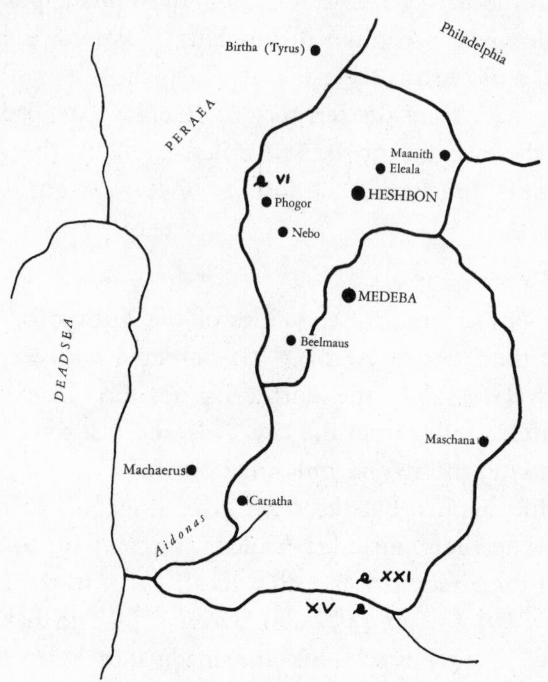

Map 23: TERRITORIES OF HESHBON AND MEDEBA

mile distant from it,[357] *Nebo* (Râs Siyâght) six miles to the west,[358] also called *Fasga* on the road to Livias, *Beelmaus* (Talmudic *Ba'al Ma'on,*[359] now Ma'in), nine miles from Heshbon, and *Maanith* (Umm el Hanafîsh) four miles on the Philadelphia road.[360] On the evidence of the milestones the area of Heshbon extended six miles on the Livias road passing Mount Nebo.[361]

Medeba

This city of Arabia was bounded on the north by Heshbon, on the

[357] *On.* 84:10.
[358] *On.* 136:7; 13; 18, 3.
[359] *On.* 46:1; Tos. *Shebiith,* 7:11; jer. *Shebiith* 38 d.
[360] *On.* 132:2.
[361] Thomsen, *ZDPV,* 1917, pp. 67-68, Nos. 229, 230.

west by the Peraea. Eusebius attributes to it *Maschana* (probably el Medîne) on the Arnon, twelve miles to the south[362] and *Cariatha* (el Qûreiyât) ten miles to the west.[363] In the south the Arnon formed the city boundary, as we can learn from the fact that north of the river, up to the twentieth milestone, the distances are counted from Medaba,[364] while south of it stands the 16th milestone from Rabbath-Moab.[365] Nabataean inscriptions found at Umm er-Rassas[366] show that this place was the residence of a Nabataean strategus, i.e. outside the limits of Medeba.

Peraea (See Map 17 on p. 165).

According to Josephus[367] this territory extended from Machaerus in the south to the borders from Pella, and from Philadelphia to the Jordan. Its northern boundary followed the Wâdi el Yâbis, including *Amathus*[368] (*Hamtan*)[369] of the Talmud, now Tell 'Amtah). In the east it excluded Ragaba, which belonged to Gerasa. Further south the boundary passed near the village of *Zia* (Kh. Zey), about which there was a dispute between the people of Peraea and the Philadelphians.[370] *Gadora* (Tell, at 'Ain Jâdûr near es-Salt), the *Gedôr* of the Mishna,[371] was the capital of Peraea, although near the border. According to Eusebius[372] *Jazer* (Kh. es-Sîr?) was situated in the Peraea, even if by way of exception its position is indicated as ten miles west of Philadelphia and fifteen miles from Esebon (Heshbon). In its southern part the Peraea bordered on Heshbon, excluding Nebo.[373] It extended as far as the Arnon and its

---

362 *On.* 126:14.

363 *On.* 112:16.

364 Thomsen, *ZDPV,* 1917, p. 50, No. 126.

365 *Ib.*

366 Clermont-Ganneau, *RAO,* II, pp. 188, 199.

367 *War* 3:2:3-47.

368 *Ant.* 13:13:3-356; *War* 1:4:2-86; *On.* 22:24.

369 jer. *Shebiith* 38 d.

370 *Ant.* 20:1:1-2. Some MS. have the corrupt version Mia.

371 *War* 4:7:3-413; *M. Arakhin* 9:6.

372 *On.* 12:3; 104:13.

373 See n. 358 above.

confluent, the *Aidonas* (Sel Heidān),[374] so as to include the fortress of *Machaerus* (el Mukâwer).[375]

Attempts have been made to define some city areas south of the Arnon on the evidence of the milestones;[376] the material at our disposal does not seem sufficient for this purpose.

---

374 Joh. Moschus, *Pratum spirituale* 155.

375 *Ant.* 13:16:3-417; 14:5:4-89; *War* 1:8:6-171; 7:6:1/3-164/179; Strabo XVI, 2, 40; Plin. *N.h.* V, 18, 72; in particular War III, 47.

376 Beyer, *ZDPV,* 1935, pp. 129-159.

PART THREE

Chapter I

THE ROMAN ROAD SYSTEM

THE general outlines of the network of roads in the Roman provinces of Judaea or Syria Palaestina and Arabia are fairly well known. A reliable summary has been published by P. Thomsen in 1917[1] and later discoveries have modified only details.[2] The chronological development of the roads has, however, been sketched only once.[3]

The inscriptions on the milestones, are, as far as they are preserved, our principal source for this purpose. The preservation of milestones has, however, been necessarily accidental, and the preservation of a legible inscription has been still more fortuitous. We must therefore eke out the evidence of the milestones from general historical knowledge and from certain logical considerations: thus it is unlikely that any Roman legionary camp would be left without a road-connection; nor would a length of road be left 'hung up in the air,' unconnected with the general network existing at the period of its construction.

The oldest Roman road in Palestine is undoubtedly that which followed the coast. Its northern sector, from Antioch to Ptolemais (Acre)[4] was certainly constructed in the early days of Nero. South of Acre the only milestones found so far are dated to A.D. 161, 193, 210, 217 and 238; the extant fragments do not, however, mention the contruction of a road and most likely they commemorate repairs only. In the coastal plain few milestones survive and we should not treat the absence of

---

[1] Thomsen, P.: Die römischen Meilentseine der Provinzen Syria, Arabia und Palaestina. *ZDPV* 40, 1917, pp. 1-103; supplemented by M. Avi-Yonah, *Map of Roman Palestine,* 2nd ed., 1940, and F. M. Abel, *Géographie de la Palestine,* II, 1938, pp. 222-231; Avi-Yonah, *IEJ* 1, 1950-1, pp. 54-60.

[2] cf. *QDAP,* 12, 1946, pp. 96-102; Hecker, *BIES,* 25, 1961, pp. 175-186 (H).

[3] Kuhl and Meinhold, *PJb,* 24, 1928, pp. 118 ff.

[4] (Nero Cl)audius (Caesar Au)gustus... (tribunicia potestate) bis... (viam?) ab Antiochia

earlier stones as a conclusive argument. It is far more likely that this important road (linking as it does the two great military bases of Alexandria in Egypt and Antioch in Syria) was completed either during the First Jewish Revolt or immediately afterwards. The march of Titus from Alexandria to Caesarea early in A.D. 70 might either have been on the new road or it might have served to fix its route. The presence of road-surveyors with the army of Vespasian is attested by Josephus.[5]

The fall of Jerusalem was followed by the establishment of a legionary camp on its ruins, held by the Legio X Fretensis. By an anomalous arrangement the civil headquarters of the newly-created 'Provincia Judaea' were not transferred to the garrison camp, but left at Caesarea, the seat of the former procurator of Judaea. A direct road linking the administrative and military headquarters of the province would naturally be required in these circumstances. The shortest line between Caesarea and Jerusalem passes Antipatris-Thimna and Gophna.[6] The milestone of Nerva found at Sha'fat three miles north of Jerusalem should obviously be assigned to this road;[7] but owing to the fact that the first fifteen miles of the road from Jerusalem to Neapolis coincide, it has been erroneously assigned to the latter.[8] Four other milestones have been found on this road near Gophna and beyond, but on none of them was the date decipherable.[9]

At the same time another road was made connecting Scythopolis (Beth-Shean) with Pella and Gerasa. This road had to be repaired under Trajan,[10] hence its original construction must have been of an earlier

(munivit? ad n)ovam colon(ia)m (Ptolemai)da. Thomsen, *op cit.* No. 922, p. 18; cf. also A. Alt, *ZDPV,* 51, 1928, p. 253 ff. An inscription erected by the inhabitants of Ptolemais and the neighboring villages in honour of Nero was found at Naharia, 17 kms. N. of Acre, *QDAP* 12, 1946, pp. 85 ff., No. 2.

[5] Josephus, *War,* 3:6:2,-118; *ib.,* 4:11:5-649-663; for the S. section of the coast road see Alt, *ZDPV,* 70, 1954, pp. 154 ff.; for the section N. of Caesarea, Avi-Yonah, *BIES* 24, 1959, pp. 36-41.

[6] Thomsen, *op cit.* (supra, n. 1): Road XXXVI, p. 76.

[7] *Ib.,* No. 263, p. 75: Imp. Nerv(a) Aug. pont. m(ax.) trib. pot...

[8] *Ib.,* p. 73 f.

[9] *Ib.,* p. 76, Nos. 267-270.

[10] *Ib.,* p. 65, No. 215: Imp. Caesar... Nerva Traianus...trib. pot. (X)VI...*refecit* per (C. Cla)udium Severum leg. Aug. pr. pr.

date. We cannot assume that these cities were connected with each other but remained unconnected with the outer world; we must presume therefore that at least one of the roads between Scythopolis and Damascus[11] was made at the same time. We may perhaps assume that the need for these roads arose from the growing economic importance of the Decapolis as well as from the necessity for prompt military assistance in the not unlikely case of another revolt.

In the days of Trajan the annexation of the Nabataean Kingdom (A.D. 106) was followed by the greatest piece of Roman road-making in the Orient, the construction of the *via nova* in the years 111—114. It was the work of Claudius Severus, the first governor of Provincia Arabia, and ran from Bostra to Aila (ʿAqaba) on the Red Sea.[12]

At that time, therefore, the Roman roads in Palestine consisted of two separate systems; the coastal road with an extension to Jerusalem, and the Arabian road, connected via Damascus with Scythopolis, Pella and Gerasa. The last named city was indeed transferred to the new province, but remained for the time being without a direct connection with its backbone, the *via nova.* These defects of the road-system were repaired by Hadrian. At the time of his death the network of Roman roads in Palestine had very nearly assumed its final shape.

In the reign of Hadrian there were two main periods of road-building activity, the first associated with the *adventus Augusti* in A.D. 130—1; the other with the revolt of Bar-Kokhba (132—135) and the measures consequent upon it. In 129 the road Scythopolis-Pella-Gerasa was connected with the Arabian road at Philadelphia, probably in prevision of the imperial visit.[13] To the same year or the following we might then tentatively assign the connection Heshbon (on the Arabian road)-Livias-Jericho-Jerusalem.[14] It was probably used by Hadrian on his return from

---

[11] *Ib.,* pp. 33-34, 70-71.

[12] *Ib.,* pp. 34-59, Nos. 67-187; Alt, *ZDPV* 71, 1955, pp. 84 ff. and Y. Aharoni, *IEJ,* 13, 1963, p. 30 ff.

[13] *Ib.,* p. 64, No. 211a.

[14] *Ib.,* p. 68, No. 230a (of 162) "...pronepotes...*refecerunt*" i. e. it was already repaired under Marcus Aurelius; see also R. Beauvery, *RB,* 64, 1957, pp. 72-101; O. Heuke, *ZDPV,* 75, 1959, p. 160.

Petra, via Jerusalem. For a continuation of his travels from Jerusalem onwards we have the evidence of a milestone (dated A.D. 130) which was found on the Jerusalem-Gaza road.[15] This line should, therefore, also be related to Hadrian's visit.

Hadrian's visit was followed by the decision to erect a Roman colony, Ælia Capitolina, on the ruins of Jerusalem, and this, in turn, was one of the causes of the revolt of Bar-Kokhba. In order to anticipate probable troubles, the Legio VI Ferrata was placed in a camp at Capercotnei, which was connected with Sepphoris (Diocaesarea) already in the 14th year of the emperor, i.e. 130/1; we may as well presume that this road was continued to Caesarea, the capital of the province (Hecker, BIES, 25, 1961, p. 176, in Hebrew). The date of the other roads connecting Legio with the sea coast and Scythopolis might belong already to the war of Bar-Kokhba which broke out in 132. The Gaza-Jerusalem road, just completed, may very likely have been used by the ill-fated Legio XXII Deioterana which came up from Egypt via Gaza and was lost in the fighting. However, as the war progressed, it must have been most useful for the Roman operations in Judaea from their south-western base. In the third year of the fighting the insurgents were finally confined to a small area in Judaea, west of Jerusalem. It has been suggested that the road connecting Beth Gubrin (later Eleutheropolis) with Hebron might have constituted part of a Roman military line encircling the area in revolt.[16] This line should, however, be extended further northwards in consideration of the Midrashic text which mentions a check of refugees from the war-area carried out by Roman guards stationed at Beth-Hôrôn, Kefar Leqîtaya (Beit Liqya) and Emmaus.[17] Recently a fragment of a Roman road was discovered at Beit Jîz, south of Emmaus.[18] It leads southwards and was presumably connected with a known Roman road from the Valley of Sorek to Beth Gubrin. From Emmaus another known road led northwards through Kefar Leqîtaya to Beth Hôrôn, and hence

[15] *Ib.*, p. 80, No. 282: Imp. Caesar... Hadrianus Aug...trib. pot. XIV.
[16] Kuhl, *PJb*, 24, 1928, p. 127.
[17] Thr. R., 1, 16, ed. Buber, 416.
[18] Reported by Dr. Z. Kallay, Jerusalem.

to the fourth mile on the road from Jerusalem to the north, thus completing the guard circuit around the insurgent area.

The last named section of this road, viz. that from Beth Hôrôn to the Jerusalem-Gophna road, followed the old 'public way' of Josephus,[19] the main road between the ancient capital and its port at Jaffa. We may assume therefore that the whole of this line, at least from Lydda, was now re-made as a Roman road. I must have been most useful as a link between the Roman bases in the coastal plain and the troops operating north and north-west of Jerusalem.

It is even possible that this road was continued further eastwards from Gophna via Aphaerema (et-Taiyibe) to Jericho. It would then by-pass Jerusalem on the north and link the Roman bases in the coastal plain (e.g. Lydda) with those beyond the Jordan (Philadelphia and Gerasa) by the way of the Heshbon-Jericho road built presumably in 130. The only extant milestone of this road may be attributed to Hadrian.[20]

When the revolt of Bar-Kokhba was finally suppressed and Beth Ther had fallen, further political and military changes occurred, which set their mark on the development of the road system of Palestine. The praetorian Province of Judaea now became the consular province of Syria Palaestina. The new legionary camp had been joined by roads (a) south-westwards to Caesarea, the capital of the province, and (b) northwards to Sepphoris, one of the centres of Galilee, which now remained the only purely Jewish region in Palestine and thus a potential centre of danger. The former road crossed the Carmel by way of the Wadi 'Ara pass. It has been well known for some time; a number of milestones were found along its route, although none could be dated.[21] It can be brought into the proper historical sequence when considered in conjunction with its northern continuation Legio-Sepphoris, along which milestones dating to the 14th year of Hadrian have recently been discovered.[22] Various other roads radiated from the new camp: one to Ptolemais (Acre) established its con-

---

[19] *War*, 2:12, 2-228.

[20] Thomsen, *op. cit.* (supra, n. 1) p. 76, No. 266, note 1.

[21] *Ib.*, pp. 69-70, Nos. 233-241.

[22] *QDAP*, 12, 1946, p. 96, No. 13.

nection with the coastal road, another to Scythopolis (Beth-Shean) joined it to the roads beyond the Jordan.[23] A third road passed Sebaste, Neapolis and Gophna and connected Legio and Ælia Capitolina, the camps of the two legions now stationed in Palestine. Up to Neapolis it is certainly Hadrianic:[24] its continuation might be assigned on logical grounds to the same scheme but so far the earliest milestone extant is of the year 162.[25] A further 'security road' was built by Hadrian from Ptolemais on the coast via Sepphoris to Tiberias,[26] affording another ready access from the coast to the heart of Galilee.

At the death of Hadrian the main road system was therefore practically complete. Later additions include the roads Damascus-Salcha-Gadara and Ælia Capitolina-Emmaus, both built under Marcus Aurelius;[27] the Bostra-Gerasa road made by Commodus[28] and the short-cut Neapolis-Scythopolis dating to the reign of Marcus Aurelius.[29] A milestone of Caracalla (unpublished) was recently discovered at Dan on the road from Tyre to Caesarea Philippi (Paneas) and another, anepigraphic one, east of Lake Hule; this may have belonged to an undiscovered road joining Caesarea Philippi and the Jordan bridge at Jisr Banat Ya 'qub. The original date of both these roads remains as yet in suspense. No data are available as regards the date of the Scythopolis-Jericho road along the Jordan,[30] or the roads south of Beersheba.[31]

This rapid survey confirms the other evidence in our possession regarding the crucial importance of the reign of Hadrian in general, and the suppression of Bar-Kokhba's revolt in particular, as the turning point in the history of Palestine under Roman rule. This fact is only too often

---

[23] Thomsen, *op. cit.* p. 69, No. 232; *QDAP* 12, 1946, pp. 101-102; see p. 141.
[24] Thomsen, *op. cit.* p. 70, No. 142.
[25] *Ib.*, pp. 73-74, No. 259.
[26] J. H. Iliffe, *QDAP,* 2, 1932, p. 120.
[27] Thomsen, *op. cit.* (supra, n. 1) p. 32, No. 66; p. 77, No. 272.
[28] *Ib.*, p. 60, No. 189.
[29] *IEJ,* 16, 1966, No. 1.
[30] For a possible branch off from this road southwards see Noth, *ZDPV,* 73 (1957), p. 38 ff.; Hippenbauer, *ib.*, 781, 1962, p. 171; Mittmann, *ib.*, 79, 1963, p. 152 ff.
[31] For these roads see now Y. Aharoni, *IEJ,* 4, 1954, pp. 9 ff., and M. Harel, *ib.*, 9, 1959, p. 175 f.

disregarded owing to a large extent to the spectacular account of Josephus. It has turned the attention of scholars to the First Revolt and has made the equally if not more serious war of Bar-Kokhba into another 'Forgotten War.'

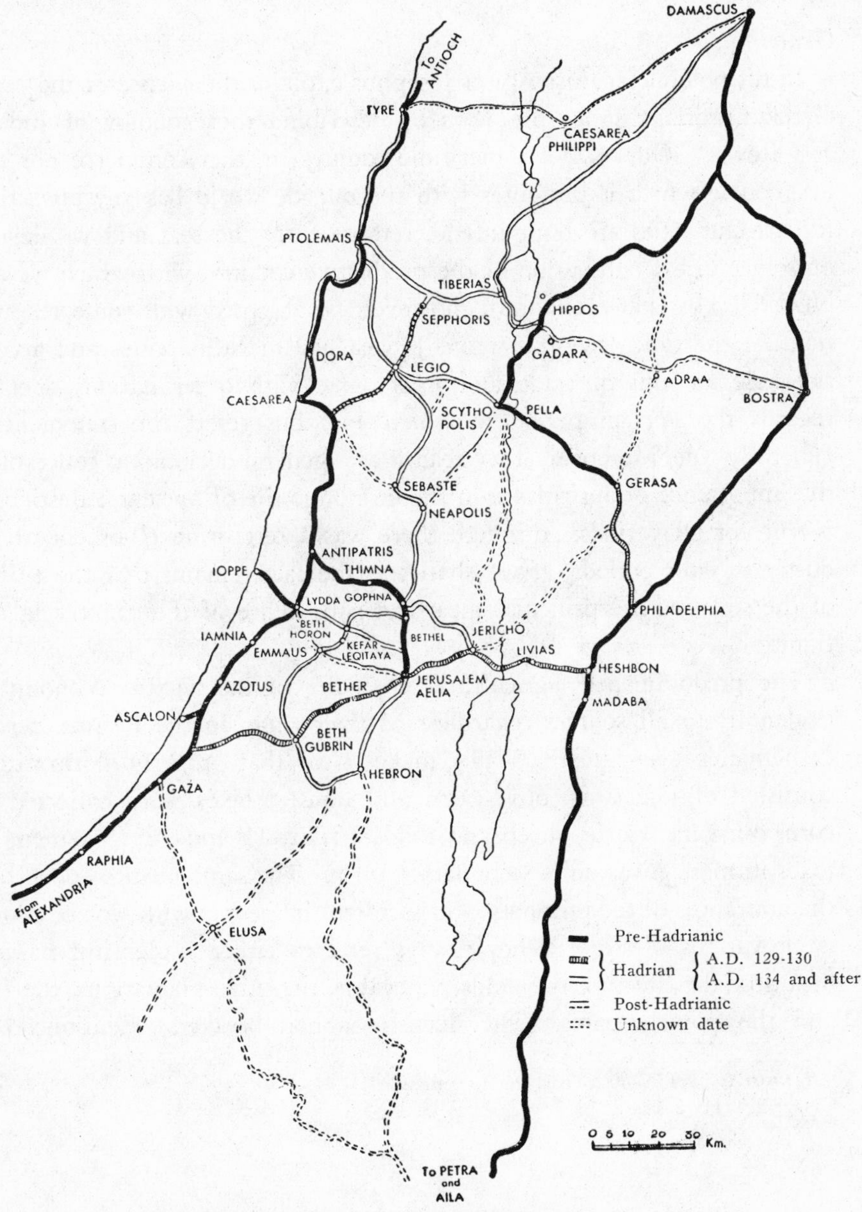

Map 24: ROAD MAP OF ROMAN PALESTINE

Chapter II
ECONOMIC GEOGRAPHY

General

In his polemic against Apion Josephus explains the silence of the early Greek historians about the Jews by describing the economy of Judaea as follows:[1] "Ours is not a maritime country; neither commerce nor the intercourse which it promotes with the outside world has any attraction for us. Our cities are built inland, remote from the sea; and we devote ourselves to the cultivation of the productive country, with which we are blessed." This statement must, however, be accepted with some reservation. At the time Josephus wrote Judaea had maritime cities and a considerable amount of trade and intercourse with other nations. Yet as regards the Persian period to which Josephus refers the statement is generally true. Moreover, if we read it as a general declaration concerning the importance of agriculture in the economic life of ancient Palestine, it is true for all periods. Although there was a certain development of industry in later periods, as we shall see, the fact remains that the tilling of the soil was the principal means of subsistence of the country in antiquity.

The predominantly agricultural character of the ancient economy is evident from all sources regardless of their time. In the Persian period Nehemiah's 'seisachteia' (5:11) makes clear that property at that time consisted of vineyards, olive-yards and houses; taxes were collected in corn, oil, wine, cattle, sheep and fowls (5:11, 15 and 18); payment of taxes in money was quite secondary (5:15). The same picture appears in the utterances of the prophets who threaten the people with woe or promise it various blessings. They always refer to either a plentiful harvest or a drought affecting the fields, vineyards, the olive plantations, the figs and the pomegranates.[2] The Jewish Sabbath-breakers, mentioned by

[1] *Against Apion* I 12-60 (Thackeray's translation).

[2] Haggai 1:11; 2:19.

Nehemiah,[3] were also engaged in exclusively agricultural pursuits. Commerce, even in such comestibles as fish, was in the hand of Tyrian merchants (Neh. 13:16). Certain professions, however, such as goldsmiths and 'apothecaries' (ointment makers) which were possibly connected with the Temple, were exercised by Jews, and formed a nucleus of craftsmen.[4]

This general picture did not change much later on. The list of 'acts of work' forbidden on a Sabbath, given in the Mishnah,[5] prohibits thirty-nine kinds of activity. Of these eighteen are connected with the tilling of the soil or making food, as against nine kinds of weaving, four of dress-making, two of building, etc. As late as the third century it was remarked in the Midrash (Eccl. R., 5:8); "He who is desirous of money and has no land—what satisfaction can he have?" It was due to these agricultural pursuits that Judaea was able in normal times to maintain itself in the seventh (Sabbathical) year during which the fields were left fallow. The balance of demand and supply was, however, rather delicate and was easily upset by a bad harvest. Then there was famine in the land and wheat had to be brought from Egypt[6] and dried figs from Cyprus.[7] The situation grew worse after the two unsuccessful Jewish wars against Roman rule. Then the Jewish authorities forbade the export of such "vital" foodstuffs as wine, oil and flour.[8] This prohibition was modified with regard to wine and oil as soon as the situation improved in the second half of the second century A.D.[9] In the third century corn could be exported as well.[10] On the other hand, the Sabbathical year was gradually restricted in area (bab. *Hulin* 6b) and finally suspended by R. Yannay in the late third century (bab. *Sanhedrin,* 26b) under the pressure of general want. The surplus of produce in that period led to occasional

[3] Neh. 13:15.
[4] Neh. 3:8, 31-32.
[5] Mishnah *Sabbath* 7:2.
[6] As happened in the time of Herod and Queen Helena of Adiabene, *Ant.* 15:9:2-307, 309; 20:2:5-51.
[7] *Ant.* 20:2:5-51.
[8] bab. *Baba bathra* 90 b.
[9] Tos. *Abodah zarah* 4:1.
[10] See below p. 202.

catastrophic falls of prices; against these public prayers were arranged from time to time.[11] The situation was especially critical during the troubled years of the general crisis in the Roman Empire during the third century. In Byzantine times the balance of trade improved due to massive imports of capital. The area under cultivation was then extended in order to provide for the needs of the increased population and the numerous pilgrims.[12]

Judaea

From the point of view of economic geography this province should be divided into three natural components: (a) the mountain (b) the coastal plain, and (c) the Jordan Valley.

A. The *mountain* around Jerusalem (the 'King's mountain' of the Talmud) was relatively poor in cultivable land, but once rich in wood.[13] Both Nehemiah[14] and Haggai[15] refer to the woods round Jerusalem, which served in one case to supply the materials for the booths on the feast of Tabernacles and the other building materials for the Temple. Pseudo-Aristeas[16] refers to the olive and fruit trees in the vicinity of Jerusalem. This statement is borne out by the Ethiopian version of the apocryphal Book of Enoch. The stories of the various sieges of Jerusalem, as told by Josephus, show that till the siege of Titus at least, the surroundings of Jerusalem were well wooded. Trees for siege operations were cut down by Herod in 37 B.C. in the suburbs of Jerusalem.[17] They seem to have been replaced by gardens in the century of peace which preceded the siege of Titus. There remained, however, enough trees on the east side of the city, between it and Bethany, to furnish the branches of trees which were strewn before Jesus on the day of his triumphal entry into Jerusalem.[18]

---

11 bab. *Baba bathra* 91 a.

12 Cf. Avi-Yonah, *IEJ*, 8, 1958, pp. 39 ff.

13 The description of Josephus (*War* 3:3:4-49) in which he lumps Samaria together with Judaea and describes both as having no deserts and rainfall "for the most part abundant" is too generalized to be of much use and is in any case not corresponding to observed facts.

14 Neh. 8:15.

15 Hag. 1:8.

16 Ps. Aristeas 112.

17 *War* 1:17:8-344.

18 Matthew 21:8; Mark 11:8.

Thus we find a garden serving as the place of Jesus' crucifixion and burial.[19] When Mary came to the tomb and saw a vague figure, she naturally believed that it was the gardener.[20] A gate in the First Wall of Jerusalem, leading northwards, was called the Garden Gate (Gennath).[21] When Titus reconnoitred outside the city, he was almost caught by an ambush laid among the garden walls in the vicinity of the Tomb of Helena.[22] Subsequently, the whole garden area, with its walls and enclosures, was razed from opposite Herod's palace to Mount Scopus.[23] The woods, which by then grew at a greater distance, were gradually cut down to furnish material for the siege machinery. At first this affected only an area of 90 stadia round Jerusalem,[24] but later on this grew to 120 stadia, eleven and fifteen miles respectively.[25] The aloe of Judaea is mentioned especially by Pliny (N.h., 27:15).

In all other respects the vicinity of Jerusalem was less favoured. There were indeed cultivable patches in the vicinity of the city; this we learn from the evidence of the Gospel of Mark.[26] It represents Simeon of Cyrene 'returning from the field' when he met Jesus carrying the cross. Josephus also mentions his former estates in the city territory.[27] The Mishnah regards the *wheat* produced at Mikhmas, NE of Jerusalem, and Zanôha, SW of the city, as of the highest quality.[28] Its quantity cannot, however, have been large, considering the smallness of the cultivable areas wedged in between the Judaean mountains.

Areas unfit to produce wheat could be used to grow *olives*. In fact, the mere number of names associated with this tree and its products show its importance. There was the Mount of Olives[29] with the 'Oil press' (Geth-

---

19 John 19:41.
20 *Ib.*, 20:15.
21 *War* 5:1:2-146.
22 *Ib.* 5:2:2-57.
23 *Ib.* 5:3:2-107.
24 *Ib.* 5:12:4-523
25 *War*, 6:2:6-141.
26 Mark 15:21.
27 *Life*, 13-76.
28 Mishnah *Menahoth* 8:1.
29 Matthew 21:1; Mark 11:1; Luke 21:37; Acts 1:12; *War* 5:2:3-70; Mishnah *Parah* 3:6.

semane)[30] at its foot, and the villages Bethzait (House of the Olive')[31] and Berzetha (Well of the Olive)[32] in the city territory. It should be noted, however, that no place in Judaea is mentioned in the Mishnah as a source of oil of the first quality.

As regards the produce of the *vineyards,* the Mishnah does accord the second place to the produce of two villages, Beth Rimah and Beth Laban, situated close to each other in the district of Thamna, i.e. in the extreme NW corner of Judaea.[33] The vine was cultivated in the whole mountain region. On the last day of the Feast of Tabernacles the daughters of Jerusalem went to dance in the vineyards near the town,[34] and vine trees were found as far south as Kefar ʿAzîz in Idumaea.[35] The pottery stamp of a wine merchant "Eleʿazar A" found in Jerusalem indicates the variety of wines available, but after 70 A.D. the vineyards passed into non-Jewish hands (jer. *Abodah zarah* 44d). Other fruit trees grown in the mountains were *figs.* The name Bethphage ('House of the Early Figs')[36] shows their cultivation near Jerusalem. The early figs of Bethany are also mentioned.[37] The figs of Keila SW of Jerusalem are contrasted with the poor kind called after Bostra and grown on the desert fringe.[38]

Some attempts were made in Jerusalem to cultivate produce which would require little ground and water, and yet be highly profitable. This included the cultivation of vegetables,[39] mushrooms,[40] and roses[41] in the gardens near the city; the rose garden was the only kind of garden allowed in the city. The irrigated plots were concentrated in the valleys south-east of Jerusalem, in particular in the Kidron Valley. The gardens

---

30 Matthew 26:36; Mark 14:32.
31 1 Macc. 7:19 (Ms.A).
32 *Ant.* 12:10:2-397.
33 Mishnah *Menahoth* 8:6.
34 *Ib. Taanith,* 4:8.
35 *Ib., Kilaim* 6:4.
36 Matthew 21:1; Mishnah *Menahoth* 11:2.
37 Tos. *Shebiith* 7:14.
38 jer. Bikkurim 63 c.
39 They were collected during the siege by the starving Jews, *War* 4:9:8-541.
40 I. Loew: *Flora d. Juden,* I, p. 303.
41 The rose gardens of Herod are mentioned in Mishnah *Shebiith* 7:6; cf. also *Maaser sheni* 2:5; the permission to grow roses in Jerusalem is recorded bab. *Baba qamma* 82 b.

were fertilized by the blood of sacrifices flowing from the Temple.[42] The 'village of Agrippa'[43] might be placed in this area, an indication of the royal estates situated there in biblical times. The name "Erebinthon oikos' ('House of the Chick Pea') for a village near Jerusalem seems to recall another local product (*War* V, 507).

Another way of putting meagre land to good use was the raising of sheep and goats. Indeed, the raising of such "small cattle" was regarded as the quickest way of getting rich.[44] After the depopulation of Judaea following upon the two revolts, there was a real danger that the herds would destroy the remnants of local vegetation. The raising of sheep and goats was, therefore restricted by the rabbinical authorities to the desert areas.[45] The sheep of Hebron were appreciated in particular.[46] The importance of this branch is evident from the widespread trade in wool and woollen garments; there was a special market for it in Jerusalem.[47] In the whole of Judaea purchase of woollen garments from women was allowed, as not subject to a presumption of theft.[48] The dyeing industry, which is closely related to the weaving of wool, was so widespread in Judaea, that in certain places even the priests had their hands dyed with woad or madder (M. *Megillah* 4:7). The raising of fowls,[49] and in particular of doves for Temple sacrifices, is also mentioned in our sources. This pursuit gave its name to the "Peristereion" rock near Siloam village.[50] The name given by Josephus to the central valley of Jerusalem (Tyropoeion or the "Valley of Cheesemakers")[51] would suggest a developed dairy industry, but the form of the name itself is highly suspect, being probably a corruption of some Hebrew name, which has not been ascertained.

---

[42] Mishnah *Yoma* 5:6; cf. *War* 5:9:4-410.
[43] Vision of Baruch, proem. (Charles: *Apocrypha,* II, p. 533.)
[44] bab. *Hulin* 84 b.
[45] Mishnah *Baba qamma* 7:7.
[46] bab. *Menahoth* 87 b.
[47] *War* 5:8:1-331; Mishnah *Erubbin* 10:9.
[48] M. *Baba qamma* 10:9.
[49] See n. 46 above.
[50] *War* 5:12:2-505; cf. Matthew 21:12, Mark 11:15.
[51] *War* 5:4:1-136, 140.

The natural resources of the mountain soil were restricted to building-stone and potters' clay—the latter especially plentiful in the mountains west of Jerusalem.[52] Jerusalem itself, situated in the midst of the mountain area, was before its destruction an important centre of economic life. This was not because of its productivity, but because it was the centre of the religious and cultural interests of the Jewish Diaspora. It was also the political centre of the Jewish state, where was spent much of the tax-money collected from the whole country. The Temple by itself supported whole groups of craftsmen: the makers of incense, bakers of shewbread,[53] weavers,[54] goldsmiths[55] and washers.[56] The associated industries included masons,[57] carpenters,[58] coppersmiths,[59] seal-cutters,[60] bakers,[61] merchants of ointments,[62] scribes,[63] and—last but not least—money changers.[64] The obligation to make a pilgrimage to Jerusalem three times a year and to spend there the moneys of the 'Second Tithe' created a demand for food which the city and its vicinity could not supply by themselves. Hence the transport of produce from Galilee to Judaea is regarded in the Mishnah[65] as an every day occurrence. According to this source money was brought to Jerusalem and taken away; but produce could not be carried away. This rule was abolished in the second century, when the question had anyhow become purely theoretical. It was only after the destruction of the city that this trend was reversed. In the second and third century A.D. the

---

[52] Such clay was found stored in stone bins in the pottery of the Tenth Legion excavated near Jerusalem in 1949.

[53] M. *Yoma* 3:11; M. *Sheqalim* 5:1; M. *Taanith* 3:3.

[54] M. *Sheqalim* 5:1.

[55] *Ib.*, 4:4.

[56] M. *Middoth* 5:3.

[57] *War* 7:2:2-26. The building of the Temple alone required 1000 transport waggons (*Ant.* 15:11:2-390) and the completion of the main building caused widespread unemployment (*Ant.* 20:9:6-219).

[58] M. *Middoth* 3:5-8.

[59] They had a special market, *War* 5:8:1-331.

[60] Tos. *Abodah zarah* 5:2.

[61] *Ant.* 15:9:2-309.

[62] Mark 16:1; Luke 24:1; John 19:39; M. *Erubbin* 10:9.

[63] bab. *Baba bathra* 14 a.

[64] Matthew 21:12; Mark 11:15.

[65] M *Maaser sheni* 2:3-5.

produce of the Oreine was sold in the markets of Caesarea.[66] In the Byzantine period the revival of Jerusalem as a centre of pilgrimage brought about another increase in demand. It was met partly by an extension of the cultivated area in the mountains, and partly from the Jordan Valley. There was also a parallel revival of industry and trade. In the fifth century we find shoemakers and calligraphers mentioned in Jerusalem in the Life of *Porphyry* of Marcus Diaconus (ed. Grégoire-Kugener, pp. 5,9). Common labourers found easily work on the many building projects (J. Moschus: *Pratum spirituale,* 97).[66a] The influx of pilgrims caused a rise in the prices of houses in Jerusalem (Justin, Nov. 40).

B. *The coastal plain of Judaea* was naturally fertile and well-watered. In Roman times the encroachment by the dunes and the extension of marshy areas had not yet made themselves felt.

To the wheat fields of this area applied probably the saying of R. Jose of Sepphoris about a Judaean *seah* yielding a five-fold yield.[67] In the drier southern parts (the Darom) barley was produced in preference to wheat. Thus it replaces wheat in the payment of alimony.[68] The 'rich wheat fields' of Joppa are mentioned by Eshmunezer King of Sidon among the gifts of the 'Lord of Kings.'[69] Jamnia and Ascalon were important centres of the wheat trade.[70] The latter city was surrounded by 'gardens', i.e. areas of intensive cultivation, including date groves,[71] its famous onions[72] and its heavy wines, which were exported in the Byzantine period even as far as to the Frankish kingdom.[73] Another centre of wine production was Gaza; its harbour (Maiumas) had a permanent colony of Egyptian wine merchants.[74] The northern sector of the Judaean plain from Jamnia

---

[66] jer. *Demai* 22 c.

[67] bab. *Ketuboth* 112 a.

[68] M. *Ketuboth* 5:8; Deut. R. 3:3.

[69] See n. 40 (Chapter I) above and Ginsberg, *JBL,* 1937, p. 142.

[70] Tos. *Ohiloth* 18 at end (Ascalon); Gen. R. 76 (Iamnia).

[71] Tos. *Shebiith* 6:36; jer. *ib.,* 39 a.

[72] Strabo XVI, 2, 29; Pliny XIX, 32, 101-5, 107; Steph. Byz. s. v.

[73] Totius orbis descriptio, 29 (ed. C. Müller: *Geogr. graec. minores* II, pp. 513-528); Gregor. Turon.: Hist. Francorum VII, 29 (*PL* LXXVII c. 434).

[74] Marc le diacre: *Vie de Porphyre,* ed. H. Grégoire-M. A. Kugener, 1930, p. 58.

to Lydda was rich in vineyards,[75] the produce of which assumed gargantuan proportions in rabbinical legends.[76] There was also an important centre of fig production between Lydda and Ono; figs were grown from Beror Hayil to Emmaus.[77] The spread of the great estates in the plains after the Jewish revolts encouraged the raising of cattle and goats,[78] which were sold at a fair held at Emmaus.[79] The dyeing industries of Lydda and the Darom were probably connected with the wool brought from the Judaean mountains; in the Darom whole townlets engaged in purple-dyeing and everybody's hands bore the marks of this trade.[80] Another industry flourishing at Lydda were the potteries, producing vessels and barrels of various shapes.[81] The proximity of the sea influenced economic life in the coastal area, in spite of the poor harbour in this coast.[82] Of the five maritime towns only two, Ascalon and Joppa were situated on the sea proper, the three others (Gaza, Azotus and Jamnia) had landing places (*epineia*) several miles from the mother city. They all engaged, however, in fishing activities. The fishers of Joppa were the mainstay of the Jewish naval activities connected with the first revolt.[83] In Roman and Byzantine times there were still Jewish fishermen there and at Jamnia.[84]

As a result of its geographic position across the via maris, the coastal area was busy with trade, and international trade in particular. One of the signs of such commercial activity were the fairs, of which those of Gaza and Ascalon[85] were the best known. The only comparative arrangement in the mountain area was the fair at the Terebinthus (Botna) which was, however, connected with a religious festival[86] and originated in

---

[75] Tos. *Eduyoth* 1:1; *Maas. sheni* 5:16.
[76] Midr. Tannaim Deut. 173; jer. *Peah* 20 b.
[77] Bab. *Ketuboth* 111b (Lod-Ono); Eccl. R. 7:12 (Emmaus); Tos. *Maas.* 2:1 (Beror Hayil).
[78] *Ib.*
[79] M. *Kerithoth* 3:7.
[80] Lydda—*Totius orbis descriptio* 31 (cf. n. 73 above); Darom—Tanhuma Nissah 8.
[81] Bab. *Menahoth* 87 a.
[82] Diodorus I, 31; Strabo XV, 2, 28; *Ant.* 15:9:6-333.
[83] *War* 3:9:1/3-414/427.
[84] Tos. *Demai* 1:11; *Petrus d. Iberer,* ed. Raabe, p. 126.
[85] Gaza—jer. *Abodah zarah* 39 d; bab. *ib.,* 11 b; Ascalon-Tos. *Ohiloth* 18:18.
[86] Sozomenus, Hist. eccl. II, 4 (*PG* LXVII, c. 941 f.); Anton. Placent. (ed. Geyer) pp. 178-9.

Hadrian's whole-sale disposal of Jewish captives.[87] A cross-section of the economic life of a coastal community is furnished by the Jewish tombstones of Jaffa (3rd-4th cent. A.D.). Among those buried (who generally belonged to the lower classes) we find the following: two bakers, a dealer in textiles, a dyer, a trader in old iron, a cumin seller, a laundryman, a fisher and a plain worker.[88] At the same time we notice among these tombstones several Egyptian Jews[89] and some Cappadocians.[90]

C. *The Jordan Valley.* The combination of an almost tropical climate and the irrigation works which were introduced into this region in the third and second century B.C. produced in the Jordan Valley and the oases of the Dead Sea region a highly specialized economy, based on the cultivation of the date palm and the balsam. Jericho begins to be identified as a "city of the palms" in the times of the Judaean monarchy.[91] Its plantations were fully developed in the Hellenistic period. In the early days of Herod they were already valuable enough to excite the cupidity of Cleopatra.[92] They were developed and extended after Herod received them back. Herod founded in the Jordan Valley the village of Phasaelis and Archelaus, his son and successor, that of Archelais.[93] The groves of the latter were irrigated by water diverted from Neara. The palms grew in the royal *phoenicon* (palm grove)[94] in an area of 18 km long. They were of several species, one of which was called the *caryotic*; it grew only here in the Roman empire.[95] The sandy and salty soil helped to preserve the Jericho dates better than those of any other kinds.[96] The oasis of

[87] Chronicon paschale (*PG* XCII, c. 613).

[88] *Sefer ha-Yishuv,* ed. Klein, 1939, pp. 82, 83, 84 (Hebrew); Frey, *CIJ* II, Nos. 902, 928, 929, 931, 937, 940, 945.

[89] *Ib.* p. 83; *CIJ* II, 895, 918, 920, 928, 930, 934, 950.

[90] *Ib.,* p. 84; *CIJ* II, 910, 025, 931.

[91] In Deuter. 34:3, Jericho is called "the city of palm trees", an obvious transfer from Hazezon Tamar.

[92] *Ant.* 15:4:2-96; *War* 1:18:5-361; Plutarch: *Antonius,* 36.

[93] *Ant.* 16:5:2-145; (Phasaelis); *Ant.* 17:13:1-340; Plin. *n.h.* XIII, 44 (Archelais).

[94] Diodor. II, 48; Strabo XVI, 2, 41; *War* 4:8:3-468-9; Tos. *Erubbin* 2:8; Tos. *Bikkurim* 2:5; jer. *Shebiith* 38 d; Bab. *Ketuboth* 110 b; Horatius, *Ep.* II, 2, 185-5; Plinius *n.h.* XIII, 38 ff.; Tacitus: *Hist,* V, 6; Trogus Pompeius XXXVI, 3.

[95] Strabo XVI, 2, 41.

[96] Pliny, *N.h.* XIII, 49.

Engeddi on the western shore of the Dead Sea also produced dates and wines.[97] Palms were still cultivated in the Jordan Valley in the late Roman and Byzantine periods.[98] The monks used to weave mats and baskets from their leaves.[99]

Owing to its unique characteristics, the most famous product of the Jordan Valley was the *balsam*, a wood resin which served for making perfumes and medicines.[100] Originally it was restricted by the shrewd commercial sense of Herod to two small plots.[101] These plantations narrowly escaped destruction during the First Revolt, a battle raging (according to Pliny)[102] around every tree; the Jews seeking to uproot and the Romans to defend the plantations. In later times the Roman treasury, out to make a temporary profit, enlarged the area of cultivation by using new methods.[103] As a result the balsam plantations extended in the fourth century from Engeddi to Livias (ha-Ramtha) beyond the Jordan.[104] According to a notice in Gregory of Tours' *cotton* grew in the Jordan Valley in the early Middle Ages.[105] In still later periods the monks on the banks of the Jordan were cultivating vegetable gardens, supplying from them Jerusalem.[106] They also grew pigs, to the disgust of the Jewish villagers who lived in the valley.[107]

The volcanic nature of the Dead Sea and its vicinity produced *bitumen,* which was valuable as material for making pitch, for caulking ships and

---

97 *Ib.* V, 73; Both Pliny and Solinus: *Collectanea* XXXV, 12 describe Engeddi as destroyed, but the latter says that the palm groves continued to flourish even after the ruin of the settlement.

98 *Totius orbis descriptio* (n. 73 above).

99 Sozomen. H. eccl. VIII, 13 (*PG* LXVII, c. 1549); Vita Johannis Damasc. 26 (*PG* XCIV, c. 456); Joh. Moschus: *Pratum spirituale* 160.

100 Diod. II, 48; Strabo XVI, 2, 41; Pliny *n.h.* XII, 111 ff.; Tacitus: *Hist.* V, 6; *War* 1:6:6-138, 361; 4:8:3-469; Pomp. Trogus XXXVI, 3; Solinus, XXXV, 5-6; Dioscorides: *De mat. medic.* I, 18; Plutarch: *Antonius,* 36.

101 Pliny, *N.h.* XII, 111. Its price is given as 300 den. a sextarius (pint).

102 *Ib.*

103 *Ib.* and Solinus XXXV, 5-6.

104 Bab. *Sabbath* 26 a.

105 Lib. De gloria martyr. XVIII (*PG* LXXI, c. 721).

106 Joh. Moschus: *Pratum spirituale,* 158.

107 *Ib.,* 92.

for mummification;[108] it was collected from rafts. The control of the supply of this material was a source of wars between the Nabataeans and the Antigonids, and later on between the Nabataeans and Alexander Jannaeus. The 'stone of Judaea' used in medicine came probably also from this volcanic region.[109]

Samaria[110]

Owing to the peculiar nature of our sources, the information available about the economic life in Samaria is much less than that regarding either Judaea or Galilee. Physically Samaria is a continuation of Judaea, presenting in cross-section the same three units: coastal plain, mountain and the Jordan Valley. However, the latter is much narrower and becomes less cultivable as one goes northwards. The coastal plain too (the Sharon area) was partly swamp and partly wood. It thus produced less than the southern part of the plain. On the other hand, the mountains of Ephraim include some comparatively large flat areas. The largest of these is the Valley of Shechem, which is well supplied with springs issuing near a geological fault. Other plains exist near Sebaste, in the Wâdi Far'a (Neel'eraba) and near Ginae on the northern border of Samaria.

The produce of *wheat* in Samaria is mentioned with reference to the valley of 'En Sôkher (Askar); the Samaritans 'on the highway' i.e. the coastal road were selling corn and peas; in Caesarea there was provided storage for wheat probably from the same source.[111] *Oil* was one of the principal products of the mountain region. It was exported mainly to Egypt, because it was not ritually pure as was the oil of the Jewish provinces in Judaea and Galilee. Both Hieronymus[112] and the Midrash Rabbah[113] mention this trade. *Wine* was produced in the Coreae area of the Jordan Valley (if this be identical with the Qeruhîm of the Mishnah).[114]

[108] Diodor. II, 48.6; Callimachus, *Fragm. hist. graec.* IV, p. 530; Strabo XVI, 2, 42, 45; Pliny, V, 72; Gallienus: *De simpl. medic. facult.* XI, 2, 10; *De symptom. causis* III, 7; Solinus I, 56; XXXV, 2.

[109] Gallienus: *De simpl. medic. facult.* X, 2, 5; Dioscorides: *De mater. medica* V, 154.

[110] This region is taken here in the geographical, and not the ethnic sense.

[111] M. *Menahoth* 10, 2; Tos. *Demai* 2:1; 4:23.

[112] In Osee xii, 1 (*PL* XXV, 923).

[113] Thr. R. v, 3.

[114] M. *Menahoth* 8:6; The other site, Hattulim, is not identified.

The production of wine in the coastal plain was extensive. Talmudic sources mention the Sharon wine[115] and Carmel wine[116] and the wine of Caesarea.[117] They also give a long list of Samaritan villages,[118] the proximity of which rendered the wine of the adjoining Jewish villages of doubtful ritual purity. This we learn of the vineyards of 'Ôgadôr, Kefar Pagesh, Bûrgatah, Birath Sôreqah (Tulkarm), 'En Kûshit and Kefar Salem.[119] Other agricultural produce of Samaria mentioned in Mishnah includes the nuts of Perekh (Beit Fûrîk), the pomegranates of Baddan (Kh.Ferwa in W. Beidân) and the leeks of Geba.[120] The 'Gardens of Sebaste' probably produced vegetables and fruits.[121] The name of Ginae ('Gardens,' *War* 3:3:4-48) refers to another such area. Caesarea produced the citrus (ethrog) which was accepted as ritually pure (Tos. *Makhshirin,* 3:1). A prominent feature of the Sharon plain was the great oak forest, *Drymus,*[122] from which the Greek word *Saronis* (meaning 'old hollow oak') is possibly derived. The Sharon served also as pasture ground;[123] calves raised there could be purchased without incurring suspicion.[124] Another produce of the area was salt, which was made on the sea coast, near the 'Tower of Salt' (Migdal Malhah).[125] Of the industrial activitiy we note only the purple dyeing of Neapolis and Caesarea,[126] and the making of beds in the latter town (jer. *Berakhoth* 6a). This populous city required imports of fish from Pelusium in Egypt and even Spain (Babyl. *Abodah zarah* 39a).

---

[115] M. *Niddah* 2:7; M. *Baba bathra* 6:2; Bab. *Niddah* 21 a.

[116] Bab. *Niddah* 21 a.

[117] jer *Megillah* 72 d; a municipal wine press is mentioned Tos. *Chil.* 18.

[118] As to the general production of Samaritan wine, see M. *Demai* 7:4.

[119] jer. *Abodah zarah* 44 b.

[120] M. *Orlah* 3:7.

[121] M *Kelim* 17:5 (Geba); *Arakhin* 3:2 (Sebaste).

[122] Strabo XVI, 2, 27-8; *War* 1:13:2-250; in LXX Isaiah LXV, 10 the word "Sharon" in the Hebrew original is translated Drymos.

[123] Hicronymus on Isaiah lxv.

[124] M *Baba qama* 10:9.

[125] jer *Demai* 22 c.

[126] *Tot. orbis descr.* 31 (n. 73 above). In the Caesarea excavations 1956 a great quantity of loom-weights was found.

Galilee

Galilee was the principal theatre of the later stages of Talmudic activity; we are therefore fairly well informed as regards its economics. One may distinguish in this province five separate economic regions, viz. the Coastal Plain, the Valley of Jezreel, the hills of Lower and the mountains of Upper Galilee, and the Sea of Galilee with its surroundings. The fertility of the whole of Galilee is highly praised by Josephus; he states that there was no patch of land left uncultivated.[127] One advantage of the Galilean economic life was that small peasant proprietors were encouraged. A typical property consisted of a field, a vineyard and an olive grove (Lev. R. 30:1). The Talmuds consider only the area of Zebulun (coastal plain and Western Valley of Jezreel) as not fertile.[128] The woods of this territory are mentioned by Josephus. Carob trees are frequently referred to in the Talmud.[129] The growth of the sycamore was regarded as the dividing sign of Upper and Lower Galilee (M. *Shebiith,* 9:2).

The principal *corn* producing areas were naturally in the plains: the Valley of Jezreel constituted a royal, later imperial estate. Its produce was stored at Beth She'arim.[130] The 'Hapharaim in the Valley' which produced the second best wheat[131] was possibly at Ophrah, identical with modern et Tayibe. The fertility of the Beth-Shean valley was proverbial.[132] The Plain of Arbel was another centre of wheat production.[133] Other such producing areas were Kefar Hittaya, as its name indicates,[134] Hûqôq and Chorazin[135] and the 'Plain of Asochis' (Biqe'at Beth Netôfah).[136] The existence of a threshing-floor is attested for nearby Kefar Sôgane, and that of millers in Sepphoris and Accho-Ptolemais.[137] The donkey caravans

[127] *War* 3:3:2-42.

[128] jer *Orlah* 62 a; bab. *Bikkurim* 65 c.

[129] Tos. *Abodah zarah* 6 (7):, 8 (Rani); jer *Maas.* 48 c (Gedru).

[130] *Life* 24-119.

[131] M *Menahoth* 8:1.

[132] Bab. *Ketuboth* 112 b.

[133] jer. *Peah* 20 a.

[134] Gen R. 5.

[135] Bab. *Menahoth* 85 a (Chorazin); jer *Pesahim* 27 c (Huqoq).

[136] Numbers R xviii, 22.

[137] Tos. *Terum* 3:28 (Sogane); Bab. *Moed qatan* 17 b (Sepphoris); jer. *Pesahim* 30 d (Accho).

which brought Galilean wheat to Tyre down Achzib way,[139] or up from the Jordan Valley,[139] were evidence that the supply of wheat in Galilee exceeded local demand. The various kinds (Sepphorene wheat, Tiberias wheat) were carefully distinguished.[140] There were special corn markets at Tiberias and Sepphoris (in the latter wheat and barley were sold in different markets).[141] All this serves as evidence of the extent of the trade in this kind of produce.

Wine produced in Galilee (and in particular in the vicinity of Tiberias, Sepphoris, Kefar Signa = Sogane, Salmin, Acchabaron and Scythopolis Beth-Shean) is mentioned by Josephus and in Talmudic sources.[142] The name of Biqe'at Beth ha-Kerem ('Valley of the House of the Vineyards')[143] now Majdel Kurûm, indicates that the grape was cultivated there too. Wine and figs were grown at Beth She'arim (Tos. *Sukkah* 2:1) and Gennezareth (*War* 3:10:7-519). Figs were grown near Tiberias (Eccl. R. 1:12), Sikhin-Sogane (Sifre Deut. 135b) and Ruma (Tos. *Errubin* 4:17); other fruits were grown in the Wadi Leimun near Acchabaron (bab. *Moed qatan* 12b).

A passage in the Babylonian Talmud points out that in Galilee wine was dearer than oil,[144] for it was the latter which was the product of that province above all others. This is stressed both by Josephus[145] and by many passages in the Talmud. One special advantage of Galilean oil was its ritual purity from the point of view of Jewish law. It was therefore much in demand by the Jews of Syria[146] and of Asia Minor.[147] Its primary fundamental importance for the economy of the region is em-

---

[138] Tos. *Demai* 1:10.

[139] Cant. R. 5:14.

[140] jer. *Baba qama* 6 d.

[141] Gen R. 79; Midr. Psalms XII, 53 a.

[142] *War* 3:3:3-45; 3:10:8-519; M *Menahoth* 8:6; jer. *Megillah* 72 d; cf. also Eccl. R. iii, 3 (Sepphoris); M Kilaim 4:4 (Salmîn); Bab. *Abodah zarah* 30 a (Acchabaron); M *ib.*, 4:12 (Beth Shean).

[143] M *Niddah,* 2:7.

[144] Bab. *Nazir* 31 b.

[145] *War* 2:27:2-592.

[146] *War* 2:27:2-591.

[147] *Sifre* 148 a.

phasized in many ways. According to the Midrash[148] it was easier to bring up a legion on olives in Galilee than one infant in Judaea. The Hadrianic persecution after the war of Bar-Kokhba did indeed temporarily reduce production, but it recovered quickly.[149] The olives of Upper Galilee were on par with wool in Judaea and calves in the Sharon;[150] the poor priest receives his due in olives in this region.[151] Teqo'a in Galilee produced the best oil in the whole country.[152] Next came Gischala,[153] whose oil produce assumed legendary proportion in Talmudic literature.[154] Other centres of production were Meirôn in Upper Galilee,[155] Sikhnîn, Jotapata, Netopha, Kefar Menôri, Sepphoris and Beth ha-'Emeq in Lower Galilee.[156] The valley of Beth-Shean produced a special variety of the olive tree.[157]

The varied soil and climate of Galilee lent itself to the cultivation of many kinds of vegetables. The villages on the borders of the Valley of Jezreel, such as Kefar 'Otnay, Simonias, Tib'on[158] had gardens in their vicinity. The higher areas grew onions (at 'Ardasqûs and Sepphoris),[159] beans, cucumbers, gourds of the porret kind and citrus (ethrog) at Sepphoris,[160] mustard at Sogane-Sikhnin[161] and Hûqôq.[162] The plain of Asochis (Beth Netôfah) supplied the greens used for oxygarum,[163] a special kind of sauce which was also exported. Flax was grown around the

---

148 Gen. R 20, 6.
149 jer. *Peah* 20 a.
150 Bab. *Baba qama* 119 a.
151 Bab. *Hagiga* 25 a.
152 M *Menahoth* 8:2.
153 Tos. *Menahoth* 9:5; jer. *Shebiith* 38 d.
154 *Sifre* 135 b.; 148 a.
155 jer. *Shebiith* 38 d.
156 M *Peah* 7:1 (Sikhnin); *War* 3:7:28-271, 3:7:29-277 (Jotapata); *Sifre* 135 b (Sepphoris); M *Peah* 7:1 (Netophah); jer. *Maas. sheni* 54 d (Beth ha-'Emeq); Tos. *Yebam.* 6:3 (Kefar Menôri).
157 M *Peah* 7:1.
158 Tos. *Demai* 5:23 (Kefar 'Otnay); Tos. *Shebiith* 7:13 (Simonias); jer *Demai* 22 c (Tib' on).
159 Tos. *Shebiith* 4:13 (Sepphoris); jer. *Erubbin* 20 c.
160 Tos. *Demai* 3:14; Tos. *Makhshirin* 3:6; jer. *Shebiith* 37 c.
161 Bab. *Ketuboth* 111 b.
162 jer. *Shebiith* 38 c.
163 M *Shebiith* 9:5.

Sea of Galilee,[164] and indeed all over Galilee;[165] one was allowed to purchase it on the same terms as wool in Judaea and cattle in the Sharon. Special products of the Jordan Valley were lupine (near Tiberias),[166] onions at Arbela, apples (including crab-apples) at Beth Yerah and edible shrub-trees (*lôtôs*) at Gennezareth.[167] The warm climate of the valley favoured the palm-tree[168] (although these never reached the extent of the groves near Jericho), as well as all kind of fruit trees. Both Josephus[169] and the Talmud grow lyrical as they describe the fertility and produce of the Gennezareth Valley. Strabo[171] attributes to it aromatic reeds and even balsam.

In comparison with its agricultural riches, the *mineral products* of Galilee were insignificant. They consisted only of sand from the shore near the mouth of the river Belus south of Ptolemais (Accho). This stretch of the coast supplied seemingly inexhaustible supplies of sand suitable for glass-making.[172] According to legend it was here that glass was discovered. The sand was mostly exported to Sidon, the great centre of glass-blowing, and possibly later on to Tiberias. In this category we may also list the famous hot springs at Hammath near Tiberias.[173]

Industry in Galilee was restricted to two main branches: textiles and vessels. From the third century onwards the fine linen of Scythopolis-Beth Shean[174] began to supersede the imports of similar goods from India by way of Pelusium in Egypt, which were used in the first century A.D.[175] This linen industry profited from the supply of raw flax grown in Galilee

---

164 Bab. *Moed qatan* 18 b.
165 M *baba qama* 10:9.
166 jer. *Shebiith* 38 d.
167 Tos. *Kilaim* 1:3; jer. *Shebiith* 6 c; jer. *Megillah* 77 a.
168 *War* 3:3:3-45; 3:10:8-517; M *Bikkurim* 1:6; jer *Hagigah* 77 b.
169 *War* 3:10:8-516-521.
170 Bab. *Pesahim* 8 b.
171 Strabo XVI, 2, 16.
172 Strabo XVI, 2, 25; *War* 2:10:1-190-1; Pliny *N.h.* V, 75; XXXVI, 191; Tacitus: *Hist.* V, 7.
173 *Ant.* 18:2:3-36; Plin. *N.h.* V, 71; Solin. XXXV, 3; M *Shabbath* 3:4; M *Negaim* 9:1; Bab. *Sanhedrin* 108 a.
174 Bab. *Ketuboth* 67 a; jer *ib.*, ii, 5.
175 M *Yoma* 3:7.

(see p. 203 above). The 'Jewish' byssus mentioned by Pausanias (V.5,2) probably also was produced in Galilee. The Scythopolis textiles are as highly praised in the *Exposito totius mundi.* In the Tariff-law of Diocletian they are valued at the highest rate.[176] Coarse cloths and sacking were produced at Tiberias[177] and at Kefar Nimra;[178] mats and leather goods at Tiberias and 'Ûsha.[179] On the other hand, we can dismiss as legendary the story [180] according to which silk was woven at Gischala in the time of Hadrian. The dyeing industry, which is closely connected with the weaving of textiles, is referred to in connection with Scythopolis, Sogane[181] and Migdal Seba'iya ('Tower of the Dyers'). The last-named place had also a weaving industry.[182]

Tanners were to be found at Tiberias (Cant. R. 1:4). The making of pottery was concentrated in certain villages, such as Kefar Hanania[183] and Sogane-Sikhnin,[184] probably because of the presence of good potters' clay in their vicinity. Glass was produced in the glass works of Tiberias[185] where a special kind of bowl (phialē) was also made.[186] The general level of craftsmanship was high in Galilee, as we can judge from the trades exercised by the Talmudic scholars; these included scribes, weavers, tanners, cobblers, potters, bakers and smiths.[187]

The Galileans were situated between two seas, the Mediterranean and the Sea of Galilee; they naturally exploited both waters. The fishers of Tiberias played an important role in the First Revolt and in later times.[188] Those of Capernaum were among the first followers of Jesus;[189] Ptole-

---

[176] Cf. n. 73 above; *Ed. Diocletiani* 27, 28; *Cod. Theodos.* X, 28, 8.
[177] Bab. *Sukkah* 20 b; Gen. R. 79.
[178] Thren. R. ii, 4.
[179] Bab. *Sukkah* 20 b.
[180] Eccl. R. II, 8.
[181] M *Eduyoth* 7:8.
[182] jer. *Taanith* 69 a.
[183] Tos. *Baba mez.* 6:3; Bab. *Ketuboth* 112 a.
[184] M *Kelim* 5:3.
[185] Gen. R. 1240; M *Kelim* 8:9.
[186] jer. *Niddah* 50 b; Bab. *ib.*, 21 a.
[187] A. Bacher: *Die Aggadah d. pal. Tannaiten u. Amoräer*, passim.
[188] *War* 3:3:5-52; 4:8:2-457; *Life,* 12; jer. *Pesahim* 30 d; Tos. *Baba mes.* 6:5.
[189] Matthew 4:17-22; 13:47 f.; 17:27; Mark 1:16 f.; Luke 5:1; John 21:3 f.

mais-Accho was the centre of sea-fishing.[190] Fishes were salted at Taricheae or Migdal Nunaya ('Tower of the Fishers')[191] for export.[192] It seems that some were even brought up in *vivaria*.[193] Another article supplied by the sea were the snails used for purple dyes; they were collected on the whole coast, at Dora[194] and from Haifa to the Ladder of Tyre, including Ecdippa.[195] Sheep and goats were raised in the woods surrounding Shezôr, and in Galilee in general (Tos. *Baba qamma* 8:14).

The Negeb

The area extending south from Beersheba to the Brook of Egypt and to the Aelanitic Gulf was in biblical times known as the 'Negeb' or 'dry land.' The annual rainfall in this region does not exceed 200 mm., and it did not amount to much more in antiquity.[196] Cultivation in this area is, therefore, restricted to areas which could be irrigated by storing the rain-water and distributing it over the fields. Agriculture in the Negeb depended, therefore, principally on the availability of labour and capital. Even in the most favourable conditions the mountains of the Central Negeb and the Arabah between the Dead Sea and Elath were cultivable only in patches. In the Northern Negeb the loess lands could be cultivated where they are free from sand dunes. The settlement of this area was thus the result of external factors. These were active in periods when some main trade routes passed this area, as happened in the Nabataean and Byzantine periods. The Nabataeans seem to have developed the methods of cultivation possible in this area. They did utilize the rain floods by damming the dry river beds and diverting the water into the fields alongside. By denuding the surface of the higher hills of stones,

---

190 Bab. *Abodah zarah* 34 b; Gen R. 3; Deut. R., vii, 6; (Ptolemais); the importance of this harbour necessitated the establishment of a customs house there (*Doctrina Jacobi,* ed. Bonwetsch, p. 77).

191 Bab. *Pesah* 46 a.

192 Strabo XVI, 2, 45; *War* 3:10:1-462-4.

193 M *Beza* 3:1.

194 Claudius Iolaus quoted by Steph. Byz. s.v. Doros.

195 *Totius orb. descr.* (see note 73 above); Bab. *Sabbath* 26 a; *Sifre* Deut. 147 a.

196 Woolley and Lawrence (The *Wilderness of Zin,* p. 32 f.) noted that the marks of past water levels in the old wells corresponded to those of the present ones.

they caused silt to collect in the irrigable areas lower down.[197] As a result we have evidence, both from literature and from the papyri found at Nessana,[198] that wheat and barley (although of a poor kind), [199] grew in the Negeb, together with vines,[200] figs and date palms. These plantations were irrigated. The small walled-in plots, which were observed near the cities, were probably producing vegetables. The many loom-weights found indicate numerous weaving establishments. The traders and (later on) the pilgrims passing through the Negeb cities were accommodated in caravanserais; the one at Nessana had sixteen beds. Baths were provided for the caravans outside the cities (e.g. at Eboda). The copper mines of Timnah (Wadi Mene'aiyye) were exploited in the Roman times, but none of the other mineral resources of the area (as known to us to-day) were made use of. The quantities of coins and the other archaeological material enable us to set up a general picture of the economic development of this area: a pioneering period in the second century B.C. to the first century A.D.; a decline caused by the Roman conquest under Trajan and the opening up of the *via nova* from Aila to Damascus, which by-passed the Negeb; and a revival from the fifth century onwards, as Byzantine trade moved inland under Arab pressure, and the pilgrims' route to Sinai was opened up.

The lands beyond the Jordan. This area can be divided into three parts: (a) the wheat and cattle lands stretching from the Sea of Galilee to the Hauràn mountains; (b) the Jordan Valley and Arabah; (c) the Trans-Jordan highlands stretching from the Yarmuk river to the Gulf of Elath. (a) The Gaulanitis Batanaea and Auranitis were opened up to cultivation but lately; witness the appeals of the Herodian Kings[201] to the inhabitants to settle down and work their land. Once settled, however,

---

[197] J. Kedar in *IEJ*, 7, 1957, pp. 178-189.

[198] Lewis, *Pal. Expl. Fund. Quarterly*, 1948, p. 102 ff.; Colt in *Archaeology*, I, p. 84 ff.; on the results of earlier researches see G. Kirk, *PEFQSt.*, 1938, p. 21 ff., 1948, p. 57 ff.; Kramer, *Excavations at Nessana*, III.

[199] The "desert" barley of average quality is mentioned M *Kelim* 17:8.

[200] St. Hilarion was received at Elusa by the inhabitants with vessels of the local wine (St. Jerome: *Vita Hilarionis*, 25).

[201] Waddington-Le Bas: *Recueil*, No. 2339; *OGIS* 424.

and strengthened by colonists from Idumaea and Babylon,[202] these regions proved most fertile. They exported wheat to Galilee and beyond,[203] raising lupine, vegetables and great herds of cattle.[204] The large estates in this area, originally Herodian, passed after the extinction of the dynasty to the imperial fiscus. In the third century the emperors of the Severan house granted them to a large extent to the Patriarch Judah I.[205] The Gaulan produced vines of which we are told the usual aggadic exaggerations; Saccae in the Hauran is also mentioned as a wine-growing area.[206] The territory of Caesarea Philippi including the Ulathah (Huleh marshes) produced rice, sesame, beans, nuts and a special kind of dates (jer. *Demai* 22d).

The Jordan Valley east of the river grew date palms at Amathus,[207] Livias and Nimra;[208] the groves extended as far as Zoar south of the Dead Sea, where also some balsam was grown.[209] For the rest of the Arabah date palms grew only sparsely in a few oases. The evidence of irrigated fields at Toloha[210] show that some kind of agriculture was practised in the Arabah as well. Probably it was meant to supply the copper mines at Phaenon. These mines were worked uninterruptedly in the Roman and Byzantine times, after an interruption in the Persian and Hellenistic period; according to Aristeas (119-20) the Nabataeans pretended they were worked-out in order to keep their independence. The

---

202 *War* 2:19:2-520; *Life* 11:54; *Ant.* 17:2:2-26.

203 jer. *Shebiith* 38 a mentions the sale of a special kind of wheat (*qôrdiqîya*) from Hippus-Susitha to Tiberias.

204 Bab. *Yebamoth* 46 a (lupine from the Gaulan); *Life* 11-58 (tens of thousands of cattle in the villages of the Batanaea); Tos. *Maas. sheni* 3:7 (vegetables).

205 jer. *Shebiith* 6 a.

206 Bab. *Sabbath* 112 a: bunches of grapes were grown as big as calves or goats. The wine of Sakutan (Saccaea) is mentioned Bab. *Abodah zarah* 58 b.

207 Cf. the story of a palm tree at Amathus which had to be fertilized by another from Jericho, Gen R. 40-41.

208 Pliny *N.h.* XIII, 44 (Livias); Tos. *Yoma* 5:4 mentions a special kind of date called after Nimrah.

209 *On.* 42:4-5.

210 Glueck: *AASOR,* XV, pp. 12-17; XVIII-XIX, pp. 149-152.

Romans sent there convicted Christians;[211] the Byzantines—whoever was regarded as heterodox at the time.[212]

The third region was the most varied in character. It included in the North areas growing wheat and barley, fruits and vegetables at Beth ha-Ramtha and Mahanaim;[213] wheat was also grown near Gadara,[214] wine at Beth-Ramtha,[215] Abila and Mahanaim; the territory of Pella,[216] Gerasa[217] and Philadelphia.[218] On the fringe of the desert small figs[219] and beans[220] were produced at Bostra. Further south began the area which excelled in small but meaty olives, which are highly praised by Pliny.[221] The Mishnah accords the second place to the oil of Ragaba in Trans-Jordan.[222] Flax was grown there, which supported the linen weavers of Gerasa.[223] At Petra ground-pines were grown, which were used to adulterate the balsam.[224] As one moves south the olive is replaced by the sesame[225] and cultivation by pasture. Strabo refers to the fact that the land of the Nabataeans was well supplied with pasturage,[226] where white fleeced sheep, large oxen and camels were raised.[227] The raising of camels in Arabia is mentioned in the Talmudic sources.[228] The gifts sent by To-

---

211 Eusebius: *Hist. eccl.* VIII, 13, 5; Id. *De mart. Pal.* XIII, 1; *On.* 114:3; 168:10; Abel: *Géographie,* I, p. 202; Glueck, *AASOR,* XV, pp. 32-35.

212 Theodoretus: *Hist. eccl.* IV, 19, 22, (*PG* LXXXII, c. 1177).

213 Targum Judges 4:5.

214 Bab. *Pesahim* 8 b; bab. *Megillah* 6 a.

215 Midr. Psalms iii (18, 1).

216 *On.* 32:16; Tos. *Shebiith* 7:17. The other Abila in the Jordan Valley also produced wine (*On. ib.*); for Mahanaim cf. Midr. Psalms, *loc. cit.* n. 215.

217 Cagnat: *Inscr. gr. ad res rom. pertinentes,* III, 1341.

218 The "Ammonite" wine served—according to the Midrash—to render the Children of Israel susceptible to the charms of the Midianite women (Numb. R. 10:3; jer. *Sanhedrin* 28 d; bab. *ib.* 106 a.)

219 jer. *Bikkurim* 63 c; jer. *Baba mezia* ii, beg.

220 jer. *Kilaim* 31 c.

221 *N.h.* XV, 15.

222 M *Menahoth* 8:2; cf. M *Bikkurim* 1:10.

223 *Suppl. epigr. graec.* VII, 827.

224 Plin. *N.h.* XII, 119.

225 Strabo XVI, 4, 26.

226 *Ib.,* XVI, 4, 18.

227 *Ib.,* XVI, 4, 26.

228 jer. *Kilaim* 26 d.

biah to King Ptolemy II included some typical desert animals, such as the onager and greyhounds.[229] The pastures began at Capitolias (Beth Rêsha)[230] in the north on the desert fringe and extended through the mountains and woods of the Gilead (Mahanaim), Machaerus where goats were raised, Moab which raised sheep and into Arabia proper.[231]

The natural resources of this area included the iron mines near Ragaba, which were worked in antiquity, the 'Iron Mountain' of Josephus,[232] and the Mishnah[233] probably refers to them. Wood grew in the Gilead region and near Machaerus (*War* 7:210). The hot springs of Emmatha near Gadara,[234] of Callirrhoe[235] and Baaru[236] were used, at least from the time of Herod to the late Byzantine times. As regards industry we hear only of a potters' guild at Gerasa, and potters' wheels at Beth Ramtha.[237] Like other parts of the country, the area beyond the Jordan underwent various economic turns. The archaeological survey of the sites undertaken by Nelson Glueck has shown that the country as a whole reached the peak of its population in Roman times. The finds at Gerasa suggest the late second century as its apogee; the effects of the annexation of the provincia Arabia in 106 and the consequent opening-up of the desert routes had by then had their effect. A secondary period of development came in the Byzantine period. The various regions were, however, affected differently. Thus Jewish Peraea seems to have been hard hit in the years succeeding the War of Bar- Kokhba.[238]

The nature of our sources does not allow us to make more than a spot-survey of ancient economics. We are without the all-over picture, which is possible only where there is plenty of statistic material available. The

---

[229] Vincent, *RB,* 1920, p. 186.

[230] Bab. *Hulin* 80 a (where Rêsha is to be read for Dwshây).

[231] M *Tamid* 3:8 (Machaerus); bab. *Menahoth* 87 a (Moab); Eusebius: *Praeparatio evang.* ix, 31-34 (Arabia); Midr. Psalms 3:18 (Mahanaim).

[232] *War* 4:8:2-454.

[233] M *Sukkah* 3:2.

[234] *On.* 22:26; Eccl. R. v, 10; Tos. *Erubbin* 6(5) : 13; Epiphanius *Adv. haer.* 30.

[235] *Ant.* 17:6:5-171; *War* 1:23:5-657; Plin. *N.h.* V, 72; Solinus, XXXV, 4; Gen. R. 37.

[236] *War* 7:6:3-180; *On.* 44:22; *Petrus d. Iberer,* ed. Raabe, p. 82.

[237] *Suppl. epigr. graec.* VII, 879 (Gerasa); Midr. Psalms iii, 18 (Beth Ramtha).

[238] *Aboth de R[illegible]i Nathan,* 27.

main sources at our disposal are of three kinds: (1) Geographers (Strabo, Pliny) who collected and digested information from other authors. They are usually more interested in stressing the unique or extraordinary than to state the (to them) obvious. (2) The historians, such as Josephus, mention economic facts only where they are of importance to their narrative; Josephus in particular tends to generalize or exaggerate; like most ancient historians he is more interested in rhetoric and the passions of the human heart than in the dry facts of production. (3) The Talmudic sources give us plentiful information, but of a very haphazard character. If a particular product is connected with some points of halachic law, or with an anecdote of the Aggadah, it is brought in. Owing to faulty M.S. transmission the information is much distorted in form. In the Christian authorities, especially to the lives of the saints and monks, economic information is only incidental. They contain, however, an as yet unworked mine of material. The pilgrim texts usually ignore economics altogether. The construction made with such faulty materials must of necessity be incomplete. It can nevertheless be regarded as correct in its main lines, especially if we consider how the essential factors of soil and climate are unchanged.

Chapter III

POPULATION

A. Composition

The eventful history of the Holy Land from the Persian to the Byzantine periods is reflected in the composition of the population in its various regions and the changes it underwent in the course of the time.

The *Jews* returning from captivity 'everyone unto his city' in the territory held by the remnant that was left in Judah as reduced by Nebuchadnezzar.[1] There were scattered Jewish settlements south of Beth-Zur till Beersheba,[2] but they seem to have disappeared in the Persian period.[3] On the other hand, Jewish settlements extended westwards into the coastal plain (Lod, Hadid and Ono) and into the mountains to the north. (Haramatha and Aphaerema).[4] Scattered settlements, the remains of the ten Israelite tribes, subsisted in Galilee,[5] in Gilead[6] and in the Tobiad lands beyond the Jordan.[7] Judah itself was purely Jewish, except for a sprinkling of Samaritans and Ashdodites,[8] of Persian soldiers[9] and Tyrian traders.[10] Most of the former left after the reforms of Ezra and Nehemiah and the dissolution of mixed marriages. North of Judaea the *Samaritans* occupied their whole province. The southern coast was inhabited by the *Philistines* (called Ashdodites in the Bible[11] and 'the Syrians of Palestine'

---

[1] Ezra 2:1; Neh. 7:6; 2 Kings 25:12.

[2] Neh. 11:25-30.

[3] Possibly in connection with the revolt suppressed by Artaxerxes (which?) Solinus, *Collectanea,* XXXV, 4.

[4] Ezra 2:33; Neh. 7:37; 1 Macc. 11:34.

[5] 1 Macc. 5:14 ff.

[6] *Ib.,* 9 ff.

[7] The land of Tobiah, the 'Ammonite servant' cf. B. Mazar, *IEJ* 7, 1957, pp. 137-145, 229-238.

[8] Neh. 13:23-24.

[9] Neh. 2:9.

[10] Neh. 13:16.

[11] See n. 8 above.

by Herodotus).[12] The *Phoenicians* extended along the coast.[13] They established also some inland colonies. We know of two such colonies, one at Marissa[14] and the other at Sichem,[15] both situated on important trade routes. Southern Judaea was occupied by the *Idumaeans*.[16] Greek mercenaries and their Egyptian wives settled at 'Athlit.[17] Greek merchants were established at Ake (Accho) already in the time of Demosthenes and Isaeus,[18] and possibly also at Dor. Beyond the Jordan lived various tribes still called by their tribal names, some of them biblical (Ammon,[19] Moab,[20] Gilead,[21] the sons of Iamre,[22] the sons of Baan[23]). The Nabataean Arabs reached from the vicinity of Gilead[24] to the coast south of Gaza.[25]

The conquest of Alexander and the rule of the diadochs naturally brought about a strengthening of the Greek element. Macedonians were settled at Samaria;[26] the cities of the Decapolis: (Dium, Hippus, Gadara, Abila, Pella, Gerasa and Philadelphia) received new names and some Greek or Macedonian settlers. The coastal Philistines and Phoenicians became Hellenized, at least as far as their upper classes were concerned.[27] In Judaea and Idumaea there were Greek garrisons[28] and officials.[29] Even

12. Hist. II, 104.
13 Ps.—Scylax (*Geogr. graec. min.* ed. C. Müller, p. 78 ff.)
14 J. P. Peters & H. Thiersch: *The Painted tombs in the necropolis of Marissa,* 1905.
15 *Ant.* 12:5:5-258.
16 Strabo XVI, 2, 34.
17 C. J. Johns, *QDAP,* II, p. 57.
18 Demosthenes: *Orat.* X 52 in Callipum, 20; Isaeus: *Orat.* IV, 7.
19 1 Macc. 5:6; 2 Macc. 4:26.
20 *Ant.* 13:13:5-374; *War* 1:4:3-89. In *Ant.* l.c. these peoples are called 'Arabs'.
21 *Ib.*
22 1 Macc. 9:36-37.
23 1 Macc. 5:4.
24 1 Macc. 5:25; 9:35.
25 Herodotus, III, 5.
26 Curtius Rufus IV, 8, 9; Eusebius: Chronicon (*GCS,* pp. 197, 199); St. Jerome: Chronicon pp. 123, 128.
27 The lower classes continued to speak Aramaic ("Syrian") both at Gaza and at Elusa (Marc le diacre: *Vie de Porphyre,* ed. Grégoire-Kugener) 68; St. Jerome: *Vita Hilarionis,* 25 (*PL* 23, c. 42).
28 *Ant.* 12:3:3-138.
29 V. Tscherikower, *Mizraim* IV-V (1937) pp. 41-2.

among the cleruchs of Tobias in the Peraea were some Macedonians and Egyptian Jews.[30] The shrinking of Phoenician influence in the Sharon was accompanied by an expansion of the Samaritans. Small groups of Jews settled in the harbour cities Joppa and Jamnia.[31]

In the beginning of the Maccabaean period the Jews of Galilee were evacuated in part, and those of Gilead as a whole.[32] There remained some Jewish elements in the Valley of Jezreel,[33] in Arbel on the Lake Gennesareth[34] and in other parts of Galilee.[35] As a result of the Hasmonaean expansion the territories of Ekron,[36] Joppa,[37] Gezer,[38] Jamnia[39] and Azotus,[40] and then Idumaea,[41] the Acrabittene,[42] and finally Galilee[43] became successively Jewish. Jewish settlements were also established in the Carmel and the Sharon forest (the 'Drymus').[44] In Judaea proper both the Greek garrisons and the Jewish Hellenizers left as soon as the Hasmonaeans became the official heads of the community of the Jews. Towards the end of the Hasmonaean period Greek officers and foreign mercenaries[45] appear in the service of Jannaeus. The eviction of the Greek settlers from Scythopolis, Gadara and Pella was temporary only.[46]

In the Herodian period the groups of the settled population were more or less stabilized. On the other hand, the greater possibilities of travel under the 'Roman peace' led to greater mobility of individuals.

---

30 P. Zen. 59003.
31 2 Macc. 12:3-4, 8.
32 1 Macc. 5:23, 45.
33 Jonathan's troops found support there when attacked by Tryphon, 1 Macc. 12:47-50.
34 1 Macc. 9:2.
35 See n. 43 below.
36 1 Macc. 10:89.
37 1 Macc. 13:11.
38 1 Macc. 13:47-48.
39 See p. 64 above.
40 It was a Jewish city in A.D. 67 (War 4:3:2-130); although it was formally detached from the Hasmonaean state by Pompey.
41 *Ant.* 13:9:1-258.
42 A toparchy of Judaea in Josephus (*War* 3:3:5-55) subdued by the Romans (*ib.*, IV, 551).
43 *Ant.* 13:11:3-318; *War* 1:3:3-76.
44 *Ant.* 14:13:3-334; *War* 1:13:2-250.
45 *Ant.* 13:13:5-374; *War* 1:4:3-88.
46 *Ant.* 13:15:4-397; 14:4:4-75; *Megillath Taanith* 21 (Ch. IV, n. 88 above).

The Herodians welcomed Greeks and invited them to their courts in Jerusalem[47] and Tiberias;[48] they also recruited some foreign troops.[49] Jerusalem was filled with Jewish pilgrims from all lands between Parthia to Rome.[50] Herod himself was purely pragmatical in his colonizing policy. He settled in Caesarea a mixed population of Greeks and Jews.[51] Jews at Antipatris,[52] Gentile cavalry veterans at Geba,[53] and Idumaeans and Babylonians in his lands beyond the Jordan; there they mixed with Syrians.[54] Under his reign Jews seem to have settled in increasing numbers in Ptolemais, Scythopolis, Hippus, Gadara and Gerasa.[55] Under the procurators Roman troops were garrisoned at Caesarea[56] and Jerusalem, and veterans were settled at Ptolemais by Claudius.[56a] Babylonian Jews (such as Hillel) and converts of the Adiabene royal family came to live in the Holy City.[57]

After the First Jewish Revolt and the destruction of the Temple there was no revolutionary change. Roman officers and soldiers[58] lived in Jerusalem with their families side by side with Jews and Judaeo-Christians.[59] It was only the War of Bar-Kokhba that brought about a radical change. By order of Hadrian, the surviving Jews were expelled from the whole municipal area of Jerusalem; even the Judaeo-Christian community had to be dissolved. The emptied area was settled by Syrians and Arabs.[60] Jewish villages were left in Judaea only in the Jordan Valley.

---

[47] *Ant.* 16:10:1-301.
[48] *Ant.* 18:2:3-37; *Life* 12-67.
[49] *Ant.* 16:10:3-314; 17:8:3-198.
[50] *Acts* 2:9-11.
[51] *Ant.* 20:8:7-173; *War* 2:13:7-266.
[52] *War* 2:19:1-513.
[53] *Ant.* 15:8:5-294; *War* 3:3:1-36.
[54] *Ant.* 16:9:2-285; 17:2:1-23-25; *War* 3:3:5-57.
[55] *War* 2:18:3-466; *ib.* 5-477, 478, 480.
[56] *Acts* 10:1.
[56a] Plin. *N.h.* V, 75; Hill, *BMC Phoenicia,* p. lxxxii f.; *QDAP* XII, p. 86 and n. 2.
[57] *Ant.* 20:1:1-2; bab. *Pesahim* 66.
[58] *QDAP* VIII, p. 54 f.
[59] Epiphanius, *De mens. et ponder.* 14, 15.
[60] J. R. Harris: *Harvard Theological Review,* 1926, XIX, pp. 199-206; Eusebius: Hist. eccl. IV, 6, 3 (*GCS* 9, p. 308).

There they were needed by the fiscus to tend the balsam plantations, now imperial property. This need explains the survival of Jewish settlements at Engaddi and Noarath into the fourth and sixth centuries respectively.[61] Another Jewish area left untouched was the Daromas in Southern Judaea. There Jews continued to live in the big villages of Anaea, Chermela, Eremmon, Jettah, Thella[62] and at Kefar 'Aziz.[63] Only after the fall of the emperor Julian did these settlements disappear (late fourth century).[64] On the coast isolated Jewish villages existed in the vicinity of Gaza[65] and the Saltus Gerariticus,[66] as well as in the cities of Gaza and Ascalon themselves.[67] Jewish settlements became denser around Jamnia, Lod, Ekron and Bene Beraq.[68] Joppa remained largely a Jewish city; it received Jewish immigrants from Egypt and Tarsus.[69] Some Jews lived also at Apollonia.[70] In the third century the Jewish community at Caesarea flourished;[71] it soon became the rival of Tiberias even in Talmudic learning. The Sharon remained a mixed area of Jews and Samaritans;[72] but the Acrabittene was definitely assimilated by the Samaritans.[73] In the North the Carmel Jews (Haifa) and those at Ptolemais, Achzib and Scythopolis stayed on.[74] Galilee remained in any case the stronghold of Judaism in Palestine from the second century onwards. After the War of Bar-Kokhba the remaining priestly clans emigrated there.[75] They were

---

[61] *On.* 86:16; Noarath *On.* 136:24; Vita Charit. *AASS* 28 Sept. VII, 578.

[62] *On.* 26:8; 88:17; 92:20; 108:8; 98:26.

[63] Mishnah *Kilaim* 6:4.

[64] Chron. ad a. 724 (Brooks) *CSSO* (*SS*) III, IV, p. 104.

[65] *Ib.*, p. 147.

[66] jer. *Shebiith* 36 c.

[67] Ambrosius, *Ep.* XL, 66 (*PL* XVI, 1154); Vita Joh. Eleemosynari *AASS* III, 121.

[68] *Sefer ha-Yishub,* I, s.v. (Hebrew).

[69] Clermont-Canneau: *Arch. Res. in Pal.* II, p. 133; *RAO* IV, p. 147; Euting: *Epigr. Miscell.* Nos. 53, 87.

[70] Euting, *ib.,* No. 80.

[71] *Sefer ha-Yishub,* s.v.

[72] Bab. *Abodah zarah* 31 a.

[73] jer. *Yebamoth* 9 d.

[74] jer. *Berakhoth* 4 d; Menologium Basilii (*PG* CXVII, 588); jer. *Shebiith* 37 a; Tos. *Terumoth* 2 end; bab. *Megillah* 24 b; M *Abodah zarah* 1:4.

[75] S. Klein: *Beitr. z. Geogr. u. Gesch. Galiläas,* 1909, pp. 102-8.

strengthened by an influx of Jews from Babylonia and Cappadocia.[76] Yet under Roman rule there was a sprinkling of Gentiles even in Galilee. The Roman overseers (lit. "oppressors"—*mesiqin*) of the confiscated lands settled in and near the Asochis plain with their families.[77] Some Syrians, Romans and Greeks lived in Tiberias. Even the Jewish patriarchs had a bodyguard of captive Goths, a gift of the emperor; they exercised police functions in the city.[78] The town of Sepphoris-Diocaesarea was held by a Roman garrison, for whose benefit a Mithraeum was set up in the vicinity.[79] Roman civilian and military officials lived there with their families.[80] The Roman garrisons, scattered over the country, were of the most mixed origins, witness the *Notitia Dignitatum*;[81] thus, Aelia Capitolina (Jerusalem) was garrisoned by Moorish cavalry. The Samaritans, who formed a kind of belt (fascia) between Judaea and Galilee,[82] profited from the vacuum created by the Jewish defeat in Bar-Kokhba's war. They spread into the southern coast, settling near Gaza,[83] Jamnia,[84] Emmaus,[85] Caesarea,[86] the Samaritan 'castra' by the Carmel,[87] and even at Tharsila in the Batanaea.[87a] The Jewish settlements in that area continued to exist, with their centre at Naveh.[88] They were, however, under strong Arab pressure in the Gaulan[89] and

---

[76] Cf. the inscription of an archisynagogue of Pamphylia found at Beth She'arim; jer. *Shebiith* 36 d; jer. *Yoma* 44 b; jer. *Sabbath* 8 a.

[77] Tos. *Ohiloth,* 16:13; *QDAP* XII, p. 88; P. *Derekh Eretz* 81.

[78] jer. *Sanhedrin* 19, 4.

[79] *Midr. Tannaim* Deut. 262; jer. *Sheqalim* 50 c; Eisler: *Orient. Literatur Zeitung,* 1909, c. 425-7.

[80] Bab. *Sabbath* 145 b.; *QDAP* XII, p. 88 f.

[81] Ed. Seeck, Berlin 1876, pp. 73, 81.

[82] jer. *Hagigah* 79 b; bab. *ib.,* 25 a.

[83] See n. 65 above.

[84] *Petrus d. Iberer,* ed. Raabe, p. 126 f.

[85] Joh. Moschus, *Pratum Spirituale* 165; cf. the Samaritan synagogue in the vicinity, at Salbit: *L. Rabinowitz Bulletin,* I, 1949, p. 26 ff.

[86] Malalas, XVIII, 232; jer. *Abodah zarah* 39 c, 44 d.

[87] Pliny, *N.h.* V, 19; *Anton. Placent.* 3; *Itin. burd.* 19, 8; Mishnah *Demai* 1:1; Thr R. i, 17.

[87a] *On.* 102:5.

[88] *On.* 136:2; Tos. *Shebiith* 4:8; L. A. Mayer and A. Reifenberg, *BJPES,* IV, p. 1 ff. (Hebrew).

[89] Bab. *Ketuboth* 112 a.

the Hauran.[90] Arab influence was also on the increase in Gerasa and other Trans-Jordan cities, as is evidenced by the inscriptions.

In the Byzantine period there was a considerable influx of pilgrims from all Christian countries.[91] Christians, Jews and Hellenes continued to mix in the bathing places and at some religious festivals (such as that near the Terebinth.[92] Monks and other settlers came from Italy, from Asia Minor (including Armenia and Iberia), Egypt and other African countries. These groups settled mainly in and around Jerusalem. Egyptian wine merchants settled in the southern ports. The Jews of Galilee maintained their positions even under Byzantine rule.[93] All the efforts of the convert Comes Joseph, even though backed by the imperial government, failed to introduce Christian worship in Diocaesarea, Capernaum and Tiberias.[94] Sepphoris-Diocaesarea in the fifth century was still purely Jewish[95] and so was the little village of Nazareth until the sixth century.[96] Jews returned in some numbers to Jerusalem and the mountains surrounding it, including the vicinity of Bethlehem,[97] were again expelled by Heraclius for joining the Persian invaders in 614, and returned only after the Arab conquest.

In surveying the development of the population trends as a whole, we note at the beginning of the Persian period a time of flux, caused by the resettlement of elements disturbed by the Assyrians and Babylonians. This is followed in the fifth and fourth centuries by a period of stability.

---

[90] Bab. *Abodah zarah* 58 b.

[91] A. Couret: *La Palestine sous les empereurs grecs,* 1869, p. 216 ff.

[92] Antonius Placentinus p. ˉ78 f.; Sozomenus, Hist. eccl. II, 4 (*PG* LXVII, 941); Eusebius, *Vita Const.* III, 41 ff.

[93] The number of places known to be inhabited by Jews in Galilee is 63 after the destruction of the Temple; in the fourth century A.D. 45 of them were still Jewish.

[94] Epiphanius, *Adv. haer.* 30, 4-12.

[95] Theodoretus, *Hist. eccl.* IV, 35.

[96] Anton. Placent. ed. Geyer, pp. 161-2.

[97] In the time of Tertullian there were no Jews left there. (Adv. Judaeos 13 (*PL* II, c. 673); St. Jerome however received lessons from a Jewish scholar (*Ep.* 84, 3). The presence of Jews in Jerusalem after the middle of the fifth century is evident from the story of the monk Barsauma (Nau *Rev. d'Or. chrét.* 1914, pp. 119-123) and the *Life of Sabas* (54, 57) of Cyrillus Scythopolitanus. The Persian invasion of 614 caused a revolt also of the Jews "in the Jerusalem mountains" (Eutychius: *Annales,* II, 5-7).

The Hellenistic period brings a fresh thaw in the rigid ethnic picture. In Hasmonaean times the movement of people becomes quite violent. Roman rule and the Herodians bring about another period of stabilization and of ethnic interpenetration, at least to a certain extent. The revolts against Rome were followed by another violent upheaval, followed by a period of rigid ethnic boundaries in the second and third centuries. In the Byzantine period there is a gradual increase in the movement of population, which continues till the Persian invasion of 614.

B. Numbers

Census-taking was well known in antiquity, but the fragmentary data which have reached us concerning Palestine do not enable us to draw definite conclusions on this subject. The few definite statements found in Josephus, or the Talmudic sources are palpable exaggerations. Thus Josephus[98] gives to understand that the population of Galilee in A.D. 67 was at least 3 million; according to Midrash Rabba on the Song of Songs,[99] the coastal plain between Antipatris and Gebath contained 600,000 towns. In view of this kind of source, one can understand why the estimate of the population of ancient Palestine varied from 700,000 (Harnack)[100] to five millions (J. Juster);[101] both are without foundation. The former simply assumed a number equal to the population of modern Palestine at the time (1902), while the latter accepted uncritically the statement of Josephus. A number of four millions has been recently suggested by F. Heichelheim, based on an estimate derived from N. Syria.[102]

We can approach the problem in two ways: (a) by utilizing the ancient data, and (b) by calculating the proportion of ancient sites

---

[98] It had 204 villages (*Life* 45-235) the smallest of which contained fifteen thousand inhabitants (*War* 3:3:2-43).

[99] Cant R i, 16; According to Strabo Iamnia and the vicinity could furnish 40,000 armed men (XVI, 2, 28).

[100] *Mission u. Ausbreitung d. Christentums,* I, 1902, p. 3, ff.

[101] *Les Juifs dans l'empire romain,* I. 1914, p. 209 ff.

[102] *Economic Survey of Ancient Rome,* ed. Frank, IV, 1938, p. 158 ff. Other scholars have suggested 2 millions (J. Beloch: *Die Bevölkerung d. gr.-röm. Welt,* 1886, p. 242 ff.; Ed. Meyer: *Handwörteb. d. Staatswissensch.* sv. Bevölkerung; W. F. Albright, *JPOS,* 5, 1925, p. 24 n.; S. W. Baron: *Social and Religious History of the Jews,* New York, 1937, I, p. 132; III, pp. 33, 39.

surveyed on the spot with the number of existing villages (taking the end of the nineteenth century as our basic datum).

We can start from the census of Nehemiah as recorded in the Bible:[103] it listed about fifty thousand men, i.e. a population of ca. 250,000 in the whole of Judah. In the Hasmonaean times Jonathan mobilized forty thousand men, i.e. the Jewish population had by then grown to about half a million. In A.D. 66 Josephus raised in Galilee also a force of sixty thousand,[104] which indicates a population of about 750,000. The revenues of Galilee being one fifth of the total revenue of Herod's Kingdom,[105] we arrive at a total of about two and a half millions. This number we can support with two other data: According to Josephus, the number of pilgrims to Jerusalem each Passover was 2,700,000,[106] which is obviously absurd. However, if we assume that Josephus considered that every Jew in Palestine literally fulfilled the biblical obligation of pilgrimage, we can take this number as the total of the Jewish population of the country. Secondly, Bar-Hebraeus[107] states that the total number of Jews in the empire under Claudius was 6,944,000. As we know that Egypt numbered one million Jews,[108] and the total for the Diaspora cannot have exceeded four millions, we are left with the same result. This maximum number seems to have shrunk to about 1½ million Jews at the time of Bar-Kokhba's war, and to about 800,000 after that war.[109] In 614 the Jews of Palestine were still able to mobilize about 20,000 men, which corresponds to a population of about 250,000. On the other hand, the Gentile population seems to have increased in the second and fourth to sixth centuries[110] A.D. almost without interruption.

No complete archaeological survey of Palestine west of the Jordan has

---

[103] Ezra 2:64-5; Neh. 7:66-67.

[104] *War* 2:20:8-583.

[105] *War* 2:6:3-95.

[106] *War* 6:9:3-425.

[107] Bar Hebreaus ed. Pocock, 1653, p. 73.

[108] Philo: *In Flaccum,* 6.

[109] These numbers can be estimated from the number of known Jewish villages before and after these events; it sank in Judaea from 105 to 42; cf. also Dio Cassius' statement as regards the numbers killed in the war (LXIX, 14), as 580,000.

[110] Eutychius: *Annales,* II, 5-7.

yet been made. A series of partial surveys (three areas in Galilee[111] and one in Judaea)[112] have shown that the proportion of Roman-Byzantine settlements to villages existing in 1900 is about 4:1.[113] In Trans-Jordan the proportion was 3 : 1 in the peak (Roman) period.[114] The population of Palestine in 1900 (which was comparable in resources and standard of life to that of ancient Palestine) was 700,000. By multiplying with four we arrive at the same result of 2,800,000 inhabitants taking the population as a whole.

---

[111] A. Saarisalo, *JPOS,* 9, 1929, p. 27; 10, 1930, p. 5 ff.; A. Bergmann-R. Kallner, *BJPES* 8, 1941, pp. 85-90 (H); N. Tsori, *Beth-Shean Valley* Jerusalem, 1962, p. 135 f. (H).
[112] Mader: *Altchr. Basiliken u. Lokaltraditionen in Südjudäa,* 1918; A. Saarisalo, *JPOS,* 11, 1931, p. 98 ff.
[113] In W. Galilee 64:19; in E. Galilee 36:6; in Judaea 18:1; it should be noted however that the Arab villages were more populated than the ancient settlements, which might have varied in the course of the Roman-Byzantine period. Hence the adjustments made above.
[114] 67 Roman, 39 Byzantine sites were noted by Glueck in 1933 and 1936-8 (*AASOR* XIV, 1934; XVIII-XIX, 1939).

Abbreviations

AASOR—Annual of the American Schools of Oriental Research.
Ant—*Antiquities of the Jews* by Josephus Flavius, ed. Niese.
Bab.—Babylonian Talmud.
BASOR—Bulletin of the American Schools of Oriental Research.
BIES—Bulletin of the Israel Eploration Society, continuing
BJPES—Bulletin of the Jewish Palestine Exploration Society.
BMC—British Museum Catalogue of Greek Coins by G. Hill (London, 1914).
DJD—*Discoveries in the Judaean Desert,* I-III Oxford.
EI—Eretz-Israel, Annual of the Israel Exploration Society.
GCS—Griechisch-christliche Schriftsteller, ed. Berlin Academy.
Hier.—Hieronymus' Latin translation of the Onomasticon, ed. Klostermann.
IEJ—Israel Exploration Journal.
IG—Inscriptiones graecae.
It.burd. (IB)—Itineriarum burdigalense, ed. Geyer in *Itinera hierosolymitana.*
JBL—Journal of Biblical Literature.
Jer.—Jerusalem Talmud.
JHS—Journal of Hellenic Studies.
JNES—Journal of Near Eastern Studies.
JPOS—Journal of the Palestine Oriental Society.
KW—H. Kohl & C. Watzinger: *Antike Synagogen in Galilaea,* Leipzig, 1916.
Life—*Autobiography* of Josephus Flavius, ed. Niese.
M—Mishnah.
Madaba Map—ed. M. Avi-Yonah, Jerusalem, 1954.
MFO—Mélanges de la faculté orientale, Université St. Joseph, Beyrouth.
MN—Mitteilungen und Nachrichten d. Deutschen Palästina-Vereins.
ND—*Notitia dignitatum,* ed. O. Seeck, Berlin, 1876.
OGIS—*Orientis graeci inscriptiones selectae,* ed. Dittenberger.
OuW—G. Dalman: *Orte u. Wege Jesu,* Gütersloh, 1924.
On.—*Onomasticon* of Eusebius, ed. Klostermann, Leipzig, 1904.
PAES—Syria. Publications of the Princeton Archaelogical Expedition.
PG—Patrologia graeca, ed. Migne.
PJb—Palästina—Jahrbuch.
PL—Patrologia latina, ed. Migne.
PSI—Papyri greci e latini (Società italiana per la ricerca dei papiri).
QDAP—Quarterly, Department of Antiquities, Palestine.
QSt—Quarterly Statement, Palestine Exploration Fund.
RAO—Recueil d'Archéologie orientale, ed. Ch. Clermont-Ganneau, 1-8.
RB—Revue biblique.
SWP—Survey of Western Palestine, 1-3, London, 1881-3.
Tab.Peut.—Tabula Peutingeriana, ed. K. Miller: *Itineraria romana,* Stuttgart, 1916.
Theodosius—Theodosius: *De situ Terrae Sanctae,* ed. Geyer: *Itinera hierosolymitana,* Wien, 1898.
Tos.—Tosephtah

Waddington—Ph. Le Bas et W. H. Waddington: *Voyage archéologique et Grèce et en Asie Mineure*: Inscriptions et Explications. Vol. III, Paris, 1870.

War—*The Jewish War* by Josephus Flavius, ed. Niese.

ZDPV—Zeitschrift d. Deutschen Palästina-Vereins

Note: The Talmudic sources (Mishnah, Tosephtah, Babylonian and Jerusalem Talmuds) are quoted by tractate; in the case of the Mishnah and Toseptah by chapter and paragraph; in the case of the Gemarah by page.

INDEXES

1. GEOGRAPHICAL

2. PERSONS AND PEOPLES

3. SUBJECT INDEX